THE BALKANS AS EUROPE, 1821–1914

THE BALKANS AS EUROPE, 1821–1914

Edited by Timothy Snyder
and Katherine Younger

UNIVERSITY OF ROCHESTER PRESS

The University of Rochester Press gratefully acknowledges support from the Institute for Human Sciences / Institut für die Wissenschaften vom Menschen (IWM) for the publication of this volume. Essays in the volume originated as contributions to two conferences in the series "The Balkans as Europe," held at the IWM in 2011 and 2014 through the generous support of the Robert Bosch Stiftung.

I ＼∨ ／∧

**Institut für die Wissenschaften vom Menschen
Institute for Human Sciences**

First published 2018

University of Rochester Press
668 Mt. Hope Avenue, Rochester, NY 14620, USA
www.urpress.com
and Boydell & Brewer Limited
PO Box 9, Woodbridge, Suffolk IP12 3DF, UK
www.boydellandbrewer.com

ISBN-13: 978-1-58046-915-9
ISSN: 1528-4808

Library of Congress Cataloging-in-Publication Data

Names: Snyder, Timothy, editor, writer of introduction. | Younger, Katherine, editor.
Title: The Balkans as Europe, 1821–1914 / [six authors] ; Edited by Timothy Snyder and Katherine Younger.
Description: First published 2018. | Rochester, NY : University of Rochester Press, 2018. | Series: Rochester studies in East and Central Europe ; 21 | Includes bibliographical references and index.
Identifiers: LCCN 2017058504 | ISBN 9781580469159 (hardcover : alk. paper)
Subjects: LCSH: Balkan Peninsula—History—19th century. | Balkan Peninsula—History—20th century. | Nation-building—Balkan Peninsula. | Nationalism—Balkan Peninsula. | Geopolitics—Balkan Peninsula.
Classification: LCC DR43 .B35 2018 | DDC 949.6/038—dc23 LC record available at https://lccn.loc.gov/2017058504

CONTENTS

A Note on Terminology

The Habsburg Empire played a central, and complex, role in the Balkans in the nineteenth and early twentieth centuries. As the structure and borders of the Habsburg Empire changed, so too did the terms used to refer to it and its constituent parts.

The terms "Habsburg Empire," "Habsburg Monarchy," and "Austria-Hungary" can be used for the entire period covered in this volume to refer to all the lands ruled by the Habsburg dynasty.

Prior to 1867, the empire was governed as a unitary state, sometimes called the Austrian Empire. The Austro-Hungarian Compromise of 1867 (in German, *Ausgleich*, literally "balancing") restored partial sovereignty to the Kingdom of Hungary. It transformed the unitary state into what came to be called the Dual Monarchy: The Kingdom of Hungary was one part. The other was the rest of the empire, officially the Kingdoms and Lands Represented in the Parliament but commonly called, simply, Austria. Cisleithania was another common but unofficial name for the Austrian half of the Dual Monarchy. It referred to the lands "this side" of the Leitha River, a tributary of the Danube.

The maps on pages ix–xvi reflect the changing boundaries and terminology.

Unless otherwise noted, all translations are the authors' own.

Maps

Europe, 1856.

Maps by Beehive Mapping.

After the Crimean War peace settlement, 1856. *Shading in vertical stripes indicates a semi-independent region.*

Kassa

Vienna . Pressburg

GALICIA

Czernowitz

Dniester

RUSSIAN
EMPIRE

Chisinau

AUSTRIA-HUNGARY

Budapest

BESSARABIA

CARINTHIA

MOLDAVIA

Ljubljana

Cluj

Drava

Zagreb

Trieste

ISTRIA

Rijeka

CROATIA-SLAVONIA

Sava

Danube

Temesvar

BANAT

ROMANIA

DALMATIA

BOSNIA-
HERZEGOVINA

Belgrade

WALLACHIA

Bucharest

Zadar

SERBIA

Sarajevo.

Danube

MONTENEGRO

Dubrovnik

Kotor

ALBANIA

Sofia

BULGARIA
Autonomous

Black
Sea

ITALY

MACEDONIA

Skopje

Plovdiv

EASTERN
RUMELIA

Naples

Turnovo

Edirne

Istanbul.

THRACE

Salonika

OTTOMAN

EMPIRE

Corfu

Aegean
Sea

Ionian
Sea

Athens.

Sicily

GREECE

Adriatic Sea

After the Treaty of San Stefano, March 1878. *Shading in vertical stripes indicates a semi-independent (autonomous or occupied) region. Light gray shading indicates full independence.*

After the Treaty of Berlin, July 1878. *Shading in vertical stripes indicates a semi-independent (autonomous or occupied) region. Light gray shading indicates full independence.*

Before the First Balkan War, 1912. *Light gray shading indicates full independence.*

Between the First and Second Balkan Wars, April 1913. *Light gray shading indicates full independence.*

After the Second Balkan War, September 1913. *Light gray shading indicates full independence.*

Europe, 1914.

INTRODUCTION

Timothy Snyder

The Balkans are commonly associated with backwardness. Why not with forwardness? There are good reasons to see the region and its constituent states as precursors of events in western Europe. Although the region, in the modern period, was less industrialized than much of the rest of Europe, the politicians and publics of the Balkans contemplated and even anticipated larger political trends.[1]

Although the honor of being the first nation-state is usually accorded to France, it is perhaps more just to treat Serbia and Greece as the first genuine nation-states. The political ideas of the early Balkan nation builders, especially among the Serbs, were not diluted by enlightened imperialism of the Napoleonic variety. The nation-states that emerged in the Balkans in the 1820s were a model for Europe, and then for the world, precisely because they were inherently adaptable and pluralistic. For example, Serbs did not propose that Serbian ideas were right for Europe and the world, but rather that what Serbs had done, others might do. The Greek model associated national revolution with both Romanticism and classicism, so that Europeans who supported Greeks against the Ottoman Empire could believe they were taking part in a universal project of liberation. These first Balkan unifications preceded the Italian and German ones by roughly half a century—hence our proposition that the historian studying European nation-states must start first with the Balkans and only then seek echoes farther west. The Italian unification, like the Greek, involved a confusion of the individual and the collective: The liberation of the nation was conceived as the liberation of a national person, principled and worthy of emulation. The German unification was more like the Serbian, its claims generally limited to those of power and folk, not universal principles. Later, in the 1920s, the Balkan model of statehood was applied throughout eastern Europe as a result of the settlements made following the First World War.[2]

The national revolutions in the Balkans did not prejudge which nations were coherent and which would gain statehood, but they did provide a model, one that is known in other, non-European, historical settings as anti-imperial or anti-colonial. The integration of Balkan nation-states, a process that began in the early nineteenth century, had to and did involve the disintegration of the Ottoman Empire. The further national integration of European territory—the Italian and German unifications, in the third quarter of the nineteenth century—had to and did weaken the Habsburg monarchy. When, in 1914, Serbia turned against the Habsburgs, all of Europe went to war, motivated in considerable measure by nationalism. The relationship between the Ottoman Empire and the national movements, and then the relationships between the older European empires and the newly sovereign Balkan states, can be understood precisely in terms that are usually reserved for discussions of global history: colonialism and anticolonialism. The Balkan states made claims against the Ottoman Empire for their independence that became familiar from the anticolonial movements of the twentieth century: the authenticity of local culture, the economic opportunities of sovereignty, the need for global recognition as a sovereign equal. The First World War was an anti-imperial war in which empires fought on both sides and after which some empires imposed anti-imperial settlements on others. Land empires—which could be touched directly by the logic of self-determination of their constituent parts—all came to an end. The logic that brought them down, however, would be extended in the twentieth century to the powers that won the First World War, which is to say to the rest of the world. In this way Balkan history exposes and breaks down the implied artificial barrier between Europe and the rest of the world, or between North and South, that defines today's discussions of post-colonialism and of global history generally.[3]

In 2011 and 2014, under the rubric "The Balkans as Europe," an international group of scholars gathered at the Institute of Human Sciences (Institut für die Wissenschaften vom Menschen), an independent institute in Vienna, for a series of workshops. The goal was not to consider our own discourses of Balkan backwardness as a European phenomenon. This has already been done, splendidly and in different ways, by leaders of the field such as Maria Todorova and Larry Wolff.[4] The goal was rather to reverse the field, to consider politics rather than discourse, and actors in the Balkans as forward-looking agents rather than as subjects of retrospective discussions. This volume, which collects six papers presented at these workshops and then revised, provides good reason to think that a sustained effort from these premises might be fruitful for historians who aim to make sense of Europe as a whole, or to place European history within a global framework.

These scholarly works demonstrate that from the beginning of the national period of Balkan history, the national has also been the European and the global. It is possible to see European history not just as a competition between nations and empires but as a field of projects of integration and disintegration—of course, integration from one perspective means disintegration from another. At a historical moment when the future of the current project of European integration is in doubt, this lesson from the Balkans is apposite. The shattering of large, durable economic units in the name of unachievable sovereignty might after all be the way of the future as well the past.

At the crucial moment of Balkan state formation, in the late nineteenth century, it was necessary to consider global economics and politics. If state sovereignty in every case involves the attempted control of human beings defined as subjects of the state, then the mass emigration from Europe during the first globalization of the late nineteenth century must have been considered a threat to the sovereignty of the states the emigrants left behind. Interestingly, as Ulf Brunnbauer demonstrates in his study of Balkan reactions to the issue of emigration, political leaders reacted to the brute fact of emigration from southeastern Europe to North America in different ways, depending upon how they understood the relationship between their own polity and the world system.[5]

At this time, Austria-Hungary was the most important and largest polity in the region. After 1867, when a constitutional compromise known as the *Ausgleich* devolved powers to the Hungarian and Cisleithanian (Austrian) halves, it was a dual monarchy, in which almost all matters of domestic policy were decided separately in Vienna and in Budapest. Both parts of the Dual Monarchy extended into the Balkans. Broadly speaking, Cisleithania (the "Austrian" part) was not governed as a nation-state, but rather as a liberal and democratizing empire where national problems were to be resolved by concessions from the center. For this reason, perhaps, the general approach to emigration was that of an open door. The Kingdom of Hungary, by contrast, was governed as a national state of the Hungarians, who were a plurality but not a majority in the territory. Consequently, Hungary did have policies to restrict emigration, although these seem to have made no difference in quantitative terms. It is, however, interesting to note that the people who did leave Hungary were for the most part members of the Slavic-speaking minorities. Whether by design or accident, emigration made Hungary more Hungarian.

In Serbia, the classic example of a new nation-state, authorities managed to arrange matters so that more people came to the country than left it. This had an obvious logic in a state that was consistently militaristic and kept a large number of men under arms. Between 1880 and 1890 Serbia witnessed a net immigration of about fifty thousand people, some of them Slavs from Austria-Hungary. Thus, even in a period without war in which emigration was largely trans-Atlantic, a certain amount of ethnic unmixing was taking place, and by design: Slavs were encouraged to immigrate to Serbia.

In Greece an entirely different policy was followed. Greek authorities understood the Greek nation to be a global nation, so they did not see emigration as a net loss. In intellectual terms, this meant that Greek leaders' image of the Greek people required thinking of them, both at home and abroad, as still members of the Greek nation. This was true in all of the other cases as well. The very concept of ethnicity, Brunnbauer maintains, developed as a result of contemplating the emigration of co-nationals to faraway places, especially the United States. If states wished to maintain cultural, political, and financial relationships with emigrants, they required terms to identify "their own" people who lived in a different polity. This was the idea of the ethnic nation. Thus the domestic project of building a nation works in an uninterrupted continuity with the foreign policy of protecting a nation. This is true whether the story is one of national death through assimilation or national health through trade. Either way, the local citizen is imagined abroad in ethnic terms.

As Holly Case reveals, this particular overlap of foreign and domestic policy was but one aspect of a larger diplomatic transformation that began in the Balkans, in which the textbook idea of sovereignty yielded, no later than the early nineteenth century, to policies designed to alter the societies of other states. Her argument requires that two dominant structures of the history of international relations be considered anew. The first is the Treaty of Westphalia, which established the principle of modern state sovereignty and is thus regarded as ideal-typical for theorists of international relations. As Case recalls, Westphalia embodied a principle of mutual recognition of sovereignty among Christian European regimes, and thus excluded the Ottoman Empire. This meant not only that unequal treaties ("capitulations") between Christian and non-Christian nations were legitimate but also that Christian powers understood the Ottoman border as a permeable membrane through which instances of their own sovereignty could intrude, establish themselves, and act.

The second notion that must be set aside, then, is the idea of nineteenth-century foreign policy as a great game of a few elite statesmen, mummified by the archaic rules of their own creation.[6] Instead, the territory of the Ottoman

Empire provided an arena where a very large number of diplomats of the lowest rank—the consuls of other states—could reinvent diplomacy as social policy abroad. These consuls had the power to bestow citizenship, which means that they created whole groups of people on Ottoman territory with a claim to protection by a foreign state—as early as 1808 some 120,000 Greeks in the Ottoman Empire were protected by the Russian Empire. By altering Ottoman society in this way, the consuls were creating the justifications for further interventions on Ottoman territory, up to and including war. In other words, what Case calls the "consular revolution" was the beginning of European practices that are familiar from a later period, such as the defense of supposedly oppressed ethnic minorities. Case demonstrates the conceptual and personal continuities between these Balkan practices and the diplomacy of the first half of the twentieth century in Europe generally.

The Balkan nation-states can themselves be seen as a product of this consular revolution, and their policies are a response to its particular structures and possibilities. They were, after all, usually created with the support of one Christian empire or another, in part because leaders in London, St. Petersburg, or, later, Berlin believed that such states would bolster the imperial order. If the Ottoman Empire was to decline, its disintegration should be managed, so went the reasoning of the great powers, so that major conflict is avoided and the interests of powerful neighbors are more or less balanced. Thus, distant diplomats, whatever their public rhetoric, in no way regarded the Balkan national revolutions as expositions of perfect sovereignty against the backdrop of Ottoman repression. On the contrary, they regarded the new states as clients that would balance other clients. So the great powers at first negotiated unequal treaties with the Balkan states, or imposed their own understandings without the presence of interlocutors from the states concerned—for example, the 1878 Treaty of Berlin, which among other things established the de facto independence of Bulgaria under Ottoman rule. The "capitulations" that the great powers had extracted from the Ottoman Empire were extended to the new states that were established on its territory. The leaders of these new states thus took two things for granted: that it was natural for states to impose their own interests by working within the societies of other states, and that full sovereignty meant some sort of equalization of these influences between the empires and the nations.[7]

The Balkan nation-states would therefore practice this kind of "consular" foreign policy against one another, the Ottoman Empire, and, finally, against Austria-Hungary. Their leaders would tend to conflate—as Dessislava Lilova and Roumiana Preshlenova demonstrate on the crucial example of

Bulgaria—the quest for full sovereignty with the content of domestic policy. Lilova makes the case that the definition of the Bulgarian nation arose in response precisely to the perception that the national territory was being explored and surveyed for exploitation by foreigners. She writes of the perception of a "deluge of foreign travelers" in the 1860s and a rhetoric of colonization in the 1870s. Bulgarian national activists believed that they must organize knowledge about their own homeland as a matter of self-defense. Maps would clothe the nation, demonstrating that the inhabitants of Bulgarian lands were not savages to be used by empires but a European people that must be treated as such. Geography seemed like the proper mode to make such arguments, Lilova argues, because its putative neutrality made its assertions seem irrefutable. At the simplest level, maps that had already been drawn by others could be enhanced with the inclusion of Bulgarian locales, written with Bulgarian orthography. Once new maps were created, they could provide the basis for statistical categories, such as population, which could then in turn become national symbols or arguments. Bulgarians preferred to make their case on the "principle of statistical majority," writes Lilova, rather than by reference to ancient history. The "priority of geography over history" seemed to be a defense of Bulgarian claims against those not only of imperialists from Europe but also of local competitors such as the Greeks. Interestingly, this entire campaign took place on writing desks: The Bulgarian intellectuals, although they called for journeys through the "terra incognita" of their own country, did not actually undertake the journeys themselves.

Likewise, in the 1860s and 1870s the Bulgarian conversation about the national economy did not distinguish between external and internal considerations. As Preshlenova argues, Bulgarian activists assumed that the abolition of Ottoman rule would automatically relieve the economic backwardness inherent in that rule. The Treaty of Berlin of 1878 had recognized the autonomy of Bulgaria, but within geographical borders that seemed unsatisfactorily restrictive to an intelligentsia preoccupied with maps, and without the formal sovereignty that might have marked a complete break with the Ottoman past. As a result, Preshlenova shows, the debate about the national economy then became identical with the debate about the achievement of full sovereignty. There was a national consensus for militarism—and thus high military budgets—as an investment in future gains of land. Meanwhile, Bulgarian politicians worked to remove what they understood as the archaic limitations on trade policy imposed at Berlin. Between 1879 and 1905 Bulgaria succeeded in regrounding its economic relations with foreign powers on the basis of reciprocal treaties. By the time Bulgaria declared its independence in 1908, the government was moving toward a full complement of economic ministries, and electoral debates included economic issues. The basic faith in militarism, however, was constant. Bulgaria joined Greece, Macedonia, and Serbia in forming the Balkan League to wage the First Balkan War in 1912, against the Ottoman Empire, to gain more land.[8]

In his reconsideration of what has been called the Serbian "Golden Age," 1903 to 1914, John Paul Newman brings home the point that Balkan militarism, on display in its purest form during that period, could serve as a general model and could change the course of European history. Already a century before the First World War, most able-bodied Serbian men had been fighting in the national revolution. Over the entire course of the existence of the Serbian state, its government was able to keep an impressively high percentage of its men under arms. In the First Balkan War, the Serbian army sent four hundred thousand men into the field. Serbia was an extreme example of the conflation of foreign and domestic policy, in that prosperity was always assumed to be a matter of controlling land that belonged to someone else: a rival nation-state such as Bulgaria, the Ottoman Empire, or Austria-Hungary.

Likewise, the Serbs were pioneers in a certain modern form of the "consular revolution," whereby they used or rather inspired national questions abroad to provoke neighbors and create the conditions for war. The assassination of Franz Ferdinand was the result of a very large number of such plots. As Newman recounts, these were the work of conspiracies within the state rather than of the state itself. In a polity legitimated by territorial growth, there was always room for disagreement about the correct means to pursue that expansion and a natural discord between civilian authorities who might want to integrate territory and military authorities who favored quick exploitation of its resources. As Newman shows, the Golden Age revealed rather than resolved these problems. Victory in the Balkan Wars brought political strife over the control of new territory, and the sense of national unity brought by triumph did not hinder yet another war in 1914—this time one that would bring in Europe, and the world. Interesting in this light is that Serbia won the First World War in two senses: It was on the side of the ultimate victors, and the victors exported the model of the nation-state northward to the rest of central and eastern Europe. Indeed, by the end of the First World War, the idea of self-determination was championed by most of the parties: not only by Woodrow Wilson and the Entente powers, but also by the Germans at Brest-Litovsk and the Bolsheviks under Vladimir Lenin. In this way, Balkan models contributed to the emergence of a new world order.

Did leaders and activists in the Balkans know that they were amplifying and accelerating trends of European and global history, or is this framework of "forwardness" an abstraction imposed from the outside? In her consideration of two moments from the intellectual history of Dalmatia, Dominique Reill suggests that people in the Balkans were fully aware of the various reciprocities, and sought to understand and exploit them. Unlike Serbia, Bulgaria, and Greece, Dalmatia was not an independent state, but rather a maritime district of Austria-Hungary, on the eastern shores of the Adriatic. Its economic debates, which she tracks through its chamber of commerce, were thus about relationships between a periphery and a center. Even so, as she shows, they were strikingly global in scope.

When arguing for the elimination of tariffs, Dalmatian businessmen and journalists looked to the example of Algeria and France. They were fully aware, as the journalism of the time demonstrates, that Algeria had been joined to France by way of a bloody colonial war. Nevertheless they could and did seize upon the form of economic agreements between Paris and its new North African *départements*, which was that of a reciprocal reduction of trade barriers between nominally equal parties. Interestingly, the obsession with reciprocity, so evident in the relationships between new Balkan states and old empires, appeared at that time in internal discussions within Austria.

Reill's second example of global perspective, the invention of the universal translation system known as Pangrafia, reveals a keen understanding of the deeper problems of global political economy as reflected in "language politics." Larger political entities seeking to consolidate imperial territory for economic integration would tend to impose one working language for purposes of trade and administration, with or without implying an attendant cultural chauvinism. In the Austrian Empire this language was German, but it was spoken well only by a minority of the empire's subjects. In Dalmatian or Istrian trade it might be Italian, which would place speakers of Croatian or Slovenian at a disadvantage. World trade would require the use of world languages, such as English, French, or Russian. In all cases, the speakers of smaller languages, even though taken together they formed a numerical majority in a region, empire, or of the world, would be forced into a position of subordination, which might encourage nationalism and rebellion. How then to have modernization without humiliation, efficiency without marginalization? A universal system of translation would allow everyone in an imperial or in the world economy to participate as equals. The project, though it was never endorsed or implemented, reveals rather deep insight into the nature of some of the core problems of modernity.

Reill's two examples can only be suggestive, but they are powerfully so: The Balkans were European and global not just in the unintended consequences of their political innovations but also in the frameworks of thought that lay behind them. This is a disturbing conclusion for those of us who might wish to think that writing or thinking in global abstractions automatically resolves political or intellectual problems; but for those attempting a plausible European or global history the Balkans might be a useful place to start. One way to write European or global history, after all, is to begin from a region such as the Balkans, not only where the grander levels of historical causality were understood and manipulated, but also where important concepts—the nation-state and anticolonialism—were invented.

Notes

1. This research agenda extends and unites some suggestions made in Mark Mazower, *Dark Continent: Europe's Twentieth Century* (New York: Knopf, 1999), and Mark Mazower, *The Balkans: A Short History* (New York: Modern Library, 2000).

2. Irina Livezeanu, *Cultural Politics in Greater Romania: Regionalism, Nation Building, and Ethnic Struggle* (Ithaca, NY: Cornell University Press, 1995), is a model study of the cultural politics of territorial expansion in the 1920s.

3. These ideas are developed in Timothy Snyder, "Integration and Disintegration: Europe, Ukraine, and the World," *Slavic Review* 74, no. 4 (2015): 695–707.

4. Maria Todorova, *Imagining the Balkans* (New York: Oxford University Press, 1997); Larry Wolff, *Venice and the Slavs: The Discovery of Dalmatia in the Age of Enlightenment* (Stanford, CA: Stanford University Press, 2001). Paul Garde, *Le Discours balkanique: des mots et des hommes* (Paris: Fayard, 2004), provides a study of discursive elements as a kind of prolegomenon for study in the field.

5. Ulf Brunnbauer, *Globalizing Southeastern Europe: Emigrants, America, and the State since the Late Nineteenth Century* (Lanham, MD: Lexington Books, 2016), unites a series of focused local studies with a long temporal range.

6. Dimitrije Djordjevic and Stephen Fischer-Galati, *The Balkan Revolutionary Tradition* (New York: Columbia University Press, 1981), make another case for Balkan ideological agency.

7. Stevan K. Pavlowitch, in *A History of the Balkans, 1804–1945* (London: Longman, 1999), uses the happy description of "empires connected across peripheries" (44).

8. For a sense of what Greeks lost by separation from the Ottoman Empire, see Gerasimos Augustinos, *The Greeks of Asia Minor: Confession, Community,*

and Ethnicity in the Nineteenth Century (Kent, OH: Kent State University Press, 1981), 75–91. Henry Roberts, *Rumania: Political Problems of an Agrarian State* (New Haven, CT: Yale University Press, 1951), is a classic attempt to integrate agriculture and high politics. See also John R. Lampe and Marvin R. Jackson, *Balkan Economic History 1550–1950: From Imperial Borderlands to Developing Nations* (Bloomington: Indiana University Press, 1982).

Chapter One

Balkan Initiatives to Make Europe

Two Cases from Mid-Nineteenth-Century Dalmatia

Dominique Kirchner Reill

Over the last two centuries, historians have committed themselves to the task of defining Europe, of defining what it is and what made (or makes) it. Scholars have adopted various approaches, from *longue durée* models tracing environmental, philosophical, and religious factors, to *courte durée* models narrating military, diplomatic, and economic developments.[1] What all of these histories share is a view that it was in Europe's power centers—Paris, Berlin, Amsterdam, Madrid, Vienna, Rome, and, yes, even London—that Europe originated. Constantine, Charlemagne, Napoleon, Marx, Metternich, Bismarck, Mazzini, and Monnet are just some of the usual figures who leap from the pages of treatises on the creation of a European order or a European consciousness. But were all the Euro-architects wielders of prestige? Were the centers of scientific innovation, religious hegemony, capital accumulation, or military might the preordained subjects in consolidating Europe's object peripheries into something grander, something European? My goal in this chapter is to show how the object of expansion, the periphery—in this case the Balkan periphery—could and did envision itself as a willing subject in making Europe, instead of just an object of the process. I do this through the example of two very different mid-nineteenth-century Dalmatian elites and their two very different plans for ways the Balkan maritime province of Dalmatia could serve as a model for Europeanization.

These elites saw Dalmatia not just as intrinsic to a Europeanizing project because the region connected western European commerce and intellectual movements through its eastern Adriatic caravan routes to the core Balkan lands that crossed over into the Black Sea and Eastern Mediterranean. They also saw Dalmatia as a microcosm of where much of the population diversity politics increasingly plaguing European communities was being played out. Dalmatia's population in the mid-nineteenth century counted about 5 percent who identified as Catholic Italian speakers (many of whom controlled local government and trade), 75 percent Catholic Slavic speakers, 20 percent Serb Orthodox Slavic speakers, with some influential micro-Sephardic Jewish and Albanian communities in some of its port towns. If Dalmatia could progress in its global outreach while peacefully negotiating its internal differences, should Europe not look to it as a useful test case for resolving similar issues throughout its many lands? The two Dalmatian elites who are the focus of this chapter, Luigi Serragli and Stipan Ivičević, believed so, and their stances remind us of the Balkan peripheries' willingness to make Europe a global core.

The Algerian Solution:
The 1851 Chamber of Commerce Resolution

In the spring of 1851, Dalmatian economic elites viewed their future within the Habsburg Empire with great unease. At that exact moment, in far-off Vienna, barons and earls around the newly anointed emperor, Franz Joseph, were trying to determine how to consolidate the territories they had come so close to losing in the revolutions of 1848–49. To do so, Vienna statesmen looked to the economy, determined to find ways to stimulate the imperial spreadsheet so that it would stop bleeding red and start showing black. The most famous of these initiatives (and perhaps the most successful) was the new Austrian *Zollverein* (customs union), which, once put into place, would abolish the tariffs imposed on trade between most of the lands controlled politically by Vienna.[2] Not all territories under Viennese supervision would partake in the union, however, and membership in the *Zollverein* was determined by the powers that be in the imperial court. The Kingdom of Dalmatia—a land controlled by Vienna since 1815 that hugged the eastern Adriatic coast from Zadar south to Dubrovnik—was one of the largest Vienna-controlled territories that had been consistently deemed unfit for inclusion in the tariff union with sister Habsburg lands. Dalmatian elites knew that Viennese statesmen could go either way as to whether Dalmatia should be included or excluded from the post-1849 *Zollverein* and all agreed that one way or another the decision would have far-reaching effects. Dalmatian elites well understood that their kingdom was poor, the second-poorest of the entire Habsburg realm, and that trade initiatives were central to advancing the province's status and its inhabitants' standard of living.[3]

Dalmatians viewed the new wave of attention that Viennese imperial over-lords were paying to economic reform as much as a moment of promise as of dread. Perhaps now the cause of the economic deficits of their underpopulated, maritime, and mountainous province would be addressed?[4] Or perhaps now what little monies they received to administer their weak infrastructures and insufficient state services would be curtailed even further? Perhaps now the new emperor with his new liberal cabinet would look to Dalmatia and invest, so that she would no longer weigh on the imperial coffers? Or perhaps now a glance at the latest Dalmatian census reports would convince the *Herren in Wien*—the gentlemen in Vienna—even more that the dilemmas of Dalmatia had to be contained, that such problems had no place in a system of free-market enterprise? No one knew which way the tide would turn, but with typical Dalmatian black humor, most expected the worst.

Businessmen, large property holders, and local community leaders through-out Dalmatia debated face to face and in their correspondence about which imperial fiscal reforms would lighten or burden Dalmatia's economic challenges. Two primary camps emerged, the isolationist and the unionist. The isolationists argued that things should remain more or less as they had been since Dalmatia's incorporation into the Habsburg Empire after the Napoleonic Wars: Dalmatia should be treated as a separate economic entity from the rest of the empire, with tariffs imposed at a set rate regardless of whether trading partners hailed from Habsburg or non-Habsburg regions. The unionists argued the opposite: Dalmatia's lack of a privileged trading status with Habsburg lands had doomed her to financial oblivion. Without a special status, her olive oil, wines, nuts, and fruits were not being "priced" to sell to her fellow northern Habsburg sister lands. As unionists saw it, without inclusion in a tariff union, Dalmatia's Mediterranean harvests had to compete with other, more enticing, Mediterranean suppliers hailing from the Italian peninsula, France, Spain, Greece, and the Ottoman Empire. Isolationists countered that Dalmatian commerce would only improve once it could compete, and that her maritime position required that she sell to any buyer. Unionists then responded that Dalmatia was too far behind to compete, but that what she could offer would sustain northern Habsburg markets' demands, and that to everyone's benefit. All the parties involved in these discussions knew that they had little say in what reforms would ultimately be introduced. For not only would Vienna make the final call, but Dalmatia itself did not have a legislative assembly, did not have any sort of effective political or economic representation, and therefore had little sway in the higher echelons of power. Hence, Dalmatians' debates about tariffs and infrastructure were geared to the ears of the military administrators of their province, in the hopes that these would inform their higher-ups of what "natives'" had to say about their potential futures.

It was in this climate that Luigi Serragli (1816–80), a member of the province's chamber of commerce, suggested that Dalmatia needed a reciprocal trade policy with Austria "along the lines of the recent French laws regarding commercial relations with Algeria."[5] When the issue was put to a vote, the chamber of commerce agreed that Dalmatia needed a policy with Austria just like the one Algeria had with France. Undoubtedly, to the modern ear, this suggestion and its endorsement seem bizarre. Did Dalmatians really want to be Vienna's Algeria? Did Serragli—an upright forty-three-year-old Dubrovnik businessman and local bureaucrat—and his colleagues who voted in favor of his idea think of Dalmatia as a land similar to the recently conquered portions of the Barbary Coast? Did Dalmatia want to be colonized by Austria as Algeria had just been by France? Or did this deliberate self-identification with France's newly vanquished "savage Other" point to an ingrained sense among Dalmatians of the role the Balkans had been assigned in Western, and Habsburg, cultural mindscapes, as Maria Todorova and Larry Wolff have suggested?[6]

Before any of these questions can be answered, we must take a moment to clarify how truly strange it was for a Dalmatian to hanker after an Algerian solution. As many scholars have argued, Algeria became part of the French Empire in a manner that few would have wished for themselves, and in a manner remarkably different from how Dalmatia had been joined to Austria. While Dalmatia had been peacefully and conclusively ceded to the Habsburg royal house by parlor diplomats at the Congress of Vienna, Algeria had been forcibly taken by the French in a bloody, costly, and drawn-out war fought against indigenous Algerians.

French claims on Algeria were not just different in kind from Habsburg claims on Dalmatia because of the discrepancy in bloodshed to enlarge empire, although the traumas of bloodshed should never be underestimated. In 1815, when the Habsburgs took up the Kingdom of Dalmatia, they cited local dynastic rights going back centuries. As such, though governed by a military administration, natives of Dalmatia were encouraged, if not prompted, to see themselves as natural subjects of their divinely-chosen monarch. In 1830, France's claim to Algeria was posited as a colonial mission *par excellence.* The liberal deputy Hypolite Passy recalled in 1834 that with the conquest of Algeria Frenchmen saw their new territory as "a soil of admirable fecundity to which streams of European population would soon flood. . . . It was an entire continent that we would summon to the benefits of industry and civilization; in a word, glory, power, wealth, all that flatters the pride, all that makes the grandeur and prosperity of nations, we would find it all, see it all grow and flourish under the African sky."[7] In essence, where Dalmatia's inclusion into the Habsburg realms signified an expansion of territory with an expansion in the number of Habsburg subjects, France's conquest of Algeria signified a colonial land grab where a "Neo-Europe," to borrow Alfred Crosby's phrase, would be colonized by a "flood" of Europeans who would wield their power with little consideration of those who currently lived under "the African sky" and exploit the country's resources for the benefit of metropolitan France.[8] Dalmatia after 1815 was considered just another Habsburg possession, perhaps a peculiar and impoverished one.[9] Algeria after 1830 was considered "a new Indies," with all the implicit racist and economically domineering traits of such an imperial relationship.[10]

Luigi Serragli and his peers in Dalmatia's chamber of commerce were hardly unaware of France's policy toward Algeria. Newspapers throughout Europe and in Dalmatia from 1830 on reported France's attack, siege, and brutal suppression of Algerian natives in order to stabilize her rule.[11] Once conquered, Algeria was nothing more or less than a colonial jewel of the French Empire. How Algeria was incorporated into France and what France's goals were for its incorporation were not a secret kept from Dalmatian eyes or ears. Journalists in such widely read papers as the populist *La Presse*, the liberal *La Revue des deux mondes*, and the conservative *Journal des Débats* reported almost daily on the parliamentary debates in Paris concerning the Algerian conquest and filled their columns with bombastic illustrated battle tales of France's heroic fighting against Algerian natives, the Berbers. Dalmatian elites had access to these articles, not just via French newspapers available in the local cafés and casinos in urban port centers, but also through their regional newspapers, such as the *Osservatore triestino* (Trieste Observer), which consistently lifted information from French news sources to fill its own columns. The press—whether the original French reports or the lifted Adriatic versions of them—regularly portrayed the prize of Algeria as farmland for France, ripe for landless or impoverished Europeans to occupy and plough. There was no doubt that Dalmatians knew that Algeria was no mere imperial province or crown land, such as their land was to Austria. Algeria was a colony, to be filled by colonizers. Did Serragli and his cohort of Dalmatian elites, then, wish the same fate for themselves?

If the question is whether Dalmatian elites wanted impoverished farmers and unemployed bureaucrats from Vienna, Vorarlberg, and Carinthia to settle Dalmatia, then the answer would be overwhelmingly negative. Throughout the entire Habsburg rule of Dalmatia, locals feared and complained about foreigners and outsiders being assigned posts within the Dalmatian administration. Land rights were also a constant bone of contention in Dalmatia.

Although there was no one agricultural system that dominated between the kingdom's capital, Zadar, in the north and the naval bases of Dubrovnik in the south, or between the island of Korčula, offshore to the west, and the inland hub of Knin, to the east, everywhere *colons*, day laborers, sharecroppers, absentee landowners, and feudal holders complained and argued about the injustices and insufficient protections offered by the Habsburg system, both to those who worked the land and to those who owned it.[12] The idea of outsiders coming in to settle Dalmatia, either its infrastructures or its lands, provoked panic, not longing. Work, good land, and a good income were hard enough to find in Dalmatia. Outsiders were definitely not welcome to come in floods to displace any locals via settlement.

If they did not desire to be conquered and they did not desire to be colonized, what, then, did Serragli and his chamber of commerce colleagues see in the Algerian solution that was better than the Habsburg solutions Dalmatians had experienced thus far? The answer, in a word, was a word: "reciprocal." Traditionally, reciprocal treaties—whether relating to tariffs, trade, or something else—are made between two separate, usually sovereign, entities. In the eighteenth century, England instituted reciprocal tariff agreements with Portugal under which the normal tariffs on Portuguese wine and English wool were abolished to counter French and Spanish competition.[13] So, too, before cementing the North German *Zollverein*, individual German states in the early nineteenth century had instituted bilateral reciprocal tariff agreements to ease mutual trade. Before 1851, France's reciprocal agreements would have not mustered much attention from a Dalmatian readership, as they followed the traditional reciprocity formulas described earlier. But what caught Dalmatians' attention about the Algerian case was that a metropole, France, instituted a reciprocal trade agreement with a subject of its own empire, Algeria—indeed, with an entity that, at least on paper, comprised three French *départements*.[14]

The new feature of this arrangement was not tariff reductions within an imperial relationship. Dalmatia herself had enjoyed reduced tariffs when selling wine to Habsburg lands throughout the 1840s. What caught Dalmatians' attention was that this "reciprocal" agreement treated each of the two trading entities as separate units, granting "exceptions" outside of the bilateral agreement specifically suited to the imperial periphery's benefit. Before the 1851 reciprocal agreement, most French goods could be sold to Algerian markets with no tariffs, while most Algerian goods had duties levied on them when they entered France. Most foreign (Piedmontese, Spanish, Ottoman, British) goods sold to or bought from Algeria also incurred tariffs at a rate proportional to mainland French duties. What this all meant was that before 1851, France had a fairly unbalanced imperial trade relationship with Algeria, mostly to France's benefit and Algeria's loss. After the 1851 reciprocal agreement, almost all French and Algerian products traded freely across the Mediterranean. Import tariffs for most items were fixed at the same level for metropole and colony, while duties placed on selling to "foreign" markets were instituted based on the interests of each entity. In other words, after 1851, France and Algeria worked within the same tariff union. As a general rule, to boost Algerian productivity, Algeria was freed from all export duties on products destined for foreign countries, excepting some products that would compete directly with French producers.[15] This in essence bolstered ties between metropole and peripheral colony, while positioning the colony's economy to reap the benefits of selling duty-free when competing with other, non-French, Mediterranean suppliers.

There is no doubt that France's change in tariff policy with Algeria was designed to stimulate a weak Algerian economy and thereby to help harmonize its inclusion within the French economy, now that it was an extended member of the grand *Hexagone*—metropolitan France. From the outset, France's designs on Algeria were as much economically driven as anything else. As the journalist and political economist André Cochut outlined in one of his several articles on the Algerian situation that were published in the *Revue des deux mondes*, most French citizens eager to include Algeria within France's empire believed that "colonization is but an affair of industry on a grand scale [*sur une échelle immense*]. What has been missing until now among all the projects so far known is precisely the minute foresight, the instinct for speculation. What are the possible means within each network [*système*] to ease the expenses on the metropole, to attract capital, to retain good workers and to constitute in Africa a population worthy enough of being called French?"[16]

In essence, France's 1851 reciprocal agreement was the answer to this question. It was an initiative of "minute foresight" aimed at attracting capital, creating employment, and easing the strains on the metropole's responsibilities to keep its imperial province's budget afloat. Seen in these terms, the 1851 reciprocal trade agreement was a development plan whereby, with the proper attention, Algeria would go from being a "cursed land" to becoming a "sister of France . . . a new France," as the French historian, journalist, and former Napoleonic officer Louis-François L'Héritier de l'Ain proclaimed.[17]

An imperial economic policy to transform a "cursed land" into a "new France"—or, more generally, a "new Europe"—was exactly what Dalmatians viewed with envy. In this vein, Serragli outlined to his colleagues how a reciprocal tariff agreement *à l'algérienne* would serve as a "transitional phase" both between the isolationist and unionist positions and between Dalmatia's status as an appendage to the Habsburg economic regime and as a fully fledged organ of the imperial system.[18] Serragli explained that a reciprocal trade agreement between Dalmatia and Austria would work as follows: All of the most important Dalmatian products would be put on the Austrian market free of tax, and the same would be the case for those from Austria in Dalmatia. Furthermore, a new tariff of 3 to 15 percent would be set up for Dalmatia for foreign imports, depending on need. On the whole, Dalmatian products would be traded tax-free outside of Dalmatia and commerce restrictions would be lifted on navigation.

A reciprocal policy allowing Dalmatia to trade freely outside of the Habsburg Empire would serve as a check to black market smuggling with Ottoman Bosnia to the east and the Italian peninsula to the west.[19] A reciprocal policy abolishing tariffs between Dalmatia and other Habsburg lands would allow Dalmatia's Mediterranean harvests to sell faster in the market squares of Prague, Lviv, and Vienna. With a reciprocal policy, capital investment into Dalmatia would be encouraged, precisely because issues of smuggling and narrow markets would be resolved.[20] In essence, members of the Dalmatian Chamber of Commerce voted for and applauded the Algerian solution because they believed that it promised to remake their economy into one "worthy of being called Habsburg," "worthy of being called European," just as France's policies promised to make the former Barbary States a land "worthy of being called French."[21]

This 1851 Algerian vote is very relevant to Balkan initiatives to unite Europe. First, it demonstrated the ability of imperial subjects on the European continent to compare their situation to that of overseas colonies. Too often, historians and theorists have categorized these histories as distinctively different, pointing to the unbridgeable gap between racialist attitudes and colonizing infrastructures that render the land-based imperial expansions of the Habsburg, Ottoman, Prussian, and Russian Empires somehow incomparable with the overseas colonial pursuits of the French, British, Spanish, Portuguese, Dutch, Italians, and Germans.[22] Serragli and the Dalmatian Chamber of Commerce did not make too much of these differences and focused instead on similarities. One European metropole (France) had initiated an economic policy with its imperial subject that struck their fancy and they proposed that their own European metropole (Austria) follow suit. For these Dalmatian elites, what was at issue was the best policy of European imperialism, whether colonial or not. In the comparability of the French and Habsburg systems, the similarity of European imperial aims to a large extent outweighed each empire's particular features.

But perhaps more important in the 1851 Chamber of Commerce vote in favor of an Algerian solution was the desire to be incorporated into empire in a manner resembling the neo-Europes taking shape throughout the rest of the globe. Historians looking at the strategies, hopes, and fears in the nine-teenth century have often explained the similarity between the goals of Balkan elites and those of their contemporaries in Britain and France by categorizing them as following the "liberal school" or "conservative school" of European thought. The omnipresence of arguments and programs using rhetoric that relied on terms such as "progress" and "Providence," "nation" and "liberty" have seemed to reveal that peripheries such as Dalmatia *followed* the trends of western Europe and tried to emulate them, often in circumstances particularly unsuitable for flattering imitation. But perhaps peoples in the Balkans wanted much more than merely to follow continental trends? Perhaps at least some of them wanted to trump the trends, wanted to be part of Europe, part of its modernization, industrialization, trade, and wealth in a more complicit man-ner than their western European contemporaries ever dreamed? Perhaps being part of an empire was not just something to be endured, but could actually be turned into a responsibility to be harmonized, to be united with Europe? Perhaps Balkan elites like Serragli and his cohort wanted to turn the tables on their subject status and require the enlightened mission of their imperial mas-ters to bear fruit and bring some sort of homogeneity of economic standards, if not status?[23] By directly pointing to France's project for Algeria, one could argue that Dalmatian elites were pushing aside old models of their expected "backward" role in Europe. Algeria was a model home of a "new France," one we have learned was not the dreamland the French had hoped it would be, but one whose design was nonetheless seen by Dalmatians as representing some-thing new: reciprocity, unity, a means to be part of an evolving Europe.

The New Cosmopolitan Art: Pangrafia

At the same time of Serragli's presentation to the Dalmatian Chamber of Commerce, another Dalmatian businessman, Stipan Ivičević (1801–71), was trying to convince Habsburg elites in Vienna that he had discovered a means to consolidate bureaucratic and commercial interactions between the empire's vast array of different national and linguistic groups, and possibly the whole world. Born in 1801 near the small port of Makarska, about sixty miles north of Dubrovnik, Ivičević—a local community leader, businessman, journalist, and amateur linguist—shared many of Serragli's concerns and convictions about Dalmatia's economic future. Like Serragli, Ivičević felt that Dalmatia's only chance for economic revival was by achieving some degree of free trade. As he succinctly put it in a letter to a friend, "Free trade with Bosnia and a free port (*porto franco*), these are our true resources. Everything else is just smoke without a fire."[24] Dalmatia, in Ivičević's estimation, needed to be transformed into a commercial haven between sea and hinterland, a hub for Mediterranean and Balkan trade. Throughout the 1848–49 revolutions and in the immediate aftermath, Ivičević stuck to a fairly consistent three-point plan for the economic revival of his province, which he outlined as follows: "Dalmatia needs to strive for: 1. Void the cordon against Herzegovina. 2. Free port 3. Political, or at least commercial, union with Bosnia." If he had been at the Dalmatian Chamber of Commerce meeting, he would no doubt have voted in favor of the Algerian solution, hopeful that it would lead to a revival of legal caravan trade with the Ottoman states and the lifting of maritime custom taxes.[25]

But though Ivičević wrote and spoke often about his position on favorable tariff arrangements for Dalmatia, this was not the project he badgered Viennese administrators about on an almost yearly basis. He had much larger projects in mind. His own strategy to center Dalmatia in imperial reform schemes was to create and disseminate his own universal system of written communication, which he called *Pangrafia universale*.[26] Pangrafia was Ivičević's lifelong passion. He began sending out exemplars of its methodology a few months before the 1848–49 revolutions broke out. Upon his death thirty years later, Ivičević was still fine-tuning it. His fixation with Pangrafia was based on what he hoped it could achieve. Overall, Ivičević's universal language system was meant to bridge divides inherent in a multilingual environment, which he believed was a way to resolve not just Dalmatia's woes, but also those of the Habsburg Empire, Europe, and perhaps even the whole world.

Ivičević believed that a universal language system would solve the troubles of his province, his empire, and his continent by ensuring that in multilingual environments—Dalmatia, the Habsburg Empire, Europe, and the world—language speakers closest to the centers of power would not enjoy privileges to the detriment of others. For example, Italian speakers in Dalmatia enjoyed obvious advantages over their Slavic-speaking compatriots, as did German speakers over everyone else in the Habsburg Empire. Ivičević, like the inventor of Esperanto thirty years later, L. L. Zamenhof, considered a universal language system to be the most fruitful means to defuse the conflicts inherent in a multilingual environment.

Ivičević's foundational concerns for Pangrafia centered around his fear of linguistic hegemony and his desire to ensure that nation formation would not translate into nation isolation. He decided that rather than develop a new language that everyone would use to communicate alongside their mother tongues it would be better to develop a formula of translation *between* different languages: a writing system that worked much like a calculator. By simplifying a grammar system and alphabet, Ivičević proposed that people use his translation tables to move between their languages and his Pangrafia, communicating through linguistic conversion and deciphering. With his translation tables at hand, people of all languages could communicate in writing. It would not be necessary for all to adopt one language—not Italian, German, English, French, or even "South Slavic" (what Ivičević termed his own, and most beloved, language group). No single group would have more control or mastery of the language of trade or government. A clear separation would be placed between languages, an *interlingua*, so to speak, allowing communication without assimilation. Ivičević argued that the only means to secure mutually beneficial interactions among Europe's peoples was to filter between languages and national groups. Thinking of his own province, he imagined Slavic speakers no longer limited to manual labor because they were incapable of utilizing the languages of governance. With Pangrafia, speakers of Italian, and German, and Slavic languages would be able to work together without any one group being privileged or disadvantaged. Ivičević identified his new science as a "sign of the Century of Progress, which will dishonor neither Dalmatia nor the entirety of Austria."[27]

Ivičević's formulaic translation scheme did not come with a newly invented vocabulary. Interestingly enough, he chose different languages at different political moments to serve as the base lexicon for his interlingua calculator. Before the 1848–49 revolutions he opted for Italian, explaining that he believed it to be "the easiest and most adaptable language . . . and understood by those who know Latin, the language of science."[28] After the 1848–49 revolutions he opted for German, for reasons he felt no need to explain. When the rulers of the Habsburg Empire showed themselves unwilling to adopt his plan, he solicited Napoleon III and Alexander II, trying French and Russian, respectively.

How would a language like Italian function as a lexicon and not a language? Simply due to the fact that in order for people to communicate between languages, all that was necessary was for them to have at hand a crossover dictionary of their language and Italian. Users of the Pangrafia system just needed to plug Italian words into the simplified Pangrafia grammar and universal communication would ensue. A Russian speaker from the Baltics could negotiate shipping terms with a Greek speaker from the Mediterranean as long as Russian-Italian and Greek-Italian dictionaries were on hand. The only benefit Italian speakers would have in this arrangement was that they would have to look up fewer words—though they would have to be careful to use standardized idioms and not dialects. Everyone would be equally advantaged or disadvantaged by their knowledge of Pangrafia's rules.

The example of Russian and Greek merchants using Pangrafia to write shipping contracts is not haphazard. From the outset, Ivičević envisioned his "new cosmopolitan art" in specifically economic terms.[29] Like any struggling businessman trying to sell his product in an increasingly globalized market, Ivičević was excited most by the commercial possibilities of connecting languages. As followers of Eric Hobsbawm and Ernest Gellner would undoubtedly appreciate, at heart *Pangrafia* was not just the key to how nations could communicate and bureaucracy could function. It also promised to resolve the problem of economic and commercial modernization in an increasingly "nationally" diverse Europe. Ivičević described his universal system as an enormous "factory of language," in which all the standardized languages and dialects of Europe would be compared and combined. Words in these "factories" were just "industrial materials," the primary materials manufactured and transformed through the subfactories of individual languages and then packaged by the superfactory, Pangrafia.[30] In Pangrafia, no local language group would be superior to the other, for, Ivičević announced, "Just as the new metric system equalizes all the measurements of the different countries, so does the system of Pangrafia equalize all of the languages."[31] To detractors who argued that the reinforcement of linguistic diversity was inviting another Tower of Babel, Ivičević responded, "Tower of Babel if you will, but not one of confusion; on the contrary, it is one of reunion."[32]

Union (or reunion, depending on Ivičević's biblical frame of mind) of Europe's increasingly divergent parts was the goal he set for his Pangrafia. And like any amateur scientist, Ivičević composed experiments to prove the validity of his discovery. His guinea pig was the population of Dalmatia itself. Ivičević believed that Dalmatia was the perfect test case for his "new cosmopolitan art" because, within the confines of this small territory, the predominantly undereducated local population were regularly forced to communicate within a linguistic environment in her tangled bureaucracy that comprised German, Italian, and South Slavic languages while also coming into contact with even more languages at her ports and along her caravan trails. Ivičević published the results of three "experiments" he had conducted using Dalmatians as his experimental subjects, confident that Dalmatia's multilingualism was a microcosm that could represent the world of greater Europe.

In the first experiment, Ivičević had a "young and talented" university student from Dalmatia study the Pangrafia system one hour a day for ten days. On the eleventh day, the student was asked "to translate into Italian, his mother tongue, an article written Pangrafically from English, a language he did not know a word of [*di cui egli non conosceva un acca*]!"[33] According to Ivičević, "The translation corresponded very well to the text."[34] The second

test was made on the same student on his eighth day of study, and "he translated very well into German (a language which he learned in school) a text
written Pangrafically from German by someone who did not know how to
properly write in German."[35] In the third case, a high school student trained
in the Pangrafic science "translated well into Italian (his school language) and
Illyrian (his mother tongue) a text written pangrafically from German: a language completely unknown to him." ("Illyrian" was considered a subset of
South Slavic; today it would be recognized as Croatian.)[36]

All three cases proved to Ivičević's satisfaction that language divides within
a multinational province such as Dalmatia (or a multinational empire) could
be avoided: Italian speakers would be able to comprehend English texts useful
in maritime commerce. German speakers—bureaucrats in Vienna—would be
able to comprehend documents written in German by those who did not have
a strong grasp of the language, such as Dalmatia's home-born administrative
clerks. And finally, German-language articles, such as Habsburg laws or military codes, would be intelligible to South Slavic and Italian speakers with no
familiarity with German, a group that included the majority of Dalmatians in
the mid-nineteenth century. "Through Pangrafia," Ivičević explained, "everyone will be able to understand each other, at least in written form." He went
so far as to boast that his "invention is perhaps more important for ideas than
steamships were for objects."[37]

Steamships were not just a metaphor Ivičević employed. The allusion to
steamships made clear that Pangrafia was meant to be as much an instrument
for the economic and administrative consolidation of a diverse conglomera-
tion of lands as a means to tie together overseas communications. The global
aims of Ivičević's project become clear when one analyzes the languages he
incorporated within his system. Though Ivičević's Pangrafia focused mostly
on European languages, including twenty-seven different tongues he believed
represented most of the communication systems of his continent, Ivičević
also included what he termed "Asian" varieties.[38] "Chinese, Persian, Hebrew,
Arabic, Turkish" headed the list of non-European languages that users of his
Pangrafic system could hope to decipher with the help of his interlingua.[39]

The inclusion of Persian, Arabic, and Turkish demonstrates how this
Mediterranean merchant had his eye firmly set on communicating with
markets to the east and south, markets ever more attainable with the expansion of steamship service of Österreichischer Lloyd (founded in 1833) to
ports in the Levant.[40] The presence of Chinese in Ivičević's bag of tricks
reveals, however, that his thinking went beyond the field of likely Dalmatian
or even Habsburg trade, but was also geared to greater European enterprises.
In fact, the English-language experiments made with Dalmatians in his case

studies and his inclusion of Chinese in his Pangrafic system make it clear that Ivičević hoped his "cosmopolitan art" would follow the paths of empires on which the sun never set. He made this point even more explicit in a letter to a friend in which he described his delight at "discovering" Pangrafia and contemplating its promise. Ivičević assured his friend that his new system could be used with great benefit "by the great European family. And then when you think about the Europeans scattered all over the world? . . . The idea is as big, as I am little."[41]

Ivičević was not exaggerating when he called his idea big. In fact, this "little" man tucked away in the study of his little Balkan crown land was trying to unite "the European family" and simultaneously unite European imperial enterprises throughout the world. With Pangrafia, fellow Europeans who spoke different national languages would no longer be forced to assimilate or isolate themselves. Grand European empires would no longer be shaken by the divisions and difficulties of their populations' linguistic diversity. The "Europeans scattered all over the world" would no longer be isolated from the peoples they were trading with, if not outright domineering. *Pangrafia*, the language superfactory, would resolve all of these dilemmas. And all that was needed was for the powers that be to promote its use.

To his considerable dismay, Ivičević's greatest passion resulted in his bitterest disappointment. Time and time again he pleaded with Habsburg elites for financial and institutional backing to launch his program. In the first years of his quest things looked optimistic. In January 1849 Ivičević succeeded in gaining an audience with members of the Academy of Sciences in Vienna, where he petitioned them to consider his Pangrafia as a possible venture for imperial backing. Ivičević explained the glories of his system to a hall of linguists and political scientists. The academy published an official report on Pangrafia indicating that "without a doubt it could offer, for its simplicity and ingenuity, a great medium for facilitating daily written correspondence between nations of different languages," but it refused to sponsor the project, citing the potentially dangerous discrepancies in using dictionaries as handbooks for universal communication.[42]

Though disappointed, Ivičević did not give up. Instead, he turned to the man he considered the true father of all nations, the young Emperor Franz Joseph. In a painfully obsequious letter written "from one Slav to the King of Slavs," Ivičević explained that his Pangrafia would eradicate miscommunication and unite the world in trade-oriented commercial harmony.[43] Now was the opportunity for Austria to lead the way, Ivičević asserted. Now was the time for the greatest Emperor of Europe to unite all Europeans. All Franz Joseph had to do was consent to have Ivičević represent him at the courts of

Europe to get their support as well.[44] Sadly, Franz Joseph never responded. Nor did any of the other crowned heads whom Ivičević contacted, crowned heads to whom he promised the means, through the example of the test cases of his Dalmatian subjects, to "draw closer and unite peoples in brotherly love [*affrattellare*] . . . and give to commerce a powerful means of communication without the wasted time of learning languages."[45] Ivičević, able to look from his office over the port of his sleepy Dalmatian town, believed he had discovered a means to take all of Europe's languages and simultaneously "infuse them together and spread them all out; like the waters into the sea, and from the sea."[46] To Ivičević's chagrin, the powers of Europe seemed blind to the promise of that kind of infusion.

Mid-Nineteenth-Century Dalmatians: Willing Architects for a New Europe

What can we learn from these two cases of mid-nineteenth-century Balkan elites who worked to incorporate their peripheral, impoverished, and powerless crown land into the designs of creating a new Europe or a newly united global Europe? First, they serve as yet another reminder that although these men were geographically and culturally located on the Balkan Peninsula, there was absolutely nothing "balkanized" about their outlooks. These activists both thought big—bigger than nationalism, bigger than Balkan intrigues, and bigger even than the vast Habsburg horizon.[47] They thought European, they thought macro, and they thought European global expansion well before the Suez Canal, the Franco-Prussian War, and the "Scramble for Africa."

Second, their cases show how they identified Europeanization as a promise to extract Dalmatia from the misery of its current subaltern position. If Europe were remade, then Dalmatia would benefit. Conversely, if the problems afflicting Dalmatia were resolved, then this would show Europe a path toward growth. By "Europeanizing" Dalmatia's infrastructures and markets through a neo-European development plan *à l'algérienne*, Austria could claim for itself an expansion of its European centers and another inlet for European wealth. By "Europeanizing" Dalmatia's linguistic divides, Vienna would have a model for resolving its own multinational headache, as would the rest of Europe. In a way, Serragli, Ivičević, and many of their contemporaries attempted to twist the very logic that Maria Todorova has shown damned them in the first place. They would stop being a "Balkan Other" by defining, expanding, and remaking Europe to include them. If they succeeded, they would be a center. If they failed, they would continue to feel as if they were "isolated even more than if they were surrounded by the Great Wall of China," a phrase coined by one of their contemporaries and countrymen, Ivan August Kaznačić, less than twenty years later, to describe what it felt like to live outside of European affairs.[48] As we know, they did fail.

Third, what these two cases show is that Euro-architects even outside the centers of political and financial power believed that the future of Europe lay in imperial consolidation and expansion. Serragli and his Chamber of Commerce voted in favor of Vienna's adopting a new form of imperialism, one that originally arose from the relationship of France with an overseas colony but that, they believed, would suit the Habsburg scene well. Ivičević set his project to resolve problems of the imperial administration as well as to help those "Europeans scattered all over the world." Toward the end of the 1848–49 revolutions, with the word "nation" on everyone's lips, it appears that nineteenth-century Europhiles were also convinced that empire was the path to progress, even at the peripheries. In fact, especially at the peripheries.

Notes

1. The literature on this topic is vast. See, for example, Robert Bartlett, *The Making of Europe: Conquest, Colonization, and Cultural Change, 950–1350* (Princeton, NJ: Princeton University Press, 1993); S. J. Woolf, *Napoleon's Integration of Europe* (London: Routledge, 1991); Anthony Pagden, *The Idea of Europe: From Antiquity to the European Union* (Cambridge: Cambridge University Press, 2002); E. L. Jones, *The European Miracle: Environments, Economies, and Geopolitics in the History of Europe and Asia* (Cambridge: Cambridge University Press, 2003); M. S. Anderson, *The Rise of Modern Diplomacy, 1450–1919* (London: Longman, 1993).

2. On the effectiveness of this Austrian *Zollverein* see David F. Good, *The Economic Rise of the Habsburg Empire* (Berkeley: University of California Press, 1984), chap. 4.

3. Konrad Clewing, *Staatlichkeit und nationale Identitätsbildung* (Munich: R. Oldenbourg Verlag, 2001), gives an excellent analysis of Habsburg containment policies vis-à-vis Dalmatia (18–140).

4. For further discussion of the economic and political situation of Dalmatia in the mid-nineteenth century, see Josip Beroš, "Stav carskog dvora prema sjedinjenu Dalmacije s Hrvatskom," *Historijski pregled* 8, no. 3 (1962): 163–75; Stijepo Obad, "Sukob talijanskih i austrijskih interesa na Jadranu u revoluciji 1848/49. godine," *Pomorski zbornik* 6 (1968): 531–36; Stijepo Obad, "Dalmacija za vrijeme izlaženja Zore Dalmatinske," *Zadarska Smotra* 44, no. 3–4 (1995): 31–38; Nikša

Stančić, *Mihovil Pavlinović i njegov krug do 1869* (Zagreb: Sveučilište u Zagrebu Centar za Povijesne Znanosti, Odjel za Hrvatsku Povijest, 1980).

5. Luigi Serragli, *Sulla Riforma doganale della Dalmazia* (Dubrovnik: Martecchini, 1851), 26. According to Serragli, "Delegates from [all of the provinces'] Chambers of Commerce, and from the agronomy societies" attended the meeting (3).

6. Maria Todorova, *Imagining the Balkans* (New York: Oxford University Press, 1997); Larry Wolff, *Venice and the Slavs* (Stanford, CA: Stanford University Press, 2001).

7. Hypolite Passy, "Rapport de la commission du budget du ministère de la guerre," *Moniteur universel,* April 10, 1834.

8. Alfred W. Crosby, *Ecological Imperialism: The Biological Expansion of Europe, 900–1900* (Cambridge: Cambridge University Press, 2004).

9. For a telling sign of how "peculiar and impoverished" Habsburg officials found Dalmatia upon initially visiting it during its first years as part of the empire, see Franz Graf Hohenwart's letter to Metternich of July 7, 1829, quoted in Clewing, *Staatlichkeit,* 62.

10. "Note de la Chambre de Commerce d'Alger en réponse au discours de M. Passy sur les dépenses de l'occupation d'Afrique, adressée aux Chambres législatives," *Moniteur universel,* May 9, 1834, cited in Jennifer Elson Sessions, "Making Colonial France: Culture, National Identity and the Colonization of Algeria, 1830–1851" (PhD diss., University of Pennsylvania, 2005), 47.

11. On the ubiquity of reports of the brutality and cost in manpower to subdue Algeria see ibid.

12. On *colons* in Dalmatia, see *Enciklopedija hrvatske povijesti i kulture* (Zagreb: Školska Knjiga, 1980), s.v. "Kolonat." On the whole, agricultural relations depended on how long the land had been held under the Venetian Republic before 1797. The *vecchio acquisto* (old acquisition) territories situated closer to the coast generally followed the *colon* (sharecropper) system predominant throughout most of the Mediterranean. The *nuovo* and *nuovissimo acquisti* (new and newest acquisitions), meanwhile, were organized either as feudal lands gifted to successful military generals or formed along the same lines as the Habsburg Empire's military border zone: in exchange for protecting against Ottoman incursions, armed families lived outside the jurisdiction of the state. Clearly, areas around Dubrovnik had their own history of agricultural relations. For an interesting discussion of Dubrovnik's commercial and agricultural position in the Early Modern Period see, for example, Francis W. Carter, *Dubrovnik (Ragusa): A Classic City-State* (London: Seminar Press, 1972), and his other works.

13. For more information on England's reciprocal treaty with Portugal, see Paul Duguid, "The Making of Methuen: The Commercial Treaty in the English Imagination," *Historia* 3, no. 4 (2003): 9–36.

14. For a concise general history of Algeria's incorporation as a French *département*, see John Ruedy, *Modern Algeria: The Origins and Development of a Nation* (Bloomington: Indiana University Press, 2005).

15. Per the agreement, export duties of any French goods into Algeria were abolished; free entrance of "a certain number" of Algerian "natural products" into France was allowed; and foreign products imported into Algeria needed to pay the same duties as if they had been imported into France via the Mediterranean ports (some exceptions to this rule existed for construction materials and products necessary for vegetable and animal reproduction, which were allowed to enter Algeria free of duties). For more information on the 1851 French-Algerian reciprocal tariff agreement, see Arthur Girault, *The Colonial Tariff Policy of France* (Oxford: Clarendon Press, 1916), 55–65.

16. André Cochut, "De la colonisation de l'Algérie: Plan et budget d'exploitation," *Revue des deux mondes* 10, no. 5 (1847): 252.

17. Louis-Francois L'Héritier de l'Ain, "Importance de l'Algérie sous le rapport de ses produits agricoles," *L'Afrique française* 1 (July 1837), cited in Sessions, "Making Colonial France," 128.

18. Serragli, *Riforma doganale*, 26.

19. Ibid., 29.

20. Serragli discusses the importance of "attracting capital investment" throughout the pamphlet, but see especially ibid., 24.

21. Cochut, "De la colonisation," 252.

22. In a very crude sense, the difference between imperialism and colonialism is usually defined with reference to Edward Said's generalization that "'imperialism' means the practice, the theory, and the attitudes of a dominating metropolitan center ruling a distant territory; 'colonialism,' which is almost always a consequence of imperialism, is the implanting of settlements on distant territory." Edward W. Said, *Culture and Imperialism* (New York: Knopf, 1993), 9.

23. For a fascinating discussion on how the "development" imperial model of mid-twentieth-century British, French, and Belgian imperialism was used by African elites as a means to demand more aid and sovereignty, if not out and out equality, see Frederick Cooper, *Africa Since 1940: The Past of the Present* (Cambridge: Cambridge University Press, 2002), 39–65.

24. Stipan Ivičević to Luigi Pavissich, April 25, 1848, in *Memorie macarensi*, ed. L. C. Pavissich (Trieste: E. Sambo & Co., 1897).

25. Stipan Ivičević to Luigi Pavissich, April 4, 1848, in Pavissich, *Memorie macarensi*. To this end, Ivičević, along with the lawyer Božidar Petranović and Ante Kuzmanić, the editor of *Zora dalmatinska*, tried to found a Dalmatian-Bosnian newspaper. Stipan Ivičević to Luigi Pavissich, May 9, 1848, in Pavissich,

Memorie macarensi; Stipan Ivičević to Luigi Pavissich, May 17, 1848, in Pavissich, *Memorie macarensi*. Ivičević also sought to convince Habsburg authorities to set up a railroad line that connected Dalmatia directly to Mostar, Sarajevo, and Belgrade. Stipan Ivičević to Luigi Pavissich, April 4, 1848, in Pavissich, *Memorie macarensi*.

26. Ivičević first described his "Pangrafia" in an 1847 letter to his friend Niccolò Tommaseo, stating that after having read and reread chapters 3 and 4 of Tommaseo's *Nuova proposta*, "by chance, some sparks [*scintilla*] came to my mind; then a ray; then a light; and I think that I have devised a System for Universal Writing that is both very easy and very reasonable [*soddisfacente*]; —not numerical, but legible like any other language." Stipan Ivičević to Niccolò Tommaseo, November 29, 1847, in Tommaseo Carteggi 92.72.11, Florence National Library. For more information on Ivičević's discovery and how it was related to the nationality question in Dalmatia before and immediately after the 1848–49 revolutions, see Dominique Kirchner Reill, *Nationalists Who Feared the Nation: Adriatic Multinationalism in Habsburg Dalmatia, Trieste, and Venice* (Stanford, CA: Stanford University Press, 2012). For a fascinating discussion of the many different forms that Dalmatian national identity could take within the autonomous movement see Josip Vrandečić, *Dalmatinski autonomistički pokret u XIX. stoljeću* (Zagreb: Dom i Svijet, 2002).

27. Stipan Ivičević to Antonio Augustino Grubissich, forwarded to Niccolò Tommaseo, November 29, 1847, in Tommaseo Carteggi 92.72.10, Florence National Library.

28. Stipan Ivičević to Niccolò Tommaseo, January 6, 1846, in Tommaseo Carteggi 92.72.7, Florence National Library.

29. Stipan Ivičević, "Pangrafia (1848)," in Pavissich, *Memorie macarensi*.

30. Stipan Ivičević to Antonio Augustino Grubissich, forwarded to Niccolò Tommaseo, November 29, 1847.

31. Ibid.

32. Ibid.

33. Stipan Ivičević, "Programma su un nuovo metodo di Pangrafia," *L'Avvenire di Ragusa* 1, no. 1 (1848).

34. Ibid.

35. Ibid.

36. Ibid.

37. Ibid.

38. Ivičević resolved the question of which dialects and languages to include with his typical pragmatism. The fourteen living languages he incorporated into his *Pangrafia* he defined as "the languages of State in Europe, which is enough

for my Chart." A comparison of how he dealt with the languages of Holland and Prussia exemplifies how he selected his "languages of State." The Prussian dialect was not included because the Prussian government used standardized German in its official missives. Holland, on the other hand, used its local Germanic dialect in laws and documents, so it was included. Pangrafia was thus an expression of the political realities of administration as much as of communication. And the presence of Illyrian and Polish—two languages that in 1847 were not official languages of state—made clear the future Ivičević envisioned for these regions. Stipan Ivičević to Antonio Augustino Grubissich, forwarded to Niccolò Tommaseo, November 29, 1847.

39. Stipan Ivičević, "Pangrafia: Introduzione," Spisi Obitelji—Stijepan Ivičević kut 2; V. Linguistika, Državni Arhiv u Zagrebu.

40. For a discussion of the expansion of the Österreichischer Lloyd line and its role in recasting the Habsburg Empire as a maritime empire, see Alison Frank, "The Children of the Desert and the Laws of the Sea: Austria, Great Britain, the Ottoman Empire, and the Mediterranean Slave Trade in the Nineteenth Century," *American Historical Review* 117, no. 2 (June 2012): 410–44; Alison Frank, "Continental and Maritime Empires in an Age of Global Commerce," *East European Politics and Societies* 25, no. 4 (November 2011): 779–84. See also Alison Frank, *Invisible Empire: A New Global History of Austria* (forthcoming).

41. Stipan Ivičević to Antonio Augustino Grubissich, forwarded to Niccolò Tommaseo, November 29, 1847.

42. Stipan Ivičević to Luigi Pavissich, February 2, 1849, in Pavissich, *Memorie macarensi*; Ivičević, "Revista del mio Sistema pangrafico del 1848," Spisi Obitelji—Stijepan Ivičević 802-II, Državni Arhiv u Zagrebu; Stipan Ivičević to Emperor Franz Joseph, March 16, 1849, Spisi Obitelji—Stijepan Ivičević 802-I-1-4, Državni Arhiv u Zagrebu.

43. Stipan Ivičević to Emperor Franz Joseph, March 16, 1849.

44. Ibid.

45. Stipan Ivičević to Niccolò Tommaseo, November 29, 1847.

46. Stipan Ivičević to Antonio Augustino Grubissich, forwarded to Niccolò Tommaseo, November 29, 1847.

47. Serragli would later be associated with the Italy-oriented Irredentist camp and Ivičević would associate himself with the proto-Yugoslav movement.

48 Ivan August Kaznačić to A. Kaznačić, September 8, 1869, RO-170/7: CXCIII/78, Državni Arhiv u Dubrovniku.

CHAPTER TWO

THE HOMELAND AS TERRA INCOGNITA

Geography and Bulgarian National Identity, 1830s–1870s

Dessislava Lilova

The key role of geography as an instrument for national identity formation is one of the specific characteristics of Bulgaria in the nineteenth century. Geography was given a prominent place in the curriculum as soon as
a Bulgarian secular education system was established. The first textbook on
the subject was published in 1835. By the end of Ottoman rule, in 1878, the
total number of geography textbooks for Bulgarian primary and high schools
had reached 38 (54 if reprints are counted). In terms of the number of textbooks, geography was second only to Bulgarian language—69 primers (or a
total of 107 with reprints)—and almost on a par with religion (31 textbooks,
or a total of 58 with reprints). Considering that the Orthodox Christian religion and the Bulgarian language were the two unquestionable pillars of the
emerging national identity, the fact that geography had an equal place in the
curriculum with those two subjects is indicative of its importance in shaping
a sense of national belonging. History was a significantly less developed discipline than geography. The educational system functioned without a textbook
on the subject until 1844, and even after that the number of Bulgarian history
textbooks (10; 16 with reprints) remained modest.

The priority of geography over history was an exception to the norm followed by European educational systems in this period. In Europe, geography
was regarded as an auxiliary discipline and usually was taught as part of other

compulsory subjects. For example, the pedagogical concept of Jesuit colleges was that history could not be understood without some geography, while geography could not be understood without some cosmography.[1] In France in the era of the revolution, geography became an elective subject that could be taught by the teachers of natural history or ancient languages, or by the librarian.[2] Still, geography was most often taught as part of history courses.[3] This was true even for the German *Realgymnasien*—secondary schools that focused on modern languages and the natural sciences—although their curricula included more classes in geography than those at the *humanistische Gymnasien*.[4] The most popular definition of geography was that along with chronology, it was "one of the two eyes of history," which explains why, during the first half of the nineteenth century, the most commonly used cartographic genre in the educational systems in France, Britain, and Germany was the historical atlas.[5] The main function of geography was to illustrate the "scenery" of antiquity.[6] The situation changed only after the 1870s, when geography gradually became an autonomous discipline. A number of European universities founded departments specialized in training teachers for schools, thereby transforming not just the status of geography in the educational system but also its ideological functions. Geography became a primary resource for the homogenization of collective imagination and for national identity formation. In the Bulgarian context this resource was mobilized rather earlier than elsewhere in Europe. In this chapter I discuss the possible reasons for this anticipatory development in Bulgaria, unusual for a small, peripheral culture.

I also analyze the persistent construction of the Bulgarian-populated lands as a "terra incognita"—a perception that seems to have remained unchanged despite the active use of geography as a nation-building instrument. Liuben Karavelov, one of the most influential leaders of the national movement, gave a glimpse of how Bulgarian intellectuals viewed their homeland in the 1870s when he wrote: "Although a number of [notes on] travels across Bulgaria, across Thrace and across Macedonia have been published in different languages in the last ten years, these lands still remain a terra incognita both for us and for the Europeans."[7] Prima facie, this conclusion is banal, since geographical knowledge about the Balkans was indeed incomplete in the mid-nineteenth century. As an ideological viewpoint, however, such a declaration is unorthodox, since it is founded on a coincidence between an internal and an external perspective on terra incognita. As a rule, those two perspectives are incompatible. As Graham Burnett shows, the very notion of terra incognita is a product of the European colonial imagination.[8] It originated as a blank spot on the map, which had to be visited, explored, named, measured, and mapped in order to become part of the known territory of an empire. Of course, the local population did not know that it inhabited an unknown land. It lived in a conglomerate of small worlds known in intimate detail. Integrating those local worlds into a large, common homeland is a key aspect of every national project. Shared cultural codes, sacred themes, or historical events are usually mobilized to this end. But Liuben Karavelov did something different. He constructed the local Bulgarian population as a collective "us" and, in speaking in its name, declared the native land to be a terra incognita. I will try to rationalize the genealogy of this vision, the reasons for its high popularity, and the results of its active ideological use.

"We Are but of Yesterday, Yet We Are Many": Geography versus History

As Maria Todorova notes, the Bulgarian national movement emerged relatively late in comparison to its Balkan neighbors, and consequently developed its strategies as a reaction to the already established projects of its Balkan neighbors.[9] Until the end of the era of Ottoman rule its efforts were focused primarily on emancipation from the powerful influence of Greek culture and nationalism. Bulgarian territorial identity was constructed with a view to making it as competitive as possible with the imagined geographies of Greek nationalism (in other words, the territories and geographies that Greek and Bulgarian nationalists envisioned for themselves overlapped). The emerging notion of the homeland became directly dependent upon the achievement of this important goal.

Robert Shannon Peckam defines the ideological foundation of the Greek territorial model as a process of "naturalizing" history.[10] According to this logic, the historical past creates the national space's integrity, which in turn guarantees the continuity of national history. In the nineteenth century, this reciprocal determinism was a *locus communis*, a common point of reference, in the imagination of the European elites, so its early and highly productive transfer into Greek culture is explicable. In the Bulgarian context, though, the concept of historical territorial right was met with resistance. Until the end of the Ottoman period it was subjected to systematic attacks and qualified as a "childish, idiotic and ridiculous" view.[11] Moreover, the Bulgarian political elite openly declared their refusal to lay claim to the boundaries of medieval Bulgaria, even though in some periods these encompassed a large part of the territory of the Balkan Peninsula. What blocked the temptation, so emblematic of Balkan nationalisms outside Bulgaria, to speculate with "historical boundaries"?

The answer lies in a specific aspect of Bulgarian history: the absence of autochthonous ancestors. The inhabitants of Bulgaria, the Slavs and the Bulgars, were not indigenous tribes; they migrated to the Balkans from their distant homelands. This peculiarity of origin is so common in the histories of various nations that it tends to be banal. In the Bulgarian case, it had acquired special meaning solely because of the conflict with the Greeks, who claimed that they had been inhabiting the Balkan lands ever since the era of Homer.

Initially, the Bulgarian elite harbored some hope that their nation's disadvantage in this conflict with Greek nationalists could be overcome by proving that its ancestors were already living in the Balkans in antiquity but were known under other names, such as Illyrians, Thracians, or Scythians.[12] The problem was that none of those versions was supported by European learning and therefore could not be used as a political argument in their territorial dispute. Thus the project of seeking ancestors in antiquity was abandoned by almost all members of the Bulgarian intelligentsia in the mid-nineteenth century. This idea continued to be supported fervently only by Georgi Rakovski, according to whom the Bulgarians were descendants of the first Aryan tribe, which had migrated from India to Europe in times immemorial. The outstanding, eccentric figure of Rakovski later acquired cult status in the national pantheon and began to be perceived as representative of the era of the Bulgarian Revival. In reality, however, his contemporaries scornfully defined his historical concepts as "old woman's tales," "a Gypsy bag," and a combined recipe for "how to plant cucumbers" and "how to make shoe polish."[13] Three reviews of Rakovski's book about the history and origin of the Bulgarians, *Nekoliko rechi o Asenyo Pŭrvomu* (A Few Words about Asen the First), that were published in 1860 were all negative. The principal criticisms of the work were that the author fantasized, disregarded of the authority of European learning, and emulated the Greek mania for historical greatness. One critic wrote: "He is so obsessed, we think, with Bulgarianness; would not this make us fall into that folly and obduracy of the Greeks who dream of swallowing up everything that exists in the world and making it out to be theirs alone? Let us be grateful only for what is ours and study it purely and well; it would be enough, we think, to elevate us and make the other peoples respect us."[14]

The anonymous reviewer's modesty is misleading. The Bulgarians indeed gave up the idea of competing with the Greeks in terms of their ancient origins, but they did not renounce their national aspirations. They simply sought to impose new rules for determining the political value of symbolic capital. In this respect, the most important task was to revoke the classical principle whereby historical heritage brought territorial dividends. This was claimed to be a retrograde, elitist, and conservative norm that had lost its validity and needed to be replaced with a demographic criterion. The principle of statistical majority was of key importance for the Bulgarian interests because its use was based on the concept that territory belonged not to its ancient past but to its present population. This changed the definition of political capital, and the new formula was crystallized with utmost clarity in the leitmotiv of Bulgarian propaganda that "we are but of yesterday, yet we are many":

> We are but of yesterday, we too can tell the Greek writers and journalists, as Tertullian told the pagans a thousand and six hundred years ago; we are but of yesterday in comparison with your praiseworthy national antiquity, and yet we have filled the cities, the villages, and even the huts both on this and on the other side of the Balkan Range. We are but of yesterday, and yet Bulgarian sweat is flowing and the Bulgarian plow is being used not only in the old lower Moesia: Bulgaria, but also in the fatherland of the sweet-voiced Orpheus: Thrace, as well as in the fatherland of the great philosopher Aristotle and of the great conqueror Alexander: Macedonia. We are but of yesterday, and so is our language in comparison with yours, whose beauty we do not want to question; and yet our language is being spoken both on the Balkan Range and along the Danube as well as along the Vardar and the Maritsa.[15]

Although it was made under pressure from concrete circumstances, the Bulgarian choice of demography as a strategic resource proved to be a proactive political move. The principle of ethnic majority gradually became a dominant factor in Balkan territorial disputes. By the last quarter of the nineteenth century, the Balkan national elites had become so obsessed with producing statistical data that Western observers started speaking of an epidemic of "morbus ethnographicus" in the region.[16] In the Bulgarian context the symptoms of this specific malaise of modernity appeared much earlier. Demography was turned into national capital as early as the mid-nineteenth century and therefore the notion of the nation as a statistical quantity was integrated into the normative core of national identity that was being shaped at the time. The unusual "immunity" to the conservative romanticism of historical geography was perhaps the most visible result, for it had direct political realization. But the rational pragmatism with which Bulgarian identity was constructed also had other consequences—less visible, but just as fundamental.

"Quantification" of Imagination:
The Nation as a Mathematical Quantity

The belief that symbolic capital was quantifiable acquired special importance. Geography proved to be an extremely productive instrument in this respect. In the first half of the nineteenth century geography was not yet an independent scientific field and dealt with positivistic systematization of knowledge about the earth, from the solar system to the atmosphere, waters, and lands of the planet to the composition and structure of the plant, animal, and human worlds. Unlike history, which was elitist and selective, geography was compilatory and encyclopedic; its practitioners were interested in all sorts of taxonomies and tried to make them as exhaustive as possible.

It was a discipline that counted, measured, and classified everything. Its taxonomic passion was a product of modernity's belief that the world is comprehensible and therefore governable because all its elements can be ordered within an appropriate scheme. This logic reduced the nation to a definite statistical number calculated by means of a mechanical procedure. The ideological projection of this number was a homogeneous community with a normative identity, such as did not exist in reality. But as Eric J. Hobsbawm explains, the census procedure itself encouraged the emergence of such a community, because it "*forced* everyone to choose not only a nationality, but a linguistic nationality."[17]

This process was usually activated by the state administration, which needed statistical data in order to adequately govern its territory. What is specific to the Bulgarian case is that nationalists tried to activate this technology of modernity on their own initiative and without state intervention. The Ottoman registers could not be used to this end: They listed population by religion and did not distinguish Bulgarians from other Orthodox Christians who were under the sultan's rule. The Balkan linguistic communities became visible only after attracting the ethnographic gaze of travelers who noticed them more out of taxonomic than out of ideological interest. It was precisely this corpus of unofficial statistical data that was instrumentalized in the Bulgarian context: Geography textbooks gave it a normative status, while newspapers and journals popularized it and motivated the collective imagination to discover the nation as a mathematical quantity.

Newspapers from the period were full of all sorts of statistical data that asserted the quantifiable form as a priority dimension of identity. Everything was calculated mathematically, both the negative and the positive aspects of the nascent imagined community. Sometimes, for example, the calculation showed that the Bulgarians did not have a feeling of a collective cause because "there is just one newspaper per two and a half million people but we still hate having to spend money on its publication."[18] In other cases the opposite seemed to be true, for according to the proportion of the population that were pupils, the inconspicuous and "tiny town of Drianovo surpasses any European land," according to amateur statistics provided by a local teacher.[19] Either way, however, statistics became the preferred form of representing the nation, and perhaps the most compelling evidence of the depth of this process is to be found in local geographical descriptions. Their appearance was the product of a large-scale campaign in the press for describing the Bulgarian-populated lands, in which dozens of authors took part, most of them anonymous.[20] They didn't extol the beautiful scenery of their small homeland in order to represent it to their fellow readers. Instead they shared local statistics: the ethnic composition of the local population, the economy of the town or village, and above all the exact number of churches, schools, pupils, teachers, reading rooms (*chitalishta*), and newspaper subscribers. Thus, the "quantification" of the local picture turned out to be the most appropriate way to integrate it into the panoramic image of the nation that became normative in the collective imagination.

It is also telling that the nation itself was projected as part of European civilization through a "numerical code" that lent ideological meanings to the quantifiable dimensions of identity. Both the scientific essence of this logic and its uses for the sake of the national project are especially evident in mathematical problems solved with the help of a globe. They are to be found in every nineteenth-century textbook on geography. Although their educational purpose was to cultivate a scientific notion of the earth, their solutions produced an ideological side effect. The basic rule of mathematical geography was that the properties of every destination were calculable. This meant that to enter into the frame of this vision, one simply needed to be located somewhere: on a particular parallel or meridian, below the zenith or nadir of the sun, in a random place with an antipode, and so on. Furthermore, solving these textbook-posed mathematical geography problems put an equal-sign between seemingly incompatible destinations, such as western Europe and northeastern Asia, Nuremberg and the Caribbean, the Hawaiian Islands and the Novaya Zemlya archipelago.[21] Although such an equation would be considered invalid in any other context, in mathematical geography it is the correct answer: for example, because at 6:00 p.m. on August 16 the sun is at its zenith in both places indicated in the problem description. In itself, this logic is neutral in content, but it possessed an ideological potential because it represented the principle of universal equality as a quantifiably provable natural law. For the Bulgarian intelligentsia, the existence of such a universal "zero point" of all identities was a strategic discovery because it eliminated, with the help of scientific arguments, the very grounds of national inferiority.

The opening paragraph of the first Bulgarian textbook on geography is symptomatic of the way this resource was used. It begins with the sentence "The Earth makes one complete rotation with respect to the sun in twenty-four hours—from which follows that when it is night for the Americans, it is day for us Europeans."[22] This statement presents a basic astronomical fact and, in this sense, it is banal. As an ideological message, however, whereby the Bulgarians are included among Europeans, it is experimental and even scandalous because the normative phrase in Bulgarian at that time was not "us Europeans." It was assumed that the right to speak in the name of Europe belonged to the leaders of progress, and the Bulgarian entry into modernity was yet to come. As one can see, mathematical geography defied this norm. Drawing on its scientific authority, mathematical geography articulated the collective European "we" not as a utopia and not even as a project, but as an elementary mode of Bulgarian identity.

This imagined geography is mapped out in Khristo Danov's atlas of 1866. It includes a map titled "A Comparison between the Major Rivers and Mountains on Earth," which is a revised version of an original map by the German geographer Johann Georg August Galletti.[23] The first change concerns the list of sixty-five mountain peaks in Europe. Whereas in Galletti's original map just three mountains in the Balkans are named, in Danov's revised version there are twenty among the sixty-five.[24] Thus, seventeen mountains in western Europe have been replaced with Balkan mountains. Furthermore, most of them are in the Bulgarian-populated lands: For example, Pirin and Rila replace Rossberg and Brenner in the Alps, Vitosha replaces Sulitjelma in Norway, and Tsarichina replaces Arbizon in France.[25] All the added peaks are situated in the lower half of the map, which shows low mountains, and that is why they do not create the impression that the Balkan Peninsula towers over the rest of Europe. Still, in comparison with the original map, the region is assigned a disproportionate presence that contains almost one-third of all mountain peaks in Europe.

The changes in the ten cities shown on the map in order to illustrate the altitude of the European settlement network are even more drastic. To this end, Galletti's original atlas uses only cities from the Austro-Hungarian Empire, while Danov's revised version uses only cities in the Bulgarian-populated lands of the Ottoman Empire: Gabrovo, Kotel, Okhrid, Plovdiv,

Sofia, Tŭrnovo, Shumen, Adrianople, Thessaloniki, and Constantinople. The smallest one among them is Kotel. Although it is a village rather than a town, it appears at the center of the map simply because it is located at the highest altitude. In the world of physico-mathematical geography this is an entirely legitimate reason, since every locale has an altitude that is measurable and mappable. In a sense, one may say that Danov's atlas tested the limits of the transformation of this politically indifferent logic into an imagined geography of the Bulgarian national project. The result was the emergence of a vision that transformed the otherwise invisible Bulgarian world into a representative part of the map of Europe.

The Shifting Boundaries of the Homeland: The Absence of a "Logo" Map

A Given the Bulgarian background, the question inevitably arises as to why the geographical imagination of Bulgarian nationalism did not use its main resource, demographic statistics, in the production of maps. Although one would expect ethnographic maps to play a key role in the visual propaganda of the notion of a national homeland, in fact a completely different cartographic model was used for this purpose. It was borrowed from the specific representation of the Ottoman Empire in Western geography, which combined political and historical elements. In practice, this means that European Turkey is represented with its actual political boundaries; its territory, however, is depicted as divided not into its then-current administrative units but into historical regions. The latter are marked with their ancient and medieval names, but their territories do not reflect a particular period; they randomly mix various layers of the historical past. That is why the regions' boundaries are provisional.

A typical example of this muddiness is provided by Bulgaria, Thrace, and Macedonia, the three regions associated with the idea of a Bulgarian homeland. Two of them, Thrace and Macedonia, had the status of provinces in both the Roman and Byzantine Empires, but their boundaries were repeatedly altered over the centuries.[26] Similarly, the lands between the Danube and the Balkan Range, designated as "Bulgaria" on European maps, were completely or partially within the domains of the medieval Bulgarian kingdom, which periodically expanded and contracted, was conquered and restored. The nineteenth-century maps, however, represent this dynamic of the territorial distribution of the Balkan lands as a synchronous snapshot made up of random fragments of the historical past, which in turn are superimposed on administrative boundaries of the Ottoman Empire.

This became the conventional representation, and the triad "Bulgaria, Thrace, and Macedonia" was eventually adopted as the geographical name of the homeland. However, only the place names were standardized; the lands they designated were treated as a territory with unclear outlines and shifting boundaries. Thus, Bulgaria didn't have a clear, easily recognizable shape. It is telling, for instance, that those regions are represented in geography textbooks from the period only by means of a list or short description of the major cities, thus giving the reader only an approximate idea of the location of the respective lands. And even those relative coordinates vary, as each textbook contains a different list of cities. The same effect is produced by geographical maps, as the boundaries of the regions on them have nothing to do with reality and reflect the cartographers' decisions. The result is that the borders of Bulgaria, Thrace, and Macedonia are inconsistently shown on the maps produced in that period.[27]

One may even say that maps had a weaker ideological effect than textbooks because they suffered from a serious structural deficiency: the absence of visual signals indicating that Bulgaria, Thrace, and Macedonia were more important than the other regions. In this respect the message of the textbooks is very clear, since the descriptions of the regions of key importance for Bulgarian identity are significantly longer than the text devoted to the rest of European Turkey. In the cartographic representation there is no such imbalance. Furthermore, there is nothing to suggest that Bulgaria, Thrace, and Macedonia constitute one continuous entity. The territory of the sacred triad is not colored, shaded, or delineated in any way. There is nothing to distinguish it from the surrounding territory so as to motivate its perception as an autonomous country with a specific shape.

Of course, it does not follow from this that the geographical maps published before 1878 did not serve the purposes of the national project. It was entirely possible to find the imagined homeland on them, provided that the observer's gaze was informed or educationally prepared in advance. The problem was, rather, that in this shape, the maps could not be used as a "logo" of the national territory, as Benedict Anderson puts it.[28] They lack the contrasting, instantly recognizable, graphic silhouette with which nations identify the image of their homeland and which lend it an emblematic status because the nation's citizens have become accustomed to seeing the geographical shape reproduced in all sorts of contexts: on "posters, official seals, letterheads, magazine and textbook covers, tablecloths, and hotel walls."[29]

In principle, every territory can be turned into a cartographic emblem, provided that it has fixed boundaries. But there were two reasons why establishing fixed boundaries proved to be an insurmountable obstacle for early Bulgarian nationalism. First, the standard maps of the period represented Bulgaria, Thrace, and Macedonia as historically formed regions, while the national elite treated them as territories formed on a demographic basis. Hence, the Bulgarian intelligentsia needed maps where the boundaries depended not on history but on the ethnic composition of the local population. At the same time, however—and this was the second reason for the absence of a geographical "logo"—the Bulgarian intelligentsia refused to use ethnographic maps made by foreigners. In fact, several ethnographic maps of the Balkans had already been published in western Europe in the first half of the nineteenth century and the distribution of the Balkan lands on most of them seemed favorable for the Bulgarian national interests.[30] Those maps were known to Bulgarian intellectuals, they were cited in support of the national cause when necessary, but not one of them was reprinted.

The refusal to use them was explained for the first time by Liuben Karavelov in his article "Zapiski za Bŭlgaria i za bŭlgarite" (Notes on Bulgaria and the Bulgarians).[31] It was first published in Russian in 1867, in the Moscow-based magazine *Russkiĭ vestnik* (Russian Herald), but the author obviously considered the issues raised in it to be of paramount importance, for in 1874 he translated the article into Bulgarian and published it without any changes in his own newspaper, *Nezavisimost* (Independence). In the article Karavelov claims that the available ethnographic studies are useless because they do not represent reality correctly and, as a rule, are detrimental to Bulgarian national interests. According to Karavelov, their flaws come from the fact that they were written by foreign travelers who do not know the region, do not speak the local languages, and are therefore easily deluded. By this logic, the only way a truthful geographical description could be produced was if Bulgarians themselves would assume the role of travelers and discover the unknown lands they inhabited. Otherwise the homeland will remain a terra incognita as much for the inhabitants as for foreigners, Karavelov concludes. And to demonstrate how a terra incognita is discovered in practice, after the theoretical introduction in his article he offers an extensive travel account.

In 1877, ten years after this article was first published, the Russo-Turkish War broke out. It led to the emergence of a sovereign Bulgarian state, and the ethnographic maps of the Balkans produced by European geographers played a key role in the talks that determined the state's borders. Until 1878, Bulgarian geographers ultimately failed to produce the country's own alternative map, and from this perspective, its strategy may be defined as a political failure. But the ten years in which the Bulgarians tried to discover their own homeland left long-lasting traces in the collective imagination. Their main result was to provide ideological resources for two contrasting but equally powerful projections of Bulgarian identity: the sense of belonging simultaneously to the power center of Europe and to the savage periphery of the civilized world.

The Discovery of Terra Incognita as a Project for Its Emancipation

What changed in this period was above all the ideological framework of the discipline of geography. It began to be perceived not as universal knowledge used for local needs but as a resource of power whose exercise had to be controlled. Or, as Petko Slaveikov explained to his readers, "Every foreigner seeks and makes notes in his studies of our countries with an aim that is different from our desires and aspirations: with a view to the interests of his fatherland."[32] In this respect he agreed completely with Liuben Karavelov and actively appealed for a native geographical production, necessary "not just for the unconditional purpose of science but also for the particular—for the moral and objective interests of the Bulgarian and his neighbor-tribes."[33]

The project for the emancipation of Bulgarian geography quickly received consensual support and was set in motion in the late 1860s and early 1870s. Almost thirty geography textbooks were published at that time, but all of them were translated from foreign originals and the development of the discipline was considered to be unsatisfactory. In 1872 the magazine *Chitalishte* (Reading Room) announced a competition for a new textbook on the physical geography of European Turkey with the explicit requirement that it had to be written by a Bulgarian.[34] The method and outcomes of geography teaching began to be treated as an issue of primary public interest. It is telling that the first question that members of the political elite asked pupils upon inspections in schools was from the sphere not of history but of geography: "How many provinces does European Turkey have?"[35] Geography teaching methods were also discussed in the press, and it was recommended that they be guided by the principle of starting from the local in order to understand the universal. Or, as a report from Thessaloniki notes with concern, "It would be regrettable if children knew how many lakes there are in Africa but didn't know the bog in Skopje or the lake in Doïran."[36] Reflecting upon the same topic, another anonymous writer concludes with alarm: "We know nothing about all this and if we do know something, we have learned it from the foreigners who know us much better than we know ourselves and who have successfully set out to take advantage of their knowledge!"[37]

Meanwhile, the Bulgarian press launched a campaign for local geographical descriptions. Already at the end of 1869, the newspaper *Makedonia* published an appeal for a nationwide compilation of a geographical dictionary of the Bulgarian-populated lands.[38] Readers were asked to describe their place of birth and send the descriptions to the newspaper; the collection was to be edited and published as an encyclopedia. The idea was met with enthusiasm and all leading print media joined in the campaign. They published instructions designed to standardize the future descriptions and constantly urged readers to contribute their own. The campaign was very emotional because, as a writer in the magazine *Letostruy* (The Flow of Years) exclaims, the alternative was "to wait for L'Zhan, Tsiprian and who knows who else to come from across the world in order to count us like sheep!"[39]

The mass use of a rhetoric that represents the Bulgarians as a herd, as a passive collective with no identity, is a distinctive feature of the campaign for local descriptions. What is distinctive in this case is that the very statistical dimension of the nation usually obscures this imagery as it implies a massive, objective presence that cannot remain invisible or be ignored. The project for the emancipation of Bulgarian geography shows, however, that by the 1870s this ideological effect was already considered to be insufficient. Both the ethnic statistics and the respective distribution of the Balkan lands continued to be important, and they determined the political priority of the geographical project. But the "numerical code" of identity was placed in a new ideological regime which was designed to increase the production of symbolic capital. Thus, the local descriptions of personal small homelands were actually embedded within the matrix of the geographical exploration of unknown lands.

The images of the mythical terræ incognitæ and their discoverers have a key place in the imagination of modernity as a triumphant symbol of will, enterprise, and ingenuity, the basic parameters through which Europe measured the difference between its civilization and the rest of the world in the colonial era. Bulgarian ideologues sought to ensure that their nation would likewise live up to those norms, and the motives for their ambition are explicable. It is more difficult to rationalize the technology of their project, which transformed the solitary European traveler into a collective of millions of local discoverers. Here is how this transformation was envisioned by one of the most active advocates of the campaign for local descriptions, the editor of the magazine *Chitalishte*, Stefan Bobchev:

It is a big shame on us that so far we have not taken the trouble to collect at least the available geographical data and to publish something like a national geography. We are not like the foreigners who have specialized associations that deliberately send people to explore different lands. We do not have— nor could we expect to have anytime soon—financial resources that could support specially appointed explorers and geographers. Our academies, our geographical associations, our specially appointed travelers, and our explorers must all be decent, clever, and judicious Bulgarians. It does not take superhuman efforts, heavy spending, or that much of a sacrifice for everyone to explore and describe the place they live in.[40]

As can be seen, the project to discover the Bulgarian terra incognita was based on a direct analogy with the activity of the geographical associations of the colonial countries. To adjust the model, three steps were envisaged: voluntary work, nationwide participation, and distribution of the territory among its millions of discoverers so that each would describe the micro-perimeter of his or her place of birth. Needless to say, this program was utopian, and not just because the unprecedented mobilization it envisaged was impossible. It was doomed to failure because of the naïve pragmatism with which geographical discovery was copied as a model, for the transformation of the homeland into a terra incognita—a land to be explored—turned out to be anything but a mechanical process.

According to Graham Burnett, geographical discovery contains an essential paradox because the geographer is simultaneously a colonial surveyor sent to draw boundaries and an explorer who has set out to cross boundaries to enter an unknown land that is, by definition, beyond the limits of the known world.[41] This means that in the classic case, the problem is how to maintain the exotic status of a terra incognita after the latter is subjected to banalizing procedures (naming, mapping, drawing of state boundaries) at the very moment of its discovery. In the Bulgarian case, though, both the paradox and the problem it created were radically different.

Here the first dilemma was that the intimately known world had to be made exotic in order to take it out of the framework of its banality and turn it into an object of geographical exploration. In other words, the potential authors of descriptions had to be taught exactly what the unique and important information was about their towns and villages, which otherwise did not produce news of public importance. To this end the initiators of the project sent them detailed instructions. Ensuring the "correct" reception of the genre proved to be much more difficult—there were no instructions on this matter, since it was assumed that readers would automatically identify as native every unknown place in the Bulgarian-populated lands, provided that it was described. Geographical discovery, however, has its own genre cliché, according to which only exotic destinations are worthy of media attention. Thus, by virtue of the very fact that it was subject to description, the local acquired the status of a mythically alluring but distant foreign land; hence, the public identified itself with the native terra incognita just as little as with tales of "the Japanese state or the land of the Hottentots," as Stefan Bobchev put it:

> But while the enlightened peoples are setting out to travel around the different parts of the universe, while they are giving up everything in order to go to distant and very distant countries and to discover, explore and get to know them closely, what are we Bulgarians doing for our fatherland? What stakes, what care, what efforts, what sacrifices are we making in order to explore our places, the places where our ancestors' bones rest, where we saw the light of day for the first time and where, finally, we are spending our lives and health? . . . Shall we tell ourselves the truth? We are doing nothing or almost nothing to trace, explore, and get to know the land we inhabit. Listening to tales of places in our lands we do not live in is just as uninteresting to us as listening to tales and accounts of the Japanese state or of the land of the Hottentots. This is what we are like.[42]

The Discovery of Terra Incognita as a Project for Its Colonization

If truth be told, Stefan Bobchev did not have objective grounds to accuse his compatriots of being "like this." It must be noted that by 1878 geographical descriptions had been submitted for more than eight hundred towns and villages in the Bulgarian-populated lands. Considering that the authors came from the readership of newspapers and magazines that had an average of 250 to 500 subscribers each, the number of people who responded to the campaign is remarkable.[43] But the expectations of the initiators of the campaign were unrealistic, so their disappointment was great and only grew over time. So did their fears of foreign studies on Bulgarian-populated lands. Whereas in the 1860s foreign travelers were seen as well intentioned but "deluded," in the mid-1870s they were already being treated as the vanguard of European colonialism which was taking advantage of the "laziness" of the Bulgarians to discover their homeland: "The foreigners who, according to their own words, visit European Turkey as a sort of California, will relieve us also of this job that is so difficult for us. They have already invaded our lands like flocks of eagles and they are scouring all parts of our place. Some of them are searching for various ore-mines; others are examining and describing the locations, the works, the abundance of our places; still others are describing the fauna and the flora that is characteristic of some areas."[44]

Thus, the presence of western European naturalists was already interpreted as an invasion and as a clear sign "that the foreigners, namely the Germans, are preparing to operate on our lands as masters."[45] In fact, not many foreign scientists were operating in the Bulgarian-populated lands at that time. Botanical expeditions were sent primarily by the Hungarian Academy of Sciences,[46] but as a whole Europe's geographical interests were focused on the colonial world and the Balkan Peninsula was not an object of special attention. If there was any indication of the growing presence of western Europe in the region, it was of an economic, not scientific, nature. Imports of European goods indeed grew: They were entitled to preferential tariffs and competed successfully with backward local industry.

This process of economic expansion into Bulgarian-populated lands was followed with growing alarm, which escalated explosively in 1866 with the opening of the first railway line in the Bulgarian-populated lands, built by the British firm Messrs. Barclay, Brothers, and Co.[47] Key figures from the Bulgarian political elite initiated a discussion in the press on the benefits and harms of railway transportation, which continued until the end of the era of Ottoman rule. This discussion was dominated by doomsday forecasts about the pending collapse of the local market under pressure from imports from Europe. According to the Bulgarian Revivalist and literary scholar Nesho Bonchev, this meant that "foreigners will hold us in our hands the way they hold the savages in America and Australia."[48] Eventually, the analogies between the state of the Bulgarian economy and the exploitation of the Indians, Africans, and Native Americans grew into a rhetorical cliché and the image of Europe as a colonial master became part of the ideological lexicon of the Bulgarian press.

The geographical debate was conducted in parallel and was strongly influenced by the way economic fears were ideologized. Furthermore, it galvanized those fears as the image of "the savages" in the colonial world entered into the national imagination by way of geography lessons.[49] Each geography textbook classified the earth's population into several large groups along a spectrum from "savage tribes" to "enlightened peoples," and defined them as universal phases of development through which all societies invariably passed. In this sense, according to the British geographer Derek Gregory, geography created an all-encompassing vision of "the world-as-exhibition" organized according to the rules of Western rationalism, from the point of view of imperial metropolises.[50] Thus, while history studied the dynamic of human advancement along "the ladder of progress," geography transformed the same process into a static picture allowing simultaneous observation of all evolutionary phases. This vision was fundamental for the imagination of modernity. For example, Edmund Burke called it "the Great Map of Mankind": "But now the Great Map of Mankind is unrolled at once; and there is no state or gradation of barbarism and no mode of refinement which we have not at the same instant under our View."[51] One may say that this was the most important "map" onto which Bulgarian intellectuals projected their nation. The irony is that after they made every attempt to position the Bulgarian nation within "civilized Europe," it ended up somewhere in "the rest of the world."

The flaw was not in the nation but in "the Great Map," yet the Bulgarian elite experienced the failure as a personal drama. Perhaps the most frank example of this is the emotional breakdown suffered by Stefan Bobchev when he visited the Rila Monastery and found there two foreign guests, a mineralogist and a zoologist. The latter turned out to be the object of ridicule on the part of the monastic brotherhood. The Rila monks called him a "fly-catcher" (*muhar*) because he loved catching bugs and flies and behaved like a child, "jumping up and down, shouting and laughing" whenever he saw "a colorful beetle."[52] For their part, the foreign scientists could not find enough words to express their admiration for the local area. They told Bobchev they found it to be "a land more blessed than the promised land, more rich than California, more poetic even than the tropical countries themselves," but added, "*Mais l'ignorance, voila ce qui est le pire* [But ignorance is the biggest problem] those people told me and gave me as an example the monks from the monastery."[53]

Bobchev himself was not at all amused that the European scientists and the Rila monks looked equally childish in each other's eyes. At that moment he himself was mentally looking at "the Great Map" on which there was a terra incognita: tropically exotic, rich as California, and biblically blessed. But it was populated by people who for some reason did not wish to discover it themselves in order to show Europe that they were not "savages." And the young patriot broke into tears of resentment.

Epilogue, or How a Terra Incognita Remained Undiscovered

The Bulgarian terra incognita indeed remained undiscovered, but not because of the population's indifference: Its status as an unknown land was simply revoked. The establishment of a sovereign Bulgarian state in 1878 led to a change in the political agenda, and the mechanisms for homogenization of the nation became centralized. State institutions mobilized ideological resources that until then had been secondary or even marginal—lofty symbolic codes, a pantheon of heroes, a festive calendar, monuments, names of streets and settlements, sites of memory, and historical, literary, and musical canons. The reform of the territorial project was part of this process, but the first indications of the character of the forthcoming change appeared as early as the 1870s. This was the decade in which the campaign to discover the Bulgarian terra incognita reached its climax, but it used a very limited range of resources: statistics, geographical maps and textbooks, descriptions of settlements, and travel notes. As a whole, the Bulgarian Revival geographical project ignored the powerful potential of poetry and it was hardly a coincidence that this is precisely where its alternative was born.

As early as 1871 there appeared an emblematic poem by Khristo Botev in which the homeland is mapped so vividly that it has the effect of a territorial "logo":

Therefore his song is sung widely
By the forests of Strandja mountain,
By the grass upon Irin-Pirin;
The honeyed pipe takes up the burden
From Stambuol to Serbia's border
And reapers, the sweet-voiced lasses,
From the Aegean to the Danube
Over Rumelia's wheat-fields . . .[54]

And whereas in Botev's poem "Haidouks" the territorial vision is not a central theme, five years later Ivan Vazov published his first collection of poems in which he gave an lesson in geography on the subject of "Where Is Bulgaria?":

Where the mighty Danube flows,
Where the Black Sea brightly dances
In the East and stormy grows;

Where the Balkan raises nobly
To the sky its mountain chain,
Where the broad Maritsa slowly
Wanders through the Thracian plain."[55]

Today every Bulgarian knows those works because both have a classic status in the national literary and musical canons. The poetry of Botev and Vazov has given form to the collective memory of the Revival and it is therefore difficult to imagine that when they emerged their territorial visions were not normative. On the contrary, they brought about a radical change in the ideological resources with which the two most important institutions of Revival modernity—the press and the educational sphere—constructed the notion of a national homeland.

Above all, statistics were revoked as relevant to territorial definitions and this eliminated the need to prove the right to "ownership" of the Bulgarian-populated lands. Thus boundaries no longer depended on the ethnic majority; they were fixed reference points of physical geography, and therefore the burden of responsibility to define them was cancelled out. In poetry, the boundaries are represented as natural, both literally and figuratively, and that is why they are not subject to contestation, let alone to shift. As a result, the impression is created of a monolithic, "natural" territorial entity that imitates a geographical map but in fact is a landscape. The new regime of representation kept the bird's eye view of the cartographic perspective, but the abstraction was transformed into a sensory vision full of lights, movements, and sounds. Hence the most important difference: The sense of belonging to the territory represented in this way is not cultivated by means of new knowledge and rational arguments. The landscape relies on spontaneous emotional identification, as it has transformed the territorial picture into an intuitively recognizable lifeworld. That is why even the endless scope of its panoramic view is incapable of turning the homeland into a terra incognita. It always creates a feeling of intimate closeness because it is seen in its entirety as if on the palm of one's hand, all its voices are heard and understand each other even without words because the people, the grass, the mountains all speak the same language.

In comparison with the rational mechanics of the "numerical code," the suggestive power of the landscape is incomparably more effective as an instrument for homogenizing the collective imagination. As an ideology, however, this type of representation is much more conservative, as well as to some extent more banal, for it reproduces the classical tradition of European Romantic nationalism.[56] It is precisely thanks to this Romantic "revolution" in the dominant geographical norm that the acquired "immunity" to the historical territorial right began to weaken progressively. Eventually, demography and history entered into a symbiosis and became the basis for an aggressive irredentist policy that pushed the Bulgarians into several wars in the twentieth century. Of course, it does not necessarily follow from this that the enlightenment rationality with which the initial notion of a homeland was created would have prevented Bulgaria's two national catastrophes. The instrumentalization of demographic statistics had its own flaws and, as we have seen, it did not prove to be effective as a strategy for overcoming the national inferiority complex. Either way, however, the first geographical project of the Bulgarian nation remained incomplete and we can only speculate about what history textbooks would have said if the Bulgarian terra incognita had indeed been discovered.

Notes

1. François de Dainville, *L'Éducation des jésuites (XVIe–XVIIIe siècles)* (Paris: Les Editions de Minuit, 1978), 427–55.
2. Daniel Nordman, "La Géographie, œil de l'histoire," *Espaces Temps* 66, no. 66–67 (1998): 44–54.
3. Ibid., 44–55. For details, see Isabelle Lefort, "Deux siècles de géographie scolaire," *Espaces Temps* 66, no. 66–67 (1998): 146–55; Olivier Dumoulin, "Les Noces de l'histoire et de la géographie," *Espaces Temps* 66, no. 66–67 (1998): 6–20; Denis Wolff, "Une rupture non consommée," *Espaces Temps* 66, no. 66–67 (1998): 80–93.
4. Hans-Dietrich Schultz, *Die Geographie als Bildungsfach im Kaiserreich: Zugleich ein Beitrag zu ihrem Kampf um die preußische höhere Schule von 1870–1914 nebst dessen Vorgeschichte und teilweiser Berücksichtigung anderer deutscher Staaten* (Osnabrück: Selbstverlag des Fachgebietes Geographie im Fachbereich Kultur- und Geowissenschaften der Universität Osnabrück, 1989), 22–45.
5. Jeremy Black, *Maps and History* (New Haven, CT: Yale University Press, 1997), 51–80.
6. Christina Koulouri, *Dimensions idéologiques de l'historicité en Grèce (1834–1914): Les manuels scolaires d'histoire et de géographie* (Frankfurt: Peter Lang, 1992), 397–400.
7. Liuben Karavelov, "Zapiski za Bŭlgaria i za bŭlgarite," *Nezavisimost* 37 (1874): 300.
8. Graham Burnett, *Masters of All They Surveyed: Exploration, Geography, and a British El Dorado* (Chicago: University of Chicago Press, 2000).
9. Maria Torodova, *Bŭlgaria, Balkanite, svetŭt: idei, protsesi, sŭbitia* (Sofia: Prosveta, 2010), 153.
10. Robert Shannon Peckam, *National Histories, Natural States: Nationalism and the Politics of Place in Greece* (London: I. B. Tauris, 2001), xiii.
11. Nikola Planinski, "'Bitka kosovopolska' ot Danail Zhivkovich," book review, *Svoboda* 37 (1870): 294.
12. For the ethnogenetic theories of Bulgarian Revival historiography, see Dessislava Lilova, *Vŭzrozhdenskite znachenia na nationalnoto ime* (Sofia: Prosveta, 2003), 201–28.

13. Dragan Tsankov, review of *Nekoliko rechi o Aseniu Pŭrvomo*, by Georgi Rakovski, *Bŭlgaria* 81 (1860): 449–50.

14. Review of *Nekoliko rechi o Aseniu Pŭrvomo*, by Georgi Rakovski, *Bŭlgaria* 79 (1860): 411.

15. *Pravo* [Truth], editorial, no. 31 (1872): 1.

16. Peckam, *National Histories*, 140.

17. Eric J. Hobsbawm, *Nations and Nationalism Since 1780: Programme, Myth, Reality* (Cambridge: Cambridge University Press, 1990), 100 (emphasis in original).

18. Petko Slaveikov, "Predposleden marsh na 'Gaidata,'" *Gaida* 15 (1864): 115.

19. Radko Radoslavov, "Drianovo," *Rŭkovoditel na osnovnoto uchenie* 6 (1874): 93.

20. See Dessislava Lilova, "Vŭzrozhdenskiat proekt za geografski rechnik na bŭlgarskite zemi," *Balkanistic Forum* 1–3 (2004): 20–25.

21. Kostaki Tŭrnovski, *Rŭkovodstvo za upotreblenie na izkustvenite zemni i nebesni globusi za uchilishtata na geografolyubitelite* (Istanbul: Pechatnitsa na v. Makedoniya, 1869), 35–38.

22. Neofit Bozveli, *Kratkoe politicheskoe zemleopisanie za obuchenie na bŭlgarskoto mladenchestvo* (Kragujevac: Knyazhesko-Srŭbska Tipografia, 1835), 3.

23. Khristo Danov, *Zempleopisatelen atlas v dvadeset i chetiri karti* (Vienna: L. Somer, 1866), 23.

24. Johann Georg August Galletti, *Allgemeine Weltkunde oder Encyclopaedie für Geographie, Statistik und Staatengeschichte* (Pest: Verlag von Konrad Adolf Bartleben, 1847), 65.

25. Pirin, Rila, and Vitosha are the names of mountain ranges, but in Danov's atlas they are given as names of individual mountains.

26. Petŭr Koledarov, *Imeto Makedonia v istoricheskata geografia* (Sofia: Nauka i Izkustvo, 1985), 52–88.

27. For a detailed analysis of place-names in Bulgarian Revival geography and their projections, see Dessislava Lilova, "Rodinata i neĭnite imena: bŭlgarskata teritorialna identichnost v epohata pod osmanska vlast," in *Istoria, mitologia, politika*, ed. Daniela Koleva and Kostadin Grozev (Sofia: Universitetsko Izdatelstvo Sv. Kliment Ohridski, 2010), 80–91.

28. Benedict Anderson, *Imagined Communities* (London: Verso, 1983), 175.

29. Ibid.

30. For a historical analysis of the ethnographic maps of the Balkans, see Henry Robert Wilkinson, *Maps and Politics: A Review of the Ethnographic Cartography of Macedonia* (Liverpool: Liverpool University Press, 1951), 1–92.

31. Karavelov, "Zapiski za Bŭlgaria."

32. Petko Slaveikov, "Narodite v Tursko," *Chitalishte* 18–21 (1871): 558.

33. Ibid.

34. Mosko Dobrinov, "Pŭrva nagrada za sustavianieto na edin uchebnik: fizicheska geografia," *Chitalishte* 13 (1872): 606.

35. Stefan Bobchev, "Bŭlgarska narodna izlozhba," *Chitalishte* 10 (1874): 269.

36. See anonymous report from Thessaloniki, "Title," *Pravo*, November 7, 1873, 3.

37. "Nashite uchiteli," *Pravo*, no. 41 (1873): 1.

38. Mosko Dobrinov, "Yavno zhelanie," *Makedonia* 6 (1869): 3.

39. "L'Zhan, Tsiprian" is a reference to the French travelers Guillaume Lejean (1828–71) and Cyprian Robert (1807–60), authors of ethnographic studies on European Turkey. See "Narodonaselenieto na Plovdivskia sandzhak," *Letostruy ili domashen kalendar* 2 (1870): 70.

40. Stefan Bobchev, "Takviz smi niĭ," *Chitalishte* 5–6 (1875): 243–44.

41. Burnett, *Masters of All They Surveyed*, 199–254.

42. Bobchev, "Takviz smi niĭ," 195–96.

43. Georgi Borshukov, *Istoria na bŭlgarskata zhurnalistika* (Sofia: Nauka i Izkustvo, 1976), 402–3.

44. Bobchev, "Takviz smi niĭ," 241.

45. Ibid.

46. See Penka Peĭkovska, ed., *Ungarski ucheni za Bŭlgaria* (Sofia: Ungarski Kulturen Institut, 2003), 351–416.

47. See Dessislava Lilova, "Evropa kato kolonialen gospodar: debatŭt za zheleznitsite vŭv vŭzrozhdenskia pechat," *Literaturna misŭl* 1 (2005): 155–275.

48. Nesho Bonchev, "Za uchilishtata," *Periodichesko spisanie* 4 (1871): 26.

49. See Dessislava Lilova, "Barbarians, Civilized People and Bulgarians: Definition of Identity in Textbooks and the Press (1830–1878)," in *We, the People: Politics of National Peculiarity in Southeastern Europe*, ed. Diana Mishkova (Budapest: Central European University, 2009), 181–206.

50. Derek Gregory, *Geographical Imaginations* (Oxford: Blackwell, 1994), 15–70.

51. George Herbert Guttridge, ed., *The Correspondence of Edmund Burke* (Cambridge: Cambridge University Press, 1961), 3:351.

52. Bobchev, "Takviz smi niĭ," 242–43.

53. Ibid.

54. Hristo Botev, "Haidouks," in *Poems*, ed. and trans. Marco Mincoff (Sofia: Narodna Kultura, 1955), 48.

55. Ivan Vazov, "Where Is Bulgaria?" in *Anthology of Bulgarian Poetry*, trans. Peter Tempest (Sofia: Sofia Press, 1980), 93.

56. For the basic characteristics of Romantic nationalism, see Miroslav Hroch, "Introduction: National Romanticism," in *Discourses of Collective Identity in Central and Southeast Europe (1770–1945): Texts and Commentaries*, vol. 2, *National Romanticism: The Formation of National Movements*, ed. Balázs Trencsényi and Michal Kopeček (Budapest: Central European University Press, 2007), 4–20.

CHAPTER THREE

LIBERATION IN PROGRESS

Bulgarian Nationalism and Political Economy
in a Balkan Perspective, 1878–1912

Roumiana Preshlenova

In this chapter I explore the correlation between the notion of liberation and attitudes to the economy in late nineteenth-century Bulgaria. The concept of "liberation in progress" is meant to imply that the reestablishment of the Bulgarian state as a result of the interrelationship of the Bulgarian national liberation movement, the Russo-Turkish War of 1877–78, and the decisions of the European Great Powers at the Berlin Congress in 1878 was not taken for granted. It was a prolonged process, not a straightforward and easy one. The enormous changes in social life included but were not limited to the establishment of a state apparatus, of new local administration, of a legal framework, as well as of economic, educational, healthcare, and cultural institutions that did not exist under Ottoman rule.

Bulgaria, like the other Balkan countries, experienced economic difficulties after emancipation from the Ottoman Empire as a result of the Berlin Congress in 1878. The Balkan countries have various but equally compelling explanations: disconnection from the large market of the Ottoman Empire, unfavorable trends in international trade, foreign competition, insufficient investments in productive spheres, lack of entrepreneurship, and so forth. I draw attention to some related yet distinct aspects of this issue. First I consider how independence—the autonomy to implement a national policy—affected attitudes to economic development and what the human, ideological, and institutional resources that informed these strategies were. A further question to be explored is how the economy was embedded in political discourse and in developmental strategies.

The relevance of these questions stems from the statements of several nineteenth-century Bulgarian politicians that society-level transformations during the crucial post-liberation era had to confront widespread illusions connected to a certain type of economic culture. The term "economic culture"—described as behaviors or attitudes toward a national economy—includes knowledge, information, and their application in the management of economic activities. Emotions and sentiments also play a key role. Since economic culture allows for different approaches to a great number of sources, it would be impossible to discuss all of them in one chapter. This examination is based mainly on texts that are relevant to specific economic problems such as statistics, parliamentary proceedings, published programs and program documents of political parties, protocols, reports, documents of professional organizations, petitions, memoranda, economic journals, and monographs from the era. Alongside these public documents, I also explore memoirs and diaries of some representatives of the political and economic elites.

The examined texts reveal a clear prevalence of political motifs, evaluations, and contexts. The wide range starts from the commonly expressed opinion, both before and after 1878, that the Ottoman Empire should be abolished as a political entity because it disregarded questions of economic advancement such as road construction, promotion of commerce and industries, and the establishment and development of professional education. It was revealed to be an economically impotent system in the nineteenth century, characterized by disorder and corruption. Until the empire's dissolution, not only Bulgarian, but also Greek, Serbian, and Romanian writings frequently discussed the impossibility of its modernization, or its inability to put an end to the feudal holdovers in its economy.[1] This view was all the more popular since many foreign observers supported it as well. Even after the emancipated Balkan economies began running into difficulties and occasional failures, this belief remained popular and gave no credence to the opinion that "Ottoman rule made possible more progress than the arrangements that accompanied self-government."[2] But in general, the idea of a national economy was not an issue in the program of national liberation before 1878, and economic writings were among the "most boring" texts in the Bulgarian press in this period.[3]

The outcomes of Bulgaria's liberation in 1878 created a serious impediment for its economic advancement due to the striking disparity between the nationalist program and its realization. The problem of identification of the nation with the territory was understood in exclusively ethnic terms, as mapped by the sultan in his decision about the foundation of the Bulgarian Exarchate of the Orthodox Church in 1870 and the referendum on this issue in territories with mixed population, subsequently confirmed by Ottoman authorities. Thus the nationalist program was based on the idea of reestablishing the Bulgarian state within the territories of the Bulgarian Exarchate, which included Moesia, Thrace, and Macedonia. Later, the Treaty of San Stefano of March 3, 1878, which ended the Russo-Turkish War, once again embodied their unification and settled the establishment of the national state within these territories.

The Treaty of Berlin, signed by Great Britain, Austria-Hungary, France, Germany (appearing as a united empire in the Concert of Europe), Italy, Russia and Turkey on July 13, 1878, was the most important international document to imply the idea of the Balkans as part of Europe. Bringing about order in this part of the continent was regarded as a priority of the Great Powers. This already implied the notion of two different "worlds" and a distinct subordination: The one had to decide about the other, which was simply "handled" internationally. The announced purpose of the Congress of Berlin was the revision of the Treaty of San Stefano of March 3, 1878, in the interest of the public law of Europe, especially as set forth in the Treaty of Paris of 1856. It is well known that its real goal was to impose upon victorious Russia the Great Powers' mandate that it retrench its conquests and spare the Ottoman Empire the coup de grace, as demanded by Great Britain and Austria-Hungary. The very manner of the (re)establishment of Bulgarian statehood as a European matter—in the absence of Bulgarian delegates to the congress—signified the nation's treatment as an object, not a subject, of European policy. It is true that participation in international affairs presumed corresponding resources, a corps of experts with the appropriate legitimacy and knowledge. A representation of the Bulgarian population before the sultan was already available in the Exarchate. But Bulgaria was not invited to the congress even as an observer, and neither were Serbia, Romania, or Montenegro, which were still lacking formal sovereignty. In this respect, the reestablishment of Bulgarian statehood fully confirms the model of the transfer of power in southeastern Europe formulated by Konrad Clewing, who states that during the nineteenth century, control over the territories detached from the Ottoman Empire was not fully transferred to the new Balkan states. This process was guided by the European powers with their right to intervene based on the Ottoman capitulations, new international treaties, or simply on their power. Some of the rights the Ottoman authorities lost went to the "Europeans" and not to the new states.[4]

As Barbara and Charles Jelavich, experts in the international system in the Balkans since the nineteenth century, have put it, the state of affairs in the region in 1870 allowed much more intervention by the Great Powers there—especially Russia, Great Britain, and the Habsburg monarchy—than at the beginning of the century. In the view of some political leaders in the Balkans, the interference of the Great Powers in their affairs was a sort of substitution for the overthrown Ottoman regime, albeit in a very different form.

The revision of the preliminary peace treaty of San Stefano, sanctioned by the Great Powers at the Congress of Berlin, envisaged the establishment of the Principality of Bulgaria only within the territory between the Danube and the Balkan Mountains with the Sanjak (administrative division) of Sofia. The rest of the territory that might have become part of Bulgaria—about 150,000 square kilometers (58,000 square miles) with a population of more than 2.5 million Bulgarians, Orthodox Christians who acknowledged their affiliation with the Bulgarian Exarchate—remained outside its borders. Among Bulgarians, this provoked strong resentment and a feeling of injustice described by dramatic views such as that "the body of the nation had been carved up on a table in Berlin by callous men to satisfy their own interests, without letting the victim be heard."[5] Deputies of the population that remained under Ottoman rule per the provisions of the Treaty of Berlin gathered in Tŭrnovo to protest against it, and the notables in the Bulgarian Constituent Assembly considered boycotting the preparation of a constitution for the same reason. Numerous petitions and demonstrations by Bulgarians from the unredeemed territories, most of all from Macedonia and so-called Eastern Rumelia, expressed their dissatisfaction. The peak of their resistance was the uprising in northeastern Macedonia from October 1878 to mid-1879. The frustration led to a change of the slogan of the Bulgarian Revival, "Liberty or Death," to one of national unification with the mobilizing and comprehensible formulation of "San Stefano Bulgaria." The first two articles of the first Bulgarian Tŭrnovo Constitution of April 16, 1879, addressed territorial frontier issues: how to maintain a common institutional framework for all Orthodox Bulgarians inside and outside the principality in anticipation of political unity.[6] Foreign observers uninvolved in the Berlin arrangements shared a similar view: "This ambition, based as it is upon a deep national sentiment, may prove stronger amidst the Bulgarians than even their passion for economy."[7] Thus, irredentism in Bulgaria became a focus in the social and state agendas after 1878, and it seemed immoral to deal with "prosaic matters" like the economy when faced with such an iniquity.

In this context, liberation could be regarded in several ways. In political terms, it is the outcome of the Russo-Turkish War of Liberation of 1877–78, which dispelled Ottoman authority over the subsequently formed territories of the Principality of Bulgaria and Eastern Rumelia, united in 1885. This is the narrowest meaning of the term. In a broader sense it included a complex of political measures taken by Bulgarian governments to abolish the clauses of the Treaty of Berlin from 1878 that restricted the sovereignty and the territory of the state. In other words, a long series of activities were intended to complete the incomplete liberation. In a sociocultural perspective, liberation implicated a wide range of state and private initiatives to abolish the signs and the sites inherited from the Ottoman past which made Bulgaria and the Bulgarians oriental, that is, non-European.[8] In terms of identity building, liberation sought the recognition of the Bulgarian state and of the Bulgarian nation as equal to other states and nations on the continent of comparable size and population. In the rhetoric of the nineteenth century, this meant becoming part of the civilized and enlightened world. Thus, all these aspects of liberation constituted a significant part of the meta-project of the new political elites for modernization or Europeanization.

This project continued that of the nationally oriented merchants and intelligentsia from the epoch called in Bulgarian historiography the Bulgarian Revival. Many of them lived in Romania, Russia, Constantinople, and Vienna, more like émigrés than members of a diaspora. Despite some mutually excluding differences between the conservative, liberal, and revolutionary circles among them, there was a broad consensus on political and religious independence, as well as on education. Economic goals were not central, and it "seemed" that national prosperity would be among the "natural" outcomes of liberation. Until the reestablishment of the Bulgarian state as a political subject, the self-organization of Bulgarian society, including economic competence, remained restricted to the private sphere, the professional guilds (*esnaf*), and the local communes concerned with the maintenance of churches and of elementary schools.[9] Bulgarian leaders' approach to the economy can be better described as the ability to survive in a personal and "national" manner in the face of alien oppression than as a strategic economic project. Intraregional, long-distance trade, and financial dealings predominantly involved networking within kinship and regional networks.

The hopes and expectation that the abolition of foreign rule would automatically bring prosperity for all Bulgarians turned out to be an illusion. The first Bulgarian governments were compelled to explain to the people why they had to pay taxes if the state was "theirs." The liberation was sufficient to release the hitherto suppressed "political instincts," as the contemporary analyst Simeon Radev put it, namely, the striving for democracy, equality, and self-government. In any case, codification of these principles did not link politics and prosperity as a goal of national development. The parliamentary democracy that was constituted lacked basic economic foundations. The political parties—in the 1880s, the Conservatives and the Liberals—showed only a general interest in the national economy. Their programmatic goals were almost identical as presented in their respective first party programs from 1882: to revive trade, to improve agriculture and transport, to distribute taxation more fairly and more uniformly. The Liberals also demanded that credit institutions be established.[10] More complex socioeconomic programs were neither thoroughly discussed nor elaborated. The economy was clearly a second-order matter, evidently if not explicitly subordinate to irredentism.

Whether the experts necessary for a large-scale strategy for economic advancement were available is a crucial question. The common economic culture of the large majority of the population was not sufficiently developed, even though around 80 percent of the population was rural and depended on predominantly self-sufficient agriculture. At the dawn of the twentieth century, less than one-third of the entire population over six years of age could read and write, and most literate people lived in towns.[11] Earlier data are even more striking, but do not exclude the population under six years. According to this data, the literacy rate in 1880 was about 3.3 percent, in 1887 it was 10.7 percent, in 1892 it was 15.6 percent, and in 1900 it was 23.9 percent.[12] On the other hand, the hitherto most wide-ranging survey in Bulgarian historiography, although not flawless, reveals that only 6.3 percent of the intelligentsia on the eve of the liberation had a university or higher school degree, mainly acquired in Europe or Russia. Moreover, two-thirds of these university or college graduates were doctors. Those with degrees in humanities, jurists, mathematicians, and clergymen were much less numerous.[13] The educational profile of the elite indicates a remarkable shortage of experts with any professional training that would prepare them to take over economic governance.

On the other hand, in searching for an explanation of the modest success of economic progress in Bulgaria in the late nineteenth century, a contemporary observer revealed a striking circumstance. Pathos, prestige, and high state salaries encouraged many if not most of the educated and economically active Bulgarians after 1878 to pursue a political career. Thus more than fifty thousand of the nation's "most productive" people were absorbed into the central, regional and local administration. This "excessive politicization" produced, in this observer's view, a noticeable lack of wealthy people who were still politically independent.[14] By the turn of the century this was regarded as one of the most serious factors that had a profoundly negative impact on the country's long-term economic progress.

The second-rank importance of the economy is further reflected in the educational structure of the political elite, which had a key role as the driving force of all radical social changes, as in all other Balkan countries with a similar social structure. This is a consideration that can be illustrated by most of the members of the Bulgarian governments in the late nineteenth and early twentieth centuries. It is not surprising that the share of graduates with a university or college degree in economics and related subjects among them was extremely low. Only 9 percent of all Bulgarian ministers between 1879 and 1915 had studied economics or administrative or political studies. Considered are all levels of education, including commercial academies which were not at a university level.[15] If this is to be expected, given the overall structure of graduates of university and higher schools, the background of the leaders of economy-related ministries is astonishing. It would hardly be an exaggeration to conclude that it was the exception rather than the rule that experts who had economics or economics-related degrees held the office of an economy-related minister. Indeed, few of them were graduates from prestigious European universities and colleges. Ivan E. Geshov graduated in finance from the University of Manchester, Hristo Belchev and Lazar Payakov studied economics in Paris, Grigor Nachovich did so in Paris and Vienna, Dimitar Hristov in Geneva, and Andrei Lyapchev in Zurich, Berlin, and Paris. As a comparison, 15 percent of Bulgarian ministers between 1879 and 1915 had a military degree, and 38 percent held a degree in legal studies. Of course, professional economic training should not be overestimated, but a minimum of economic education should be required at least for ministers of finances and trade. The relatively high rate of educated jurists was in any case a feature of modern European democracies. In the view of Max Weber, who regarded them as the fifth level or type of professional politicians in a historical perspective, they were typical for western Europe as an independent social layer and belonged together with the political parties.[16] Political rather than professional staff occupied the lower levels of power, too. Only 5 percent of state employees in Bulgaria in 1911 had an economy-related education in the broadest sense of the term. This includes all those who were trained in economic subjects—had studied state administration, finance, social or commercial, handicraft, or industrial sciences.[17] The widespread patronage networks in southeastern Europe certainly came at the cost of competent and politically neutral administrators, although this phenomenon was not unique to this region.[18]

In the first decade after the liberation, most efforts were dedicated to the establishment of the state apparatus. Even then, the economy was not a priority. The Constituent Assembly in Tŭrnovo (February–April 1879) established only six ministries: Foreign Affairs and Religion, Education, Internal Affairs, Justice, War, and Finances. Economic ministries had not been allowed in order to trim the budget. Thus, until 1882, the Ministry of Finances—with its Customs Department and Accountancy Court in control of the state budget—remained the only economically relevant institution in the central administration. The minister of education was responsible for agriculture and received reports on the state of affairs in the different regions. A meta-economic Ministry of Public Buildings, Agriculture and Trade existed, but only provisionally, from 1882 to 1885.[19]

A significant institutional change occurred only after the First Bulgarian Agrarian and Industrial Exhibition in 1892. Organized by the government, and in line with a popular nineteenth-century trend, the exhibition was intended to demonstrate national unity and the progress of native production. All the participants in the exhibition came together in a meeting, chaired by a prominent politician, economist, and banker, Ivan E. Geshov, to discuss the evident economic problems of the country: poor labor conditions, inefficient taxation, primitive production techniques, unfavorable foreign trade agreements, lack of banking and professional education, weak native industry, and so forth. Necessary measures to improve the situation were clearly articulated during the meeting. This gave rise to a number of institutions key to a modern economy In 1893, two new ministries were added to the Bulgarian governmental structure: the Ministry of Trade and Agriculture and the Ministry of Public Buildings, Transportation, and Communications. Then, in 1911, on the eve of the Balkan Wars, separate ministries were created for finances; trade, industry, and labor; agriculture and state estates; public buildings, transport, and public works; railways, mail, and telegraphy. Furthermore, chambers of commerce and industry were established in 1895 in the most significant commercial centers: Sofia, Varna, Ruse, and Plovdiv, and in 1907, Burgas. The chambers were tasked with studying the economic situation in their respective regions, collecting statistical data, and submitting evaluations of the associated business circles.[20]

It would be fair to interpret the nineteenth-century adoption of certain elements of modern Europe as evidence of a path toward modernization that, especially when considered alongside the adoption of foreign political institutions, mediated or not, was "inorganic" to the Balkans' own course of development. Admittedly, the transformation and the adaptation of Balkan societies lagged far behind their modernized political infrastructure and legal frameworks. The disparity between the imported elements and the still very traditional environment allowed for doubts and speculations. It nourished a long-lasting political and intellectual debate in Bulgaria as well as in Serbia, Greece, and Romania regarding the proper path of development. The goal to be like modern Europe while retaining freedom and independence—to autonomously reproduce foreign patterns in the Balkan economic and cultural environment—had clear implications on both state and public levels. There are other questions regarding who imported what patterns, what were the means of transmission, who were the mediators, and so forth. In any case, countries on the periphery of Europe were not passive recipients of influences emanating from the major core cultures, but were dynamic and critical participants in a process of institutional and cultural selection, exchange, and adaptation.[21]

The constitution of an economic framework, starting from an institutional zero level in 1879 to the establishment of a state apparatus following European templates and the elaboration of a modern statutory base, was accompanied in public discourse by a leitmotif regarding the issue of the disproportionately large expense of state employees. The related problem of reducing state expenditure on administration, and of taxation as the main source of this expenditure, dominated the programs of all political parties from the 1880s.[22] This leitmotif was continuously heard in the press, in literature, and in economic and political essays. A number of interrelated narratives were clustered together: state employees as a burden on the population, enrichment at the expense of the state and the people, corruption, the state as an estate, and so on. In everyday language, these narratives were all expressed in terms of the metaphor of a dinner at the state table. It is worth remembering that Bulgarian governments changed thirty-four times during the first thirty-four years of autonomous and independent existence, from July 1879 to December 1913 (some governments were subsequently reconstituted). These frequent changes not only produced political instability, which had a negative impact on the economy, but were also led to turnover of state employees at the higher and lower levels of administration, increasing the impression of coterie-like rule and corruption. In one way or another, the misuse of the state as provisional personal property shaped the image of state servants as a social category, and of most politicians. This was contrary to Max Weber's thesis about politics as a vocation, a notion that shaped the idea of liberation as well:

> He who strives to make politics a permanent *source of income* lives "off" politics as a vocation, whereas he who does not do this lives "for" politics. Under the dominance of the private property order, some . . . very trivial

preconditions must exist in order for a person to be able to live "for" politics in this economic sense. Under normal conditions, the politician must be economically independent of the income politics can bring him. This means, quite simply, that the politician must be wealthy or must have a personal position in life which yields a sufficient income. This is the case, at least in normal circumstances.[23]

The identification of state employees as a principal problem for economic policy had many implications. Probably the most serious among them was the strong awareness of the absence of political morals, understood as a breach of the social contract. In other words, damage was done to the common feeling of equality that was based on a strong traditional egalitarianism in Bulgaria and Serbia at that time, arising from their specific social structure. Both countries had been deprived of an aristocratic stratum in the course of the Ottoman conquest and what followed. It is no accident that the Law of Criminal Prosecution of Ministers, augmented by the Law of Criminal Prosecution of Profiteer State Officials, was elaborated and took effect on January 18, 1895, before the Commercial Code was established, which treated business, associations, deals and bankruptcy and was intended to create a modern normative framework for economic activities.[24] Another no less serious implication is that during the first two decades after the liberation, the issue of state officials as a burden and evil for society took the place of a genuine economic debate, or at least dominated this debate. In this sense it supplanted the elaboration of an essential national economic manifesto. This could be conservative—which, in the view of Rumen Avramov, it should be—or liberal, which would correspond to the general "spirit" of the political environment in Bulgaria at that time, shaped as it was by liberal nationalism, "that peculiar brand of liberalism that fused the notions of popular sovereignty and citizenship with the ethno-cultural frame of national romanticism" that "was subjected to 'traditionalist' reinterpretations and adaptation which were meant to serve local needs and expectations."[25] Economic and cultural advancement for the new political elite was contingent upon the creation of a favorable political environment whose main attributes would be national sovereignty, representative government, and civil rights.

For a long time, the national economy was driven by inertia and had no explicitly formulated project. Ad hoc reactions often prevailed over strategic plans. This is true even in the case of the two successful governments of the National Party (Narodna Partiya), which represented the most educated part of the elite. The administrations of the conservative prime ministers Dr. Konstantin Stoilov (1894–99) and Ivan E. Geshov (1911–13) both left a remarkable legacy with their competent economic policy. For example,

Stoilov's cabinet significantly improved the institutional and statutory control of the state budget and taxation, established model farms as a step toward the modernization of agriculture, promoted the emerging network of Raiffeisen cooperatives, and made progress in constructing railways, roads, and ports. It also introduced modest state protectionism for nascent industry by means of particular laws, similarly to Romania and Serbia at that time, and by means of import tariffs determined in trade agreements from 1896 and 1897. The National Party had emphasized the economy as a priority in its program and electoral campaign, but it had highlighted the main goals of establishing order and the rule of law, "to spare state money and punish the abusers," and reducing or abolishing some taxes.[26] It is evident that the practical achievements of the government went far beyond these populist, programmatic goals that appealed to a broader public. The politics of the second government were similar, although in a series of articles the prominent and well-educated prime minister, Ivan E. Geshov, set out his general views, took a stand against exhortations for excessive savings, and raised the need for new foreign loans and far-reaching public construction.

The programmatic and electoral features of the National Party, like those of the other political parties at this time, can be explained if one considers the political culture of the society. The electorate was incapable of understanding complicated economic messages and arguments. Demonstratively reacting to moral and social requirements was a clearer message than publicly setting out a comprehensive economic project. A convincing example of this was the reaction to the deteriorating economic situation in Bulgaria after the 1880s. The influx of cheap foreign industrial production, undermining traditional native handicrafts, aroused growing concern. The political reaction was the law of 1897 that obliged policemen, soldiers, and all state and local officials and deputies to wear clothes and shoes made out of native materials and manufactured by native producers during their working hours.[27] The official reason for this measure was to promote native industry. Its absurdity, first and foremost, as well as the proof of the materials' origin, not to mention the verification procedures, were frequently ridiculed by contemporaries. The economic effect was questionable, but the political impact was certain. The message to the population was that if the state apparatus prospered and profited from the nation, it had at least to show patriotism in economic terms by wearing "national" products. This internal nationalism was well matched to the situation of a poor state, "neglected by history."

Until the turn of the century, even purposeful economic policy was not preceded by a broad and adequate publicizing of its goals and methods beyond populist pledges, and tended to confirm the sense of a lack of social equity and inclinations instead of channeling them into a forward-looking, consistent national project. The formulation of concrete economic problems alongside vague statements of people's prosperity ran parallel to the pluralizing trend of political parties and took programmatic shape only after the small economic spurt at the beginning of the twentieth century. Whether the formulation of economic intentions was a result of the upswing or of the maturity of the political elite is a question that requires further exploration. The process of elaborating and formulating economic positions within political parties' general programs is evident from their published documents: in the Radical-Democratic Party's program in 1906 and 1911; the Young-Liberal and the National Parties' in 1908; the Liberal Party's in 1910; and the National Liberal Party's in 1911. An exception is the Democratic Party, which formulated its economic views in its 1895 and 1903 programs. Only the Agrarian Union of Aleksandăr Stamboliyski, a political organization of the peasantry and one of the strongest peasant parties in the Balkans, was founded with clearly articulated economic interests and demands.[28] But, albeit belatedly, the conceptualization of economic attitudes, together with expanding literacy, accounted for growing electoral activity. It is indicative that 43 percent voted in 1901, increasing to 54 percent in 1911. It is also the case that a peak in electoral participation, especially in urban areas, was brought about by the failure to achieve national unification during the Balkan Wars in 1912–13. In 1914 more than 67 percent of the electorate participated in the parliamentary elections.[29] There are no exit poll data to confirm the conclusion that the elaboration and dissemination of more concrete economic goals in the political parties' programs after the turn of the century was directly linked to growing participation in parliamentary elections. Presumably three factors—increasing literacy, the crucial phase of irredentist policy, and a stronger sense of involvement in economic affairs—accounted for this development.

The perceived failure of political parties in the late nineteenth century to obliged even the elites to reveal their intentions on how to run the national economy and to elaborate concrete proposals in their programs provoked bottom-up activities. One sign of this was the meeting at the First Bulgarian Agrarian and Industrial Exhibition in 1892 and, in 1895, the establishment of the Bulgarian Economic Society, comprising industrialists, teachers, lawyers, doctors, clerks, journalists, and others of varying political orientations. One of the two commissions within the society was mandated "to organize the struggle against foreign products" and emphasized access to the Ottoman market as a precondition for Bulgarian economic advancement.[30] Finding a

successful formula for the so-called Eastern markets, including Greece, continuously dominated economic debates as an alternative to intense competition
with Europeans. Under the slogan "Prefer the Native," the society established
branches around the country; its members represented the most educated and
most economically knowledgeable segment of Bulgarian society.[31] Their fundamental task was to draw society's attention to the country's poor economic
state. Public lectures, discussions, and a journal further outlined the means to
overcome economic backwardness. Despite the society's initially quasi-belli-
cose rhetoric, it managed to carve out a public space for discussing economic
problems. The *Journal of the Bulgarian Economic Society* won recognition as
the most respected economic publication in Bulgaria in that time.[32] A number
of less important newspapers and journals worked toward the same goal. The
debate about the best means to improve the Bulgarian economy overtly manifested a clash between traditionalism and modernity that had been hidden
under the surface of the initial push toward economic nationalism.

Discussions relating to the Bulgarian National Bank (BNB) revealed a similar anxiety. The bank had been established in newly independent Bulgaria in
1879. Many public figures, invited to comment on the mission of the bank,
pointed out the danger of foreign economic domination: "Bulgarian merchants with their scanty capital will remain mere observers while the foreigners will use the country's resources, as happens in Serbia and Romania."[33]

Such animosity toward different forms of foreign presence and intervention could be found, first and foremost, in the economy-related rhetoric of all
liberal political parties in Bulgaria at that time. At their most extreme, they
warned against foreign states, banks, companies, influx of population, loans,
and goods. Apprehension of foreign domination was inherent in conservative
parties, too, although it was expressed in a more moderate way.[34]

It would be simplistic to interpret this attitude as xenophobia; rather, it
stemmed from concern regarding a latecomer's prospects of development in a
market dominated by foreign economies. Later debates on the reform of the
Bulgarian National Bank as a private company and on railway construction
clearly revealed a predominantly negative attitude toward the involvement of
private capital in the country's economic development: Absolute state sovereignty had to be protected against any foreign interference at any cost, including deterring badly needed foreign investment. Insecurity was intensified
because Russian diplomacy had been geared toward exploring various channels in an effort to establish political and economic domination.

Consequently, Bulgarians were chronically, and justifiably, fearful that their
newly liberated country would be turned into a *gubernia*, a province of Russia.

Indeed, several railway construction projects and attempts to found banks or enterprises using an influx of Russian capital, personnel, or know-how failed because they were viewed as suspect. The speculative character of those most interested in the BNB and the railways, as well as the Great Powers' rivalry in the Balkans, also contributed to this mistrustful disposition. In any case, the fact remains that it hampered the influx of investments to an extremely poor economy and thus slowed down its improvement. Railways, meanwhile, were built to meet strategic military needs rather than to facilitate exports. In addition, Bulgaria, like the other Balkan states, adopted the system of state railways to ensure control over its own territory.

After the reestablishment of the Bulgarian state, a significant part of the Turkish population left their homes and property in Bulgaria. Thus, after 1879 the idea of independence similarly marked the transfer of land from Muslim to Bulgarian ownership. The abandoned land was taken over by or sold to Bulgarians, or later distributed by the Bulgarian government to landless peasants and Bulgarian refugees from other parts of the Ottoman Empire. In 1910, only 11 percent of the population in Bulgaria was Turkish.[35] The distribution of large Ottoman-owned private estates (*chifliks*) to landless Bulgarian peasants was aimed particularly at enabling self-sufficiency, thus ensuring that independent small proprietors would be the main feature of Bulgarian agriculture.[36] This led to a predominantly self-sufficient agriculture with low production, although some progress was made in comparison to the earlier stage.[37] Demonstration farms were established in all twenty-two districts in Bulgaria, and data on modern agricultural equipment reveal increased importation of ploughs, harrows, harvesters, threshing machines, corn huskers, winnowing machines, grain cleaners, and viticultural spraying machines between 1893 and 1902. Even so, a recent survey of Bulgarian statistical data from the era reveals stagnation in per capita GNP between 1879 and the 1930s.[38]

Economic planners also sought to reduce imports of industrial products. They regarded this as the main factor in the ruin of traditional native handicrafts, which lost even the internal market to cheaper, modern European goods—not only machines and equipment but also everyday consumer goods. The insight that Bulgarian artisans were for a long time incapable of transforming their trade in accordance with new market requirements changed this attitude somewhat. On the other hand, industrial imports often accounted for a negative foreign trade balance and engendered a drain on national financial resources. In both aspects industrial imports were to be reduced by increasing national industrial production. There was a rough consensus in the late nineteenth century in Bulgaria, Serbia, and Romania to proceed with industrialization,[39] but with active state intervention by means of protectionist policies with explicit laws for encouraging nascent industries (1883, 1894, 1895, 1905) and via tariff protection. But the consensus was precarious because these policies failed to bring about structural changes in agriculture, which remained extensive, and thus did not increase agriculture's low productivity. The attraction-repression effect that European economic modernity had on Balkan societies produced a corresponding adoption-rejection response. Efforts in Bulgaria, Romania, and Serbia to promote industrial advancement in the late nineteenth and early twentieth centuries by implementing protective legislation implicitly recognized the economic superiority of industrial development in the outside world. This resulted from the perception that the latter had "sufficient and cheap capital and facilities" to supply even raw materials at much better prices than native producers could.[40] Such administrative encouragement in the form of tariff protectionism thus aimed to create better conditions for nascent local industries, hampered by historical circumstance. Nevertheless, its main goal was to achieve greater independence from foreign industrial imports and a more favorable trade balance.

Western European economic power was viewed not only as a threat to but also as a template for the development of the Balkan countries' economies, even although the latter was taking place at a different pace and in much more unfavorable conditions. But the economic nationalism of this period did not really aim at autarchy in the sense of isolating the Balkans. Rather, efforts to protect native production corresponded entirely to the general trend of commercial protectionism in the late nineteenth and early twentieth centuries, when nationalism had cast its spell in most European countries. Of course there was a desire to catch up, as demonstrated in Romania, Serbia, and Bulgaria with laws that explicitly provided administrative encouragement to nascent industries. At the time, catching up seemed merely a matter of moving quickly along a predetermined path, although it later became evident that the course of the path was not in fact that predetermined.

There was a firm consensus regarding expenditures for military purposes in preparation for national unification while the economy and other social spheres were neglected.[41] Intentionally disregarding its economic backwardness, Bulgaria and the other Balkan countries spent disproportionate sums on the military and related purposes: roughly 10 percent of the relevant budgets, and additional extra-budgetary sums, funded to a great extent by foreign loans.[42] This went hand in hand with respect for Western progress and faith in the still very strong tradition of the Enlightenment and its universality, nourishing the hope to achieve an Enlightenment society at some point.

Insofar as an economy-related strategy was unanimously and continuously pursued, it concerned abolishing the "humiliating" restrictive clauses of the Treaty of Berlin, intrinsic to the idea of liberation and firmly embedded in a prevailing perspective on international affairs. In this case, the national and the transnational must be regarded as conditioning and supplementing each other because this aspect of Bulgarian nationalism and its European predetermination are interconnected.

The partial transfer of administrative powers from the Sublime Porte (the central government of the Ottoman Empire) to the national states in the Balkans by the Great Powers, and under their supervision, implied a division of political subjects in Europe into fully sovereign—if not oversovereign—and semidependent. The intention of the Concert of Europe was to "guide" the immature, newly established Balkan states and to prescribe some of the most important state principles. Some stipulations of the Treaty of Berlin nevertheless exclusively favored the signatories, including the Sublime Porte. For example, the Great Powers imposed on Bulgaria the obligation to bear a part of the public debt of the Ottoman Empire. Bulgaria was also required to take over the Ottoman government's duties and obligations regarding the Rustchuk–Varna Railway as well as the engagements that the Sublime Porte had contracted with Austria-Hungary and the railway company for the operation of the railways of Turkey in Europe, with respect to the completion, union, and operation of the lines placed upon her territory (Articles IX, X). The latter conditions were also imposed on Serbia (Article XXXVIII).

If the limited sovereignty granted to Bulgaria can be viewed as concern about the immaturity of its society, the clauses imposing the Ottoman foreign trade regime on it cannot. According to Article VIII,

> The Treaties of Commerce and Navigation, as well as all the conventions and agreements concluded between foreign Powers and the Porte, and which are now in force, are maintained in the Principality of Bulgaria, and no change can be made in them with regard to any one Power until she has given her consent thereto. No transit duty shall be levied in Bulgaria on merchandise passing through the Principality. The subjects and citizens and commerce of all the Powers shall there be placed upon a footing of perfect equality. The immunities and privileges of foreign subjects, with the rights of jurisdiction and of consular protection, which have been established by the Capitulations and usages, will remain in full force, as far as not modified by consent of the parties interested.[43]

According to the capitulations, European traders in the Ottoman Empire were exempt from local prosecution, local taxation, local conscription, and the searching of their domicile.[44] These restrictions concerned the Great Powers' economic and political privileges without making corresponding concessions for Bulgaria. Serbia also inherited the trade regime of the Porte until the conclusion of new arrangements (Article XXXVII).

It took the political elite in Bulgaria almost thirty years to abolish the so-called regime of capitulations imposed by Article VIII of the Treaty of Berlin. If the restrictions for Serbia's foreign trade envisaged a period until the conclusion of new arrangements with her partners, the corresponding restrictions for Bulgaria were not limited in time until a Great Power had given consent thereto. From the very beginning Bulgarian governments contemplated abolishing these stipulations in one way or another. A formal and explicit but incomplete breakthrough was the hard-won right to conclude trade agreements independently of the Sublime Porte. On the occasion of the expiration of the Ottoman conventions from 1861–62, Bulgarian governments invited foreign contractors to negotiate new ones at the beginning of the 1880s. After several failed attempts, Stefan Stambolov's cabinet succeeded in signing agreements first with Great Britain (1889), then with other Great Powers (Germany, Austria-Hungary, Italy, and France) and with smaller states (Belgium and Switzerland). The contracting parties mutually provided each other the clause of the most favored nation. This formal recognition of foreign trade independence from the Ottoman Empire accounted for a decrease in state revenues from import duties of about five hundred thousand leva per year.[45] A more general observation emphasizes the fact that the new trade agreements put an end to the validity of the Ottoman agreements with the European states with regard to Bulgaria. In all negotiations henceforth, Bulgarian governments insisted on this mutuality and reciprocity, as well as on the abolition of the one-sided privileges the Great Powers granted themselves in the Treaty of Berlin.

The next achievement in overcoming the juridical status of inequality in foreign trade was agreements with the main European states in 1896–97. They explicitly set out equal treatment of the contracting parties' citizens with regard to commerce and industrial activities as well as navigation. In addition, Bulgaria founded its own trade agencies in Thessaloniki, Bitolja, and Skopje in 1897.[46] With these representations, along with diplomatic representations, the country expanded its scope of action in international trade independently of the formal supremacy of the Ottoman Empire.[47]

The status of sovereign participant in international economic forums was further confirmed by Bulgarian participation in the First International Agrarian Congress in Rome in 1905. The last remnant of the restrictions—the immunities and privileges of foreign subjects, with the rights of jurisdiction and of consular protection—was abolished in the trade agreements of 1905. Thus, Bulgaria started the new century as a fully sovereign nation in international trade. The archaic and degrading formulation of the capitulations disappeared from her commercial treaties even before the official declaration of independence from the Ottoman Empire in 1908. In any case it was a symbolic victory and came at the expense of the economic interests of the nation.

A concise retrospective analysis by a Bulgarian economist, Hristo Mutafov, appeared in the *Journal of the Bulgarian Economic Society* in 1910, immediately after the so-called fat years. This journal was the most prestigious and nonpartisan economic journal at that time. The analysis sums up the peculiarities of nationalism with regard to economic policy as well as national self-perception in this context. Mutafov combines competence with sober criticism, far from the typical, everyday journalistic nihilism, as seen in the following passage:

> If we want to compare to the Western cultural countries in every respect then we must have the ambition to catch up with them, especially with respect to economic power, not only in the number of guns and cannons. . . . We have to be modest indeed. We have been living a free life for only thirty years. The accumulation of wealth, the development of productive forces, which in other countries has lasted for centuries, this is something we cannot hope for. . . . In our geographical position, in the wealth of soil, and in frugality we do not measure up badly. But we lack that wide range of national-economic policy which has given strength to manufacturing and trade in developed countries. We talk about labor organization, about increasing productivity, investing capital in national production, finding and winning markets, organization and expansion of commercial and industrial credit along with agrarian credit, conducting a systematic and appropriate agrarian and commercial policy which should not be content with half measures, which does not wipe out today what was created yesterday, etc. . . . The few economists in the country are aware of the importance of such activities. They have repeatedly pointed them out. However, there are no statesmen to allot to them the same importance and, by implementing them, to lay down the solid foundation of a strong national-economic organism."[48]

Whatever label is used to describe Bulgaria's economic situation—growth without structural change (per Alexander Gerschenkron); evolution without development (per Michael Palairet)—the Bulgarian economy remained over-shadowed by incomplete liberation. Primarily, what continued to mobilize social activity was nationalist sentiments, or popular irredentism, in Mark Mazower's words. By the time of the Balkan Wars in 1912–13, Bulgaria was liberated with regard to the formal status of sovereignty in some aspects of politics and foreign trade. But large territories with predominantly Bulgarian populations remained outside the state boundaries. This meant that the drive for national unification still served as the strongest bond between the elite and the masses. From a sociocultural perspective, many of the oriental signs and the sites inherited from the Ottoman past were removed in the cities. The towns nonetheless retained a shape close to oriental ones, with the exception of the central parts of the capital and several other cities. A large majority of the population (excepting a small elite) did not change its lifestyle, which remained within the bounds of a traditional, extremely modest existence.

Recent scholarship stresses that transfers of ideologies and models is an asymmetrical communication between the core and the periphery. As Roumen Dashkalov and Diana Mishkova have argued, "Imports (transfers) cannot be expected to function like the models in their original context, and divergen-cies and transmutations due to mixing with the local practices are normal."[49] Local conditions put their stamp on the adapted templates. International (regional and European) conditionality must also be taken into consider-ation. It seems therefore reasonable to avoid hegemonic comparisons between Western and non-Western development in this context. Such comparisons were not eschewed late nineteenth-century Bulgaria, as is evident from pub-lications from this period. The sense of lag and lack, analytically subsumed in the notion of backwardness was a dominant trope not only in eastern Europe, as Maria Todorova has pointed out.[50]

The belief that wealth and independence were inextricably linked contin-ued to enjoy strong support in Balkan societies into the late nineteenth cen-tury. Freedom was recognized as a necessary condition for economic stability and prosperity and vice versa, although experience showed that many other prerequisites were also crucial in achieving these economic goals. The econ-omy gradually emerged as a matter of great social significance in the building up of a modern state. By the eve of the Balkan Wars, the nationally minded political elite in Bulgaria had visibly progressed in its grasp of economic poli-cies as a systematic and important state activity that was much more complex than balancing incomes and expenses. This insight was closely related to the nationalists' belief that the survival of the nation in an internationally highly competitive political and economic environment was inextricably linked to national unity, in the broadest sense of irredentism plus acceleration of economic progress. The economic growth during the first decade of the twentieth century resulting from internal stabilization, growing involvement in international trade, and massive foreign investment in 1905–6 transformed the economy from being the backdrop for national development to being its focus. The public debate on economic issues expanded and there were some that the particular economic culture of poverty—one shaped by a reflex to save instead of investing in forward-looking, well-planned, and large-scale projects—was being overcome. Rationality as an attribute of economic behavior occurred more often in the activities of the political elite.

However, until the First World War, Bulgaria and the other Balkan states were too absorbed by their quest to remediate their incomplete liberation from the Ottoman Empire. For them, the nineteenth century, in other nations a period of accelerated economic growth, turned into a prolonged age of irredentism. To a greater or lesser degree, the resulting circumstances undoubtedly deflected social attention from improving conditions and prospects for economic progress. The preoccupation of the elite with the unfulfilled national ideals, whatever the slogan—full independence, San Stefano Bulgaria, or liberation and unification—absorbed a lot of social energy and resources, which were diverted from potential economic progress. Unfortunately, the first decade of the twentieth century, successful in many aspects and marked by a steady if not spectacular economic mini-spurt, ended in the Balkan Wars. They revived and perpetuated the dominance of the idea of national unification over pragmatic economic policy and incited Bulgarian politicians to sacrifice the country's economic interests again after an uninterrupted decade of successful recovery after the difficult initial phase of sovereign life.

Notes

1. Ivan Ilchev, *Rodinata mi—prava ili ne: Vŭnshnopoliticheskata propaganda na balkanskite strani (1821–1923)* (Sofia: Universitetsko Izdatelstvo Sv. Kliment Ohridski, 1995), 381.

2. Michael Palairet, *The Balkan Economies c. 1800–1914: Evolution without Development* (Cambridge: Cambridge University Press, 1997), 1. Some representatives of the most conservative or evolutionist political current of the Bulgarian elite, the Turcophiles, also claimed national rights and the principle of nationality.

Their Turcophilism was provoked by concerns about the integrity of the Bulgarian ethnos in the wake of radical and premature revolutionary actions.

3. It was explicitly stated in an article that appeared in *Turtsia*, October 23, 1871, "The economic issues are among the most boring topics for our readers of any rank. . . . Policy is our soul," cited in B. Mintses, "Dŭrzhavnopoliticheskite i sotsialnostopanskite idei v bŭlgarskata doosvoboditelna literatura," *Sbornik za narodni umotvoreniya, nauka i knizhnina* 16–17 (1900): 44.

4. Konrad Clewing, "Staatensystem und innerstaatliches Agieren im multiethnischen Raum: Südosteuropa im langen 19. Jahrhundert," in *Geschichte Südosteuropas: Vom frühen Mittelalter bis zur Gegenwart*, ed. Konrad Clewing and Oliver Jens Schmitt (Regensburg: Verlag Friedrich Pustet, 2011), 467. See also Georgi P. Genov, *Bŭlgariya i Evropa: San Stefano i Berlin 1878* (Sofia: Bŭlgarska Istoricheska Biblioteka, 1940).

5. Marin V. Pundeff, "Bulgarian Nationalism," in *Bulgaria in American Perspective: Political and Cultural Issues*, ed. Marin V. Pundeff (Sofia: Universitetsko Izdatelstvo Sv. Kliment Ohridski, 1993), 27. See also Mark Mazower, *The Balkans* (London: Phoenix Press, 2000), 90–91.

6. Edda Binder-Iijima and Ekkehard Kraft, "The Making of States: Constitutional Monarchies in the Balkans," in *Ottomans into Europeans: State and Institution-Building in South-Eastern Europe*, ed. Wim Van Meurs and Alina Mungiu (London: Hurst, 2010), 10.

7. Edward Dicey, *The Peasant State: An Account of Bulgaria in 1894* (London: John Murray, 1894), 176.

8. For more on this issue see Maria Todorova, *Imagining the Balkans* (New York: Oxford University Press, 1997).

9. Plamen Mitev, ed., *Sŭzdavane i razvitie na moderni institutsii v bŭlgarskoto vŭzrozhdensko obshtestvo* (Sofia: Kooperatsiya "IF-94," 1996).

10. Veska Nikolova and Dimitŭr Sazdov, eds., *Programi, programni dokumenti i ustavi na burzhoaznite partii v Bŭlgaria 1879–1918* (Sofia: Nauka i Izkustvo, 1992), 19–76.

11. G. Chankov, "Gramotnost na naselenieto v Bŭlgaria," *Uchilishten pregled* 1–2 (1926): 7, writes that the exact rate in 1900 according to Bulgarian statistics is 29.8 percent.

12. Kiril Popov, *La Bulgarie économique 1879–1911: Étude statistique* (Sofia: Impr. de la Cour, 1920).

13. Nikolai Genchev, *Bŭlgarskata vŭzrozhdenska inteligentsiya* (Sofia: Universitetsko Izdatelstvo Sv. Kliment Ohridski, 1991).

Liberation in Progress 75

14. Boncho Boev, "Vŭtreshen pregled: Kliuch kŭm bŭlgarskiya ikonomicheski zhivot prez minaloto stoletie," *Spisanie na Bŭlgarskoto ikonomichesko druzhestvo* 10 (1901): 705.

15. The following analysis is based on data in Angel Tsurakov, *Pravitelstvata na Bŭlgaria 1879–1913* (Sofia: Geya Libris, 1996), and Tasho Tashev, *Ministrite na Bŭlgaria 1879–1999* (Sofia: Akademichno Izdatelstvo Prof. M. Drinov, 1999). The results are close to those in Dobrinka Parusheva, *Pravitelstveniyat elit na Rumŭniya i Bŭlgariya vtorata polovina na XIX i nachaloto na XX ve* (Sofia: Institut za Balkanistika, Bŭlgarska Akademiya na Naukite, 2008).

16. Max Weber, *Politik als Beruf* (Munich: Duncker & Humblot, 1919), 23–24. On the modernizing role of the administrative elite in Bulgaria see Wolfgang Höpken, "Beamte in Bulgarien: Zum Modernisierungsbeitrag der Verwaltung zwischen staatlicher Unabhängigkeit und Balkan-Kriegen (1879–1912)," *Südost-Forschungen* 54 (1995): 219–50.

17. Estimated from data in *Statisticheski godishnik na Bŭlgarskoto Tsarstvo: 1911* (Sofia: Dŭrzhavna Pechatnitsa, 1914), 444–45.

18. Dobrinka Parusheva, "The Web of Power and Power of the Webs: Political Elites in Romania and Bulgaria in the Late Nineteenth Century and Their Networks," in *Society, Politics and State Formation in Southeastern Europe during the 19th Century*, ed. Tassos Anastassiadis and Nathalie Clayer (Athens: Alpha Bank Historical Archives, 2011), 141–76.

19. The analysis of the development of the governmental structure is based on data in Veselin Metodiev and L. Stoyanov, *Bŭlgarskite dŭrzhavni institutsii 1879–1986* (Sofia: Dŭrzhavno Izdatelstvo "D-r Petŭr Beron," 1987). See also Veselin Metodiev, "Nachalnata istoriya na izpŭlnitelnata vlast v Bŭlgaria," in *120 godini izpŭlnitelna vlast v Bŭlgariya*, ed. Georgi Markov (Sofia: Gutenberg Publishing House, 1999), 28–29, 33.

20. Roumiana Preshlenova, "Im Vorhof zur Macht: Wirtschaft und Öffentlichkeit in Bulgarien 1878–1914," in *Öffentlichkeit ohne Tradition: Bulgariens Aufbruch in die Moderne*, ed. Harald Heppner and Roumiana Preshlenova (Frankfurt: Peter Lang, 2003), 153–57.

21. This issue is theoretically regarded in, for example, Michael Werner and Bénédicte Zimmermann, "Beyond Comparison: Histoire croisée and the Challenge of Reflexivity," *History and Theory* 45, no. 1 (February 2006): 30–50. On the Balkan case see Diana Mishkova, "Liberalism and Tradition in the Nineteenth-Century Balkans: Towards History and Methodology of Political Transfer," *East European Politics and Societies and Cultures* 26, no. 4 (November 2012): 668–92; Wolfgang Höpken, "Institution-Building, Political Culture and Identity in Bulgaria: The Challenge of 'Europeanization,'" in *Bulgaria and Europe: Shifting Identities*, ed. Stefanos Katsikas

(London: Anthem Press, 2010), 23–32; Holm Sundhaussen, "Institutionen und institutioneller Wandel in den Balkanländern aus historischer Perspektive," in *Institutionen und institutioneller Wandel in Südosteuropa*, ed. Johannes Papalekas (Munich: Südosteuropa-Gesellschaft, 1994), 35–54.

22. Nikolova and Sazdov, *Programi, programni dokumenti*.

23. Max Weber, "Politics as a Vocation," *From Max Weber: Essays in Sociology*, ed. H. H. Gerth and C. Wright Mills (London: Routledge, 1991), 84–85.

24. Maria Manolova, *Parlamentarnoto upravlenie v Bŭlgaria 1894–1912* (Sofia: Akademichno Izdatelstvo Prof. M. Drinov, 2000), 24, 43.

25. Rumen Avramov, "Neosŭshtestveniyat konservativen manifest v Bŭlgaria," in *Stoyan Bochev: Kapitalizmŭt v Bŭlgaria: Ikonomicheski tekstove (1911–1935) i lichni spomeni*, ed. Rumen Avramov (Sofia: Fond. Bŭlgarska nauka i kultura, 1998); Mishkova, "Liberalism and Tradition."

26. Veska Nikolova, *Narodnata partiya i burzhoaznata demokratsiya: Kabinetŭt na Konstantin Stoilov (1894–1899)* (Sofia: Nauka i Izkustvo, 1986), 93–96. See also Veska Nikolova, "Vŭzgledi i stopanska politika na narodnata partiya, 1894–1912," *Izsledvaniya po bŭlgarska istoriya* 10 (Sofia, 1990); Veska Nikolova, *Narodnata partiya 1894–1920: Mezhdu konservatisma i liberalisma* (Veliko Tŭrnovo: Vital, 2004).

27. Velichko Georgiev and Staiko Trifonov, eds., *Istoriya na bŭlgarite 1878–1944 v dokumenti*, vol. 1, *1878–1912* (Sofia: Izdatelstvo Prosveta, 1994), 487.

28. Nikolova and Sazdov, *Programi, programni dokumenti*; Dimitrina Petrova, *Bŭlgarskiyat zemedelski naroden sŭyuz: 1899–1914* (Sofia: Fond. Detelina, 1999); John D. Bell, *Peasants in Power: Alexander Stamboliski and the Bulgarian Agrarian National Union, 1899–1923* (Princeton, NJ: Princeton University Press, 1977).

29. Tatiana Kostadinova, *Bulgaria 1879–1946: The Challenge of Choice* (New York: Columbia University Press, 1995); *Statisticheski godishnik*, 429.

30. Boncho Boev, "Po sŭstavyaneto na druzhestvoto," *Spisanie na Bŭlgarskoto ikonomichesko druzhestvo* 1 (1896).

31. "Izvestiya ot druzhestvoto," *Spisanie na Bŭlgarskoto ikonomichesko druzhestvo* 1 (1901): 63–68.

32. Preshlenova, "Im Vorhof zur Macht," 158–60.

33. *Bŭlgarska Narodna Banka: Sbornik dokumenti*, vol. 1, *1879–1900* (Sofia: Bŭlgarska Narodna Banka, 1998).

34. Nikolova and Sazdov, *Programi, programni dokumenti*.

35. *Statisticheski godishnik*, 48.

36. Georgiev and Trifonov, *Istoriya na bŭlgarite*, vol. 1, 417–43.

37. Roumiana Preshlenova, "Austro-Hungarian Trade and the Economic Development of Southeastern Europe before the First World War," in *Economic*

Transformations in East and Central Europe: Legacies from the Past and Policies for the Future, ed. David F. Good (London: Routledge, 1994).

38. Martin Ivanov and Adam Tooze, "Convergence or Decline on Europe's Southeastern Periphery? Agriculture, Population, and GNP in Bulgaria, 1892–1945," *Journal of Economic History* 67, no. 3 (2007): 672–703.

39. John R. Lampe, *The Bulgarian Economy in the Twentieth Century* (London: Croom Helm, 1986), 39.

40. Dnevnik (stenograficheski) na VIII obiknoveno narodno sŭbranie, I redovna sesiya, XLIV zasedanie (December 19–20, 1894).

41. Cyril E. Black, "The Process of Modernization: The Bulgarian Case," in *Bulgaria, Past & Present: Studies in History, Literature, Economic, Music, Sociology, Folklore & Linguistics,* ed. Thomas Butler (Columbus, OH: American Association for the Advancement of Slavic Studies, 1976), 111–31.

42. Boev, "Kliuch kŭm bŭlgarskiya ikonomicheski zhivot," 627–29.

43. "Treaty of Berlin, July 20, 1878," http://archive.thetablet.co.uk/article/20th-july-1878/11/the-treaty-of-berlin.

44. On the regime of capitulations, see Şevket Pamuk, *The Ottoman Empire and European Capitalism 1820–1913: Trade, Investment and Production* (Cambridge: Cambridge University Press, 1987).

45. G. K. Svrakov, "Bŭlgarskata mitnishka tarifa za vnosnite stoki v neinoto razvitie," *Godishnik na vissheto tŭrgovsko uchilishte Varna* 9 (1935–36): 13, 16; *Istoria na finansovata i kreditnata sistema na Bŭlgaria,* vol. 3, bk. 2, *Ot osvobozhdenieto do 9.IX.1944* (Varna: G. Bakalov, 1983), 171ff., 176ff.

46. Elena Statelova and Vaska Tankova, *Konstantin Stoilov v politicheskiya zhivot na Bŭlgaria* (Sofia: Izdatelska Kŭshta Anubis, 2001), 263–65.

47. Despite Bulgaria's status as a semisovereign state, Bulgarian diplomatic representations were founded in Constantinople, Belgrade, and Bucharest (1879), Vienna (1889), St. Petersburg and Athens (1896), Paris and Cetinje (1897), London and Rome (1903), and Berlin (1904). In 1908, Bulgaria also had trade representatives in Edirne and Dedeağaç.

48. Hristo Mutafov, "Nasheto stupansko razvitie," *Spisanie na Bŭlgarskoto ikonomichesko druzhestvo* 14, no. 6 (1910): 410.

49. See, for example, Roumen Daskalov and Diana Mishkova, eds., *Entangled Histories of the Balkans,* vol. 2, *Transfers of Political Ideologies and Institutions* (Leiden, Netherlands: Brill, 2014), xi–xii.

50. Maria Todorova, "Modernity," in *Modernism: The Creation of Nation-States, Discourses of Collective Identity in Central and Southeast Europe 1770–1945: Texts and Commentaries,* vol. III/1, ed. Ahmed Ersoy, Maciej Górny, and Vangelis Kechriotis (Budapest: Central European University Press, 2010), 21.

CHAPTER FOUR

EMIGRANTS AND COUNTRIES OF ORIGIN

The Politics of Emigration in Southeastern Europe until the First World War

Ulf Brunnbauer

Emigration and the State

On October 4, 1913, the foreign minister of the Kingdom of Montenegro, P. Plamenić, dispatched a note to Labuda Gojnić, the interior minister:

> Lately, a new wave of emigration of our citizens to America has begun. They descend in whole groups to different places in the Bay of Kotor in order to continue to Trieste. From reliable sources we have learned that most of them have no passport at all and some of them have old ones, which are not valid anymore. Our emigrants, out of all emigrants from different countries, suffer the most because they receive no protection from anywhere. They fall into the hands of speculators, who trade with them and dispatch them on the ships of the Austro-Americana [steamship line]. It would be helpful if our border authorities strictly control each emigrant's border crossing, and return those who do not have a valid passport. Moreover, all persons who are in contact with emigration agents should be monitored as closely as possible.[1]

Writing a month later, the foreign minister expressed his suspicion that the Austrians were facilitating Montenegrin emigration:

> I have learned that the Austrian border authorities use various means to facilitate Montenegrin emigration to America and are in collusion with the

steamship company Austro-Americana. They distribute secret propaganda for emigration. Because of that, ever more young Montenegrins emigrate from Montenegro, which impairs our army. Small groups of Montenegrins without passports arrive in Kotor, Risan, and Budva [towns in Austrian territory] and receive documents from the Austrians for the continuation of their journey.[2]

The Montenegrin ministers' correspondence exemplifies the pre-1914 wave of overseas emigration from the Balkans, which became a major governmental concern across southeastern Europe. Bureaucrats from across the region felt that the movement of people across state borders constituted a problem and jeopardized salient state development goals. Governments started to worry about emigration for a number of reasons. Their main concern was that emigration would challenge one of the state's fundamental claims: that the state enjoyed sovereignty over its people. This included the expectation that citizens felt an emotional attachment to and loyalty toward their state. How could this claim be maintained if people left in order to live thousands of miles away? Was this not an embarrassment to a state that portrayed itself as the manifestation of the nation's destiny? As in other parts of Europe, the fact that mass emigration from southeastern Europe occurred in parallel to nation and state building intensified these concerns.[3]

The politics of emigration have so far received less scholarly attention than immigration politics. Nancy L. Green and François Weil assert that this imbalance reflects the fact that "most migration history is written from where we are: the countries of immigration, past and present."[4] Yet the state, its regulations, and agents were important factors in shaping emigration as well. States developed specific policies of exit and addressed emigrants with legislation and decrees. Mark I. Choate points out the comprehensive polices by which Italy, after unification, handled the many emigrants from Italy. Through these measures, the government aimed to retain emigrants' loyalty to country and nation, increasing the inflow of migrant transfers, and facilitating their return.[5]

In contrast to Italy, the southeastern European states' emigration regulations have yet to be systematically explored. The literature on the politics of emigration in the Balkans concentrates on forced emigration. The research on "ethnic cleansing" in nineteenth and twentieth century Balkan history is extensive.[6] Ethnic cleansing has been described as an instrument of radicalized nation building in a region where nationalist designs clashed with multiethnic populations. Especially during and immediately after war, different regional governments repeatedly expelled various minority groups in order to achieve their goal of ethno-national homogeneity.[7] As Tara Zahra shows in her seminal 2016 work on mass migration from eastern Europe and its significance for concepts of the free world, "Emigration policy became an explicit tool of new and more violent forms of nation building and population politics."[8] In peacetime, too, minorities often felt pressure from government and society to leave their country.[9]

Governments not only pursued the emigration of minority groups as a goal, but also used emigration as a tool to achieve certain goals related to nation and state building. To that end, governments and experts sought to wrest control over voluntary as well as forced migration. For example, current research on interwar and socialist Yugoslavia discusses official efforts to establish at least symbolic control over labor emigration.[10] Although the dispositions that would shape emigration regimes throughout the twentieth century were laid down before 1914, the role of overseas emigration for the emergence of specific emigration policy provisions has yet to be discussed systematically.

In this chapter I argue that analysis of the politics of emigration provides insight into the ways political elites conceptualized the state and its functions. Emigration policies reshaped the function of state machinery and the relationship between the state and citizen. Political elites and public opinion often viewed emigration as a threat to the imagined and physical boundaries of the polity on which they projected their claim of sovereignty. But governments also began to use emigration as a safety valve for social discontent and to selectively encourage people to leave, depending on these people's place in the developmental and international agenda of the state. Zahra even calls the emerging politics of exit "one of the most consequential political discoveries of nineteenth-century European states."[11] Aside from this, state response to any salient social phenomenon—such as mass emigration—is necessarily a relevant issue in its own right. Pre-1914 southeastern Europe is an excellent subject through which to analyze these issues since the governments in the region pursued a diverse range of responses to emigration, ranging from laissez-faire to outright prohibition of emigration.

Case studies from southeastern Europe therefore challenge the notion of an "exit revolution," which Aristide R. Zolberg posits to have taken place in nineteenth-century Europe.[12] Zolberg argues that European countries tended to liberalize their exit rules as a result of liberal economic policies but also as a response to perceived demographic and social pressures. However, as this study shows, an opposing tendency was also growing out of many modern states' desire to control population movement and maintain sovereignty over territory *and* people. Not all European states shed the physiocratic legacy, which assumed that the size of a country's population was one of its most important sources of wealth.[13]

The bureaucrats of the modern state shared the view that the very act of border crossing required state redress. State governments tended to perceive the movement of people across borders as a threat to their strategies of controlling people. As Charles Tilly argued, the modern state prefers sedentary subjects who can more easily be counted, taxed, drafted into the army, sent to school, and otherwise controlled.[14] Under the regime of territoriality, modern bureaucracies viewed border control as one of their most important tasks.[15] This necessitated the implementation of coherent methods of identification for people who wanted to cross state borders and the concentration of cross-border movement at designated points.[16] These attempts to control emigration engendered transnational administrative interactions, as sending, transit, and destination countries tried to force other state governments to honor their particular rules. The United States, receiving the largest total number of immigrants during this period, was particularly eager to see its rules of entry enforced at the point of embarkation, especially after the US Congress started banning specific groups from immigrating.[17]

In effect, a variety of salient concerns fed into emigration policies. Nationalism was another political practice and ideology that shaped emigration policies but was also influenced by emigration. Green and Weil claim, "Defining emigrants was part of a larger process of defining citizens (and their obligations), national character, as well as the notion of a cultural nation."[18] Thus, many national activists viewed the emigration of co-nationals as a loss to the nation's viability. Other dissenting voices saw emigration as a way to spread the nation's global influence or emphasized the economic benefits of migrant transfers. State governments became concerned about emigrants' homeland-oriented activities, adding another transnational dimension to state practices. One of the important factors for official and public perceptions of emigration was the dominant self-image of the polity, be it a multiethnic empire or a homogeneous nation-state. Another factor was intergovernmental competition. Civilian government and the military often took different views vis-à-vis emigration, and the actions of local government often differed from those of central government. Would-be migrants, for their part, found myriad ways to circumvent state rules, which then often prompted governments to enact new, more restrictive measures. As a result, governments' attempts to control their citizens' movements often led to the state becoming more interventionist.

Political Responses

Southeastern European societies were traditionally very mobile, but at the end of the nineteenth century migration patterns shifted from regional destinations toward the Americas.[19] The reasons for this change were manifold: the crisis of farming in the Balkans, compounded by the unequal distribution of land; the rise in natural population growth; the negative consequences of the grape pest phylloxera for wine production; the absence of industrial development; the linking of southeastern Europe to the central European railway network.[20] Not all parts of southeastern Europe were equally affected by these transformations, but many were. At the same time, there was tremendous pull coming from the Americas, especially the United States. The rapid industrial expansion of the late nineteenth century created an almost insatiable demand for cheap immigrant labor, especially in physically demanding but poorly paid jobs in heavy industry and mining, for which it was increasingly difficult to recruit white native-born American workers. Wages for the immigrants might have been very low and working conditions extremely arduous but migrants could nonetheless reasonably expect that they would earn much more money than at home and be able to save to send money back home and to pay for their own planned return.[21]

Immigrants from Austria-Hungary were the largest group of foreign citizens arriving in the United States in the early twentieth century. From 1876 to 1910, almost 4 million people emigrated from Austria-Hungary, roughly in equal numbers from Austria and Hungary.[22] One of the Habsburg regions particularly affected was the Kingdom of Croatia and Slavonia, whence more than 200,000 emigrants left between 1899 and 1914 (85 percent of them went to the United States).[23] Greece and Montenegro recorded high rates of emigration as well. From Greece, an estimated 310,000 individuals emigrated overseas between 1896 and 1915 (95 percent of them to the United States).[24] From Montenegro, reasonable estimates put the number of emigrants for the same period at more than 20,000 (10 percent of the total population).[25] The mass exodus only stopped with the outbreak of the First World War, followed by the most important destination countries' imposition of stringent immigration restrictions in the early 1920s.

The diversity of southeastern Europe's political landscape at that time makes the region a perfect case study for discussing emigration policies. The northern parts of southeastern Europe, including a long stretch of the Adriatic coastline, belonged to the Dual Monarchy, whose two constitutive parts developed different legal systems after the 1867 *Ausgleich*, the Austro-Hungarian Compromise. Croatia was part of Hungary but enjoyed certain levels of autonomy in addition to possessing its own diet (*sabor*, or assembly) and governor. On former Ottoman territory emerged six eventually independent nation-states: Greece (independent since 1831), Serbia (1878), Montenegro

(1878), Romania (1878), Bulgaria (autonomous as of 1878; independent in 1908), and Albania (1913). Until the First Balkan War, the Ottoman Empire still ruled large parts of the central Balkans.[26] It would be easy to assume that imperial and nation-state emigration policies diverged as a result of their different multinational or homogeneous concepts of belonging. Yet the reality was more nuanced.

The Habsburg Empire

The Dual Monarchy of Austro-Hungary provides a fascinating case study for the discussion of emigration policy. Not only was it a major country of emigration, but due to its dualist nature the political responses in the two constitutive units diverged significantly. Nevertheless, a shared aspect was the fact that in both realms, the emigration rates differed significantly among the nationalities. Although this does not mean that the imperial governments pushed members of nondominant groups into emigration, this pattern of differential emigration rates did affect state perception of and reaction to emigration. Significant differences in the emigration rates of specific nationalities, of which the government kept track, strengthened government officials' and interested publics' tendency to look at these social phenomena through the lens of nationality.

In Cisleithania (the "Austrian" half of the empire), the 1867 constitution stipulated that the "freedom of emigration is restricted by the state only in the way of military service."[27] This marked a reversal of previous imperial emigration patents, which had outlawed emigration.[28] From 1867 until 1913 Austria pursued an open-door exit policy. But in around 1890, this became a matter of political concern when annual emigration reached and then surpassed fifty thousand people.[29] In the ensuing Austrian emigration debate, two major factions were in opposition. The first, comprising the liberal-minded Ministry of Trade and representatives of steamship lines, craftsmen, and farmers, defended the freedom to emigrate, highlighting its positive socioeconomic consequences. The two major political parties with mass support, the Christian Social Party and the Social Democrats, also defended freedom of movement, while urging the government to actively combat the economic reasons behind emigration.

The opposite faction in this debate, represented especially by the Ministry of War, called for restrictions. Its members portrayed emigration as a "danger for our army, therefore for our power; for our agriculture, therefore for our national wealth."[30] Army officials particularly deplored the added difficulties to carrying out conscription when so many conscripts were abroad. In addition, landowners in areas such as the province of Galicia demanded restrictions on emigration, fearing that the exodus of the rural poor would deprive them of cheap labor.[31]

In view of the intensity of the debate and the rising numbers of emigrants, the government could not ignore the issue. In his throne speeches of 1897, 1901, and 1907 to the Imperial Council (*Reichsrat*), Emperor Franz Joseph I promised new legislation on emigration.[32] The government did introduce a bill on emigration in parliament in 1904, which included restrictive clauses. But because of severe criticism in a parliamentary enquiry, particularly from liberal members of parliament, the bill never made it to the floor. A new government initiative for a law on emigration in 1908 did not make it into the *Reichsrat* at all.[33] So Cisleithania, while a top supplier of emigrants, remained without specific legislation on emigration, and a designated state service was not established. The Austrian government did not even produce its own official counts of emigrants.[34]

The army, though, continued to pressure the administration to stop the exodus of young males. In 1912 the government complied, releasing new regulations for military recruitment that included the provision that males over the age of seventeen were required to receive a special permit from the authorities if they wanted to emigrate.[35] With increased political and military tensions in the wake of the Balkan Wars and thanks to the skillful exploitation of a scandal about large-scale transportation to America of young men who had not fulfilled their compulsory service, the army eventually gained the upper hand. The government began to intensify border controls and, after the failure to pass a restrictive law on emigration through parliament, implemented new administrative restrictions.[36] In January 1914 the minister of the interior issued various directives declaring that men from seventeen to thirty-six years of age were not allowed to leave the country unless they could prove that they had finished their military service or were exempt from it.[37] To ensure compliance, the government created an extensive network of controls at the border and at railway stations. The Austrian police direction in Vienna set up the Central Office for the Monitoring of Emigration, which was the first centralized state organ dealing with emigration. Despite challenges from *Reichsrat* deputies, who criticized the new rules limiting emigration as a violation of the constitution, the new controls became effective as of March 1, 1914.[38] On the eve of the outbreak of war, the imperial government declared a complete foreign travel ban for any potential recruits.[39]

Reflecting the different nature of its state, Hungary's response to mass emigration was markedly different from Austria's. In Hungary, the political elite considered their country a national state, in contrast to the composite nature of the Austrian part of the monarchy. As a result of the clearly nationalizing nature of government policies in Hungary, the country passed a law on emigration in 1903, thus following the example of other European countries that had passed legislation dealing specifically with emigration (Switzerland in 1888; Germany in 1897; Italy in 1901). Hungary also produced detailed annual statistics on emigration.[40] Such official production of knowledge is always a good indicator for a state's perception of problems. Although the law did not actually ban out-migration, the government's greater focus on emigration compared to that of Austria highlighted the connection between nationalism and emigration.

The Hungarian 1903 Law on Emigration, described by contemporaries as "the most drastic of its kind," defined an emigrant as someone who went abroad for a "continuous period of life."[41] Article II of the law contained restrictions on the emigration of specific population groups, such as conscripts without proper permission from the authorities; persons against whom criminal procedures or arrest warrants were pending; people who did not have sufficient money for transportation or who did not fulfill the entry requirements of the country of destination; and people whose voyage was paid by a foreign government or private person for the purpose of colonization. Articles V and VI charged the Ministry of the Interior with outlawing emigration to any country where the life, health, "morality," or property of emigrants from Hungary would be threatened. The law also dealt with the business of emigration, outlawing advertising and regulating practices of transportation and the activities of transport companies. The law also established the Emigration Fund, which supported emigrants in need. The government promised to guarantee a safe channel for the transfer back to Hungary of migrants' savings through Hungarian banks.[42] The main aim of the Hungarian law, then, was to bring emigration under the government's strict control. Its restrictive language was designed to placate large landowners, who had urged the government to ban emigration.[43] Despite its seemingly restrictive language, the law did not reduce the number of emigrants. In 1904, when the law became effective, more people emigrated from Hungary than ever before (70,488 compared to 68,457 in 1903). Between 1905 and 1907, the annual number rose to more than 160,000 emigrants each year.[44]

The government generally subscribed to liberal economic policies and abstained from actively restricting emigration. Any government-imposed restriction on emigration would have been difficult to enforce because the border between Hungary and Austria was not patrolled. The Hungarian government had earlier learned from local authorities' unsuccessful attempts to control people that there was little it could do to reduce the number of emigrants.[45] The government also viewed emigration as a safety valve for social and ethnic tensions. In internal communications, government bodies stressed that persons from non-Magyar nationalities left in disproportionate numbers (around 70 percent of the emigrants from Hungary were non-Magyars), which facilitated the overarching goal of Magyarization.[46] This stance can be seen in 1907, when Prime Minister Sándor Wekerle sketched an "action program for the support of the return of Hungarian emigrants from America" and made it clear that this solely concerned Hungarian speakers.[47]

The government's intentions underlying the Law on Emigration were revealed by Prime Minister Kálmán Széll in the parliamentary debate: The bill aimed to render emigration beneficial for Hungarian economic interests. According to Széll, control over emigration would consolidate and redirect the stream of emigrants through the Hungarian sea port of Fiume (today's Rijeka).[48] To the government's frustration, prior to 1903 almost all emigrants from Hungary left via German or Dutch ports.[49] Based on the new law, Hungary concluded an agreement with the Cunard shipping company, granting it the sole license for transport of Hungarian emigrants, from Hungarian ports. Cunard promised to service the Fiume–New York connection with at least two ships monthly. In return, the Hungarian government guaranteed a minimum of thirty thousand emigrants per year and, in the case of less than thirty thousand passengers, promised to pay an indemnity of 100 crowns per "missing" passenger. The government also instructed local authorities across the country to issue passports only to emigrants who would leave from Fiume. To facilitate the process, emigrants enjoyed a discount on train tickets to Fiume. At government expense, the port facilities in Fiume were modernized and a hostel for up to two thousand emigrants was built.[50]

With these measures, the Hungarian government achieved a substantial increase in the number of passengers embarking from Fiume, yet most emigrants from Hungary continued to leave from North Sea ports. The severe resistance to the agreement with Cunard by the powerful North Atlantic Pool—the cartel of the most important transatlantic shipping companies—was one major reason behind this. Upon hearing about the agreement with Cunard, the North Atlantic Pool dramatically lowered its prices for steamship tickets to America, forcing Cunard to reduce its ticket prices as well, which made the whole operation unprofitable.[51] The German government also intervened on behalf of the cartel, pressuring the Hungarian government into signing an agreement in 1905 prohibiting the imposition of any measures preventing emigrants from traveling through Germany.[52] Articles in German and American newspapers portrayed the treaty between Hungary and Cunard as a violation of the US law that prohibited the immigration of contract workers.[53] The American press accused the Hungarian government of wanting to get rid of "unwanted" elements.

With a new Law on Emigration, passed in 1908, the Hungarian government made a second attempt to challenge the preeminent position of the North Atlantic Pool in the emigration business. The law stipulated that government licenses for the transportation of emigrants would be awarded only to companies that agreed to observe Hungarian law and accepted Hungarian officials' supervision in their ports. The Hungarian government entered into protracted negotiations with the cartel, during which the cartel fended off most of the Hungarians' demands. They reached an agreement only in 1911, in which the only concession the cartel made was to observe Hungarian law in their business activities *in* Hungary and to make a one-time contribution of one hundred thousand crowns to the Hungarian Emigration Fund.[54]

The second nationalizing tendency of Hungarian emigration policies concerned ethnic mobilization. One of the Hungarian government's major fears in respect to emigration was the political impact of non-Magyar émigré organizations in America on their co-nationals in Hungary. The American Slovak community in particular was a thorn in the side of Magyarization. Slovaks from Hungary recorded particularly high rates of emigration. Once in the United States, they were exposed to intense national agitation by numerous Slovak organizations and publications, whereas in Hungary expressions of Slovak national identity were suppressed. Booker T. Washington commented in 1912, "The Slovak or the Croatian who comes to America does not at once lose his interest in the political and social struggle of his native land."[55] Washington and other observers noted the strong sense of national belonging that was nurtured by national organizations among the emigrants from Hungary, where their compatriots at home were exposed to policies of Magyarization.

The Hungarian government viewed the non-Magyar emigrants in similar terms: It feared that Slovak (and Croatian and Serbian) returnees would distribute pan-Slavic or national, or socialist, propaganda in Hungary. These fears were aggravated by the fact that a significant share of emigrants from Hungary did return. To monitor this potential problem, the government ordered local authorities to produce detailed statistics about returnees and to observe their activities.[56] The government also frequently banned Slovak and other non-Magyar publications brought from the United States.[57] In 1902, the Hungarian government started the ill-fated "American Action," in which the state began subsidizing pro-government émigré organizations and sending loyal priests to emigrant parishes in America. The government's ultimate goal was to maintain "the sentiment of belonging" to Hungary among the emigrants. Through these methods, Hungary tried to extend its Magyarization policies across the Atlantic. Yet the Hungarian government was caught in the contradictions of its own policies: On the one hand, the emigration of Slovaks reduced their number in Hungary, about which the government was not displeased, while on the other hand, the government had no means to suppress anti-Hungarian agitation in America; nor could it prevent its citizens from returning.

The salience of debates and policies of emigration for the articulation of nationalist concerns can also be illustrated by the Kingdom of Croatia and Slavonia, which was part of Hungary but enjoyed a degree of self-government after 1868. Perennial disagreements with the Hungarian government about the extent of Croatian autonomy shaped political debate in Croatia. Other often disputed issues included the relationship between Croats and Serbs in the kingdom and Croatian nationalists' demand to unify Croatia with Dalmatia. In short, politics and press at the turn of the century were saturated with debates about the nation.

Unsurprisingly, mass emigration to America, which started in the early 1890s, became an important issue in public and political debates, and local newspapers reported on emigration as a standard feature. They warned readers about the unfortunate fate of emigrants in America and deplored the loss of able-bodied young men. But newspapers also informed readers about Croatian emigrants' associations in America. Members of the Croatian diet took up this issue as well. There were at least seven interpellations by diet members between 1900 and 1914, in which they criticized the government's inaction with respect to emigration.[58] One of the most ardent critics was Stjepan Radić, leader of the Croatian Peasant Party, who alleged that while whole regions were emptied of adult Croats, "tens of thousands of Magyar and German settlers" would replace them.[59] There were only few voices in the Croatian debate on emigration that stressed its positive effects as manifested in the massive inflow of migrant savings.[60] Encapsulating these sentiments in 1912, the Serb community leader in Croatia, Laza Horvat, gave a speech inciting listeners to "remember what I tell you: *America is the grave of our people, it is a new Kosovo, the abyss, and not the salvation of our people.*"[61]

Concerned about emigration's impact on local population, the Croatian government took several steps to discourage the process. In 1883 it placed the emigration under police supervision. After that, the government repeatedly issued decrees outlawing the business of emigration agents (the frequency of such decrees is evidence of their ineffectiveness). A major decree on emigration, issued in 1901, regulated the business of travel agencies.[62] The decree prohibited encouraging "workers and peasants to emigrate, verbally or with brochures, steamship line itineraries or other advertising material." But the many ads by steamship companies and travel agencies in newspapers suggest that this provision was not enforced. The government established an emigration office under its department for internal affairs. They also set up the government-administered Emigration Fund to assist destitute emigrants. After Hungary passed its Law on Emigration in 1903, the Croatian government drafted its own law, which in 1906 was brought before the Croatian *sabor*.[63] Most of its thirty-one clauses included regulations of the transportation of emigrants by steamship companies, which the Holland-America Line and the Hamburg-America Line protested against.[64] Following other countries of emigration, such as Italy, where governments tried to build links with compatriots abroad, the bill stipulated that the government take measures to maintain emigrants' attachment to Croatia. Exemplifying early efforts to create loyal diasporas, the authors of the bill explained that the state should help the emigrants "morally and materially, so that their love and affection for their home-country would be kept alive."[65] Voices of experts in the provincial government recommended strengthening contacts with Croatian and Serbian emigrant organizations in America and subsidizing their publications in order to counterbalance "revolutionary writing in the press."[66]

Although the bill was introduced in the diet three times—1906, 1910, and 1914—the government could not get it through. It never even made to the floor because Croatian lawmakers simply did not have competency in this area of legislation. Instead, Croatia had to accept Hungarian legislation. The governor (*banus*) of Croatia could only issue decrees regulating administrative and technical issues concerning emigration.[67] In November 1913, trying to influence the situation, the governor decreed that conscripts and reservists were only allowed to leave the country with written permission and after payment of a security deposit of one hundred to one thousand crowns.[68] These restrictions apparently had effects: The number of Croatian emigrants declined immediately and stayed low until war broke out.

Thus, only under pressure from the army in a time of heightened international tensions were real restrictions on emigration enacted in the Habsburg

Empire. The only deviation from this pattern concerned emigration to Brazil, which was the fourth most important destination for emigrants from Austria-Hungary: sixty-four thousand Austrian and Hungarian citizens emigrated to Brazil between 1876 and 1910.[69] The government of Brazil and its federal states actively promoted immigration for the purpose of colonization of the countryside, promising support and land. Yet Austro-Hungarian consuls in Brazil frequently reported on extremely poor conditions of immigrants. Many immigrants from Austro-Hungary were not given land, but were forced to work on large farms known as *fazendas*, whose owners faced labor shortages after the abolition of slavery in 1888. Wanting to protect their citizens, Austrian officials repeatedly declared bans on emigration to Brazil when consuls warned about conditions there.[70] The government was especially concerned as emigration to Brazil was usually for permanent settlement, whereas emigrants to North America typically intended to return. However, local authorities sometimes pursued a different agenda. In a country where municipalities were responsible for supporting the poor, local officials considered emigration—even to Brazil—as a way to reduce the financial burden of poverty relief.[71] Reports from different parts of the Dual Monarchy suggest that local municipalities tried to dump poor locals in the Americas, and some of them failed to enforce the ban on emigration to Brazil.

The Nation-States

The debates and attempted policy measures in Croatia and Hungary indicate nation-building elites' concerns regarding emigration. These governments were particularly concerned with population size of the nations they were trying to build, given the association between population and political power. In addition, the national states in the region were relatively young. With only a few years or decades of internationally recognized sovereignty, their youth increased their sensitivity about losing citizens to other sovereign domains. Despite these similar concerns, there were significant differences between the emigration regimes of the diverse Balkan states, resulting from differences in migration patterns, institutional set-ups, and distinctive ideological foundations of the nations.

The situation in Montenegro and Serbia provides a particularly interesting example for the bilateral dimension of migration policies. Montenegro, a country of barren karst lacking almost any industrial development, continually hemorrhaged people, initially mainly in the direction of Serbia, which itself was sparsely populated until the late nineteenth century.[72] The Serbian government invited settlers from neighboring countries to clear and farm previously unused land. The government of Montenegro, in turn, encouraged emigration as one of the few ways to prevent starvation in the country.[73] The historian Đoko Pejović asserts that a powerful motive for Prince Nikola, who reigned from 1860 to 1918, to continually stress the brotherhood of Montenegrins and Serbs was to keep Serbia's door open for immigrants from Montenegro. Nikola's expansionist foreign policies toward Ottoman territory and plans to drain the Lake of Scutari stemmed from the same goal of securing more arable land.[74] Consequently, it came as a blow to the Montenegrin government when the Serbian government closed its borders to settlers from Montenegro in 1882.[75] The Serbian minister of foreign affairs explained his government's decision by stating that uncultivated land was running out.[76]

This justification was not credible in view of the fact that Serbia had passed its Law on Colonization, which encouraged immigration, only two years earlier. Rather, the Serbian government used immigration policy as leverage in its attempts to force the Montenegrin ruler to accept Serbian preeminence in the effort to unify all Serbs of the Balkans. Serbian immigration policies vis-à-vis Montenegro corresponded to the ups and downs of the bilateral relations between the two countries.[77] In the early 1880s, relations were notoriously bad. Serbia supported opposition to the Montenegrin Prince Nikola: He backed the return of the deposed Karadjordjević dynasty to the Serbian throne.[78] When relations warmed, Serbia again permitted Montenegrin immigrants, most of whom settled in regions newly acquired by Serbia from the Ottoman Empire, from which the majority of the Muslim population had been expelled.[79] Settlers received land, tax breaks, and guns so they could guard the border with the Ottoman Empire.[80] Relations between Serbia and Montenegro repeatedly deteriorated and then improved again, leading to a continuous seesaw in immigration policy. In 1907, for example, the Serbian prime minister, Nikola Pašić, once again informed his Montenegrin colleague that no land was available in Serbia for immigrants from Montenegro.[81]

One of the major consequences of the repeated closures of the Serbian border was the redirection of the migration stream from Montenegro to the United States, which during the 1890s became the most important receiving country for Montenegrins. This led to a change in the migration pattern from permanent settlement of whole families in Serbia to predominantly temporary migration of young males to the United States. Throughout these shifts, the Montenegrin government continued its open-door emigration policy. Only when the Montenegrin state prepared for war against the Ottomans did it attempted to curtail emigration. In 1911, the Ministry of War issued

instructions to the local military authorities explaining the restrictive regulations for the emigration of conscripts.[82] Some of the government's other
measures included a temporary suspension of issuing passports, the confisca-
tion of the passports of returnees (to prevent them from leaving again), and
actions against private emigration agents.[83] The government used the semi-
official newspaper, *Glas Crnogorca* (Voice of Montenegro), to disseminate
anti-emigration propaganda, frequently reporting about the difficult fate of
Montenegrin citizens in the United States.[84] Journalists also pointed to raised
aspirations created by emigration which the country could not possibly fulfill:
"Our modest peasants were used to be satisfied with so little," but after migration to the United States, they do "not settle anymore for polenta."[85] However,
since emigration from Montenegro continued more or less unabated, governmental efforts to restrict departure to America appear not to have had much
effect. This was a result of the extremely weak administrative capacity of a state
that could not effectively police its border.

The frequent *Glas Crnogorca* reports about Montenegrin citizens in the
United States had the effect of firmly bringing emigration to the attention
of the public; the press presented emigrants as continuing to be part of the
Montenegrin community. The first issue of *Glas Crnogorca* in 1871 contained the obituary of a Montenegrin emigrant in the United States.[86] The
newspaper regularly printed information on how much money Montenegrin
emigrants donated for laudable domestic causes—usually the renovation of
local churches. The paper also celebrated Montenegrin emigrants who organized homeland associations in the United States.[87] Through these articles
one can see firsthand the home country's expectation that emigrants would
send money to support their families and communities, to behave well, and to
remain loyal to their ruler and their country.

As indicated earlier, in contrast with Montenegro, the Serbian government
was decidedly pro-immigration, and anti-emigration for its own population.
As the relationship with Montenegro shows, the Serbian state had gratefully
received settlers from its neighboring countries for decades.[88] Special decrees
and laws facilitated immigration. The first, regarding colonization in 1862,
regulated the award of Serbian citizenship to settlers and guaranteed them state
support.[89] April 1880 saw the publication of the Law of Settlement of Foreign
Colonists, whose purpose was to repopulate the territories of the former sanjak
of Niš, which the Congress of Berlin awarded Serbia in 1878.[90] These policies
attracted a significant number of farmers—usually but not always Orthodox
Serbian speakers from Montenegro.[91] In contrast to Montenegro, other
states were not as supportive of the emigration of their citizens to Serbia. The

Habsburg monarchy worried about peasants from Croatia moving to Serbia and demanded that the Serbian government stop this.[92] Passport protocols from different Croatian districts suggest that in the 1880s, the Croatian government issued the majority of passports for emigration to Bosnia or Serbia.[93] Apart from farmers, Serbia also attracted a significant number of professionals, traders, and entrepreneurs, many of whom were Serbs from the Dual Monarchy. Total immigration numbers for Serbia are not known, but the historian Holm Sundhaussen calculates a net immigration to Serbia of 55,308 persons between 1880 and 1890 alone.[94]

Serbia's anti-emigration stance only became evident in the mid-1900s, as there had previously been no significant emigration. Until then, there were few long-distance emigrants from Serbia at all; most migrants were seasonal workers who returned each year. The number of emigrants to the United States only began to increase at the end of the 1910s, but remained low by regional standards. This change can be attributed to deterioration of the economic situation in Serbia, the increasing scarcity of fertile land, and the penetration of Serbia by emigration agents. However, the government reacted quickly to stop the flow. The government raised fees for passports to prohibitive levels. As a result, before the Balkan Wars the number of overseas emigrants from Serbia was only about three thousand.[95]

Bulgaria followed a similar policy, promoting immigration while restricting emigration of ethnic Bulgarians (but not members of minorities). In 1880 Bulgaria passed the Law on the Resettlement of Depopulated Lands, which encouraged ethnic Bulgarians to come to Bulgaria and settle on land abandoned by Muslims during and after the 1877–78 Russo-Turkish War.[96] Additionally, in the decades after the war Bulgaria supported the immigration of presumed co-nationals, mainly from Macedonia and Thrace, and did not impede the emigration of Turks and Greeks.[97] When the first signs of significant overseas emigration appeared around 1905, the minister of the interior promptly decreed that workers who wanted to leave for America were not to receive a passport unless they could prove that they would return within a month.[98] Would-be migrants proved capable of circumventing the provision, and the government introduced new restrictions on the issuing of passports for presumptive emigrants in 1906.[99]

Nonetheless, emigration to the United States continued to increase. In 1907, more than seventeen thousand Bulgarian citizens left for America, more than in any previous year. The military concerns discussed earlier regarding loss of manpower in a period of military buildup plagued policy makers. In response, in December 1907 the National Assembly passed one of the most restrictive emigration laws of the period.[100] It outlawed or limited emigration for nine categories of people, including reserve recruits, who were only allowed to leave if they made a deposit of one thousand to five thousand leva—a prohibitive sum. The emigration law also granted the government the right to stop emigration to any country for "social" reasons or if the well-being of the emigrants was at risk.[101] As an additional measure, in 1910 the minister of the interior instructed district authorities to invalidate passports of travelers suspected of wanting to travel to America.[102] Emigration out of Bulgaria was not totally stopped, but the numbers continued to be relatively low: Between 1908 and 1912, 18,653 individuals are recorded as emigrating from Bulgaria, out of a population of 4.3 million in 1910. In the same period, more than 60,000 people left Croatia, which had a population of 2.5 million.[103]

The Kingdom of Greece pursued completely different emigration policies than its northern neighbors. The Dillingham Commission, which the US Congress established in 1907 to study immigration, also analyzed emigration conditions in Greece. The commission concluded that "no restriction [was] placed upon emigration."[104] Greek citizens enjoyed the constitutional right to cross their country's borders.[105] The Greek state did not keep emigrant records and emigrants did not have to request official permission to leave. The difference can be explained by the specific conceptualization of nationhood in Greece, which saw the Greek nation as a global one and embraced ethnic Greeks living around the world, in contrast to that of the Bulgarian and Serbian understanding of nationality as much more closely linked to territory.

Economic conditions in Greece were also different: Greek society looked back on a long tradition of traders, seafarers, and migrant workers. Political interest in emigration intensified only at the beginning of the twentieth century, when the annual number of immigrants to America from Greece surpassed ten thousand, and the press urged the government to curb emigration. In 1906 the Greek Chamber of Deputies established a commission to study the causes and consequences of emigration. Its report included a draft bill for a Law on Emigration, but it was never passed.[106] The report is striking for its emphasis on the beneficial consequences to Greece of emigration. It stressed that most emigrants did not leave permanently and that they regularly sent money to Greece:

> Moreover, [the emigrant] utilizes his savings in foreign lands in the improvement and development of his property at home. . . . Not only does he not forget his obligations to [his family], but when fortune smiles upon him he considers it his first duty to send them means for their own support and also for the maintenance and improvement of the family property. By nature

ambitious, and, above all else, anxious for the good opinion of the people in his village, he attends to the settlement of his debts, and, having a firm determination to return and live in his own country, he sends there all the savings of his labour abroad to be deposited in the usual manner, or for the purpose of purchasing real estate or making loans to his fellow villagers.[107]

The commission maintained that "the districts furnishing the largest number of emigrants were among the most prosperous, owing to the money coming back into the country. Thus the commission recommends the government protect this source of national wealth. . . . All the benefits . . . from emigration will continue only so long as close relations are maintained between our country and our fellow-countrymen across the ocean."[108]

The government heeded the commission's advice, viewing emigration as a social safety valve with the additional effect of reducing the number of poor within the country and increasing money inflow to Greece. Instead of imposing restrictions, the government debated how best to maintain the bonds between the emigrants and their homeland in order to encourage them to continue sending money and eventually to return. For this purpose, the government established the Panhellenic Union in the United States.[109] The state maintained its stance on emigration, as can be seen in the failure of another emigration bill in 1912, never voted on by parliament, which did not include any clauses discouraging emigration. Throughout the twentieth century the government would impose restrictions on emigration during periods of military conflict, but also lift them immediately after the end of hostilities.

One major reason for the tranquillity of the Greek government was that emigration was not considered to be harmful per se. The historian Ioanna Laliotou asserts that "the transterritorial conception of the national subject was a constitutive element of modern Greek nationalism from the moment of its genesis and thereafter."[110] Where the Serbian and Bulgarian governments viewed emigration as a loss to the nation, the Greek government framed it as the extension of the inherently transterritorial Greek nation across the Atlantic. The Greek community in America was simply another part of an age-old Greek diaspora, which intellectuals and politicians thought revolved around the Greek state.[111] The Greek government viewed Greek emigrants as representatives of Hellenic culture in America. This also explains why Greek observers were not particularly worried about emigration as such but rather about the possibility that Greek emigrants' behavior could injure the honor of Greek culture. This pertained especially to the *padrone* system in the United States: a notorious mechanism for recruiting boys from Greece to travel to

America and blatantly exploiting their labor. Greek observers viewed the *padrones* as a stain on the Hellenic nation.[112]

Emigrants and Intermediaries

Government measures were an important part of the reality of emigration regimes but still were just one part, not the whole. States may have imposed rules to guide, limit, or support emigration, but migrants were creative in finding ways to circumvent such rules. As is still the case today, state regulations concerning migration were often bypassed, undermined, or simply ignored. State action, by imposing rules or restrictions on movement, ultimately motivated emigrants to resort to illicit means to achieve their goals; the government then used this behavior to justify additional measures for control. The situation in Hungary regarding the port in Fiume illustrates this progression: Fiume was the only place where the Hungarian government could enforce its rules concerning exit, so emigrants preferred to travel from a North Sea port, although this was technically illegal. Thus, the restrictive clauses of the Hungarian Law on Emigration ended up being self-defeating. Fiume never became the primary point of departure for emigrants from Hungary.

Migrants usually planned their departures with significant support from travel agencies, relatives, and friends. A huge network of interlinked business interests supported them, including steamship companies and travel agents and their subagents. They hoped to secure a slice of the huge emigration business; their tentacles reached into the most remote corners of the region. Emigration agents and steamship companies were not the main cause of massive overseas emigration, but they greatly facilitated the transportation of millions of Europeans to the Americas in the three decades prior to the First World War. The amount of attention government officials devoted to emigration agents and steamship companies demonstrates their importance in the process of migration. Agents of steamship companies and their intermediaries were usually the first to feel state attempts to regulate emigration. In most countries concerned, governments repeatedly issued decrees that outlawed the active facilitation of emigration.[113] The Hungarian minister of trade even issued decrees in the 1880s and 1890s ordering postal officers not to deliver brochures advertising emigration or letters that contained prepaid tickets and to report intended recipients' names and addresses to the authorities.[114] The interior minister of Montenegro instructed local authorities to arrest "as foreign unscrupulous agents" all those who praised life in the United States.[115]

Yet these myriad decrees and measures did not achieve their intended aims. Stricter rules typically meant an increase in the number of illegal border crossings and of forged documents. Even the comparatively efficient Austro-Hungarian bureaucracy was on the losing side of the struggle. The Austrian minister of trade, Dr. Rudolf Schuster von Bonnott, conceded to the parliament's budget commission in 1913 that "the continuous circumvention and the planned violation of existing laws and other regulations have become an outright characteristic of the emigration business."[116] The Hungarian prime minister and minister of the interior, Count Khuen-Héderváry, reported in 1911 that despite "the most energetic measures"—1,968 people were punished for violations of the ban on the encouragement of emigration—the business of illicit agents continued unabated.[117] The enterprise was so profitable that punishment did not deter agents. Large agencies, such as Missler in Bremen, Klaus in Buchs (Switzerland), and Gergolet in Genoa, operated networks of hundreds of subagents. The latter were often influential people in their villages, such as tavern keepers, officials, or even priests, who received a commission for each successfully solicited migrant. Unable to reach the companies operating abroad, local state authorities could only prosecute these subagents, but this barely affected the agency abroad.

These companies' adaptability and their impact on emigration routes can be clearly seen in an Austrian example. Most emigrants from Austria took ships from ports in Hamburg or Bremerhaven, so they had to pass through Germany. In 1905, the Prussian police tightened transit restrictions, and police controls on both sides of the border became more vigilant. In response, emigration agencies readily redirected the flow of emigrants.[118] In a matter of months the small town of Buchs in Switzerland, just across the border from the Duchy of Liechtenstein, became one of the major transit centers for emigrants from east-central and southeastern Europe. The main reason for the selection of Buchs was the absence of effective border controls between Austria and Liechtenstein.[119] Emigration agencies also tried to conceal the destination (in this case, Buchs) of their passengers by issuing train tickets for short segments of the journey in order to minimize police suspicion.[120] Some agencies went even further. The Viktor Klaus Agency disguised emigrants to America as seasonal workers.[121] Another example of emigration agencies' creativity can be found in Montenegro. In 1911, the interior minister instructed district authorities, who issued passports, to find out where emigrants to America were acquiring the money for transit. The government wanted to stop would-be migrants from going into debt and also to prevent US-immigration officials from sending emigrants back, which would occur if the American border controls discovered that the individuals had been solicited through debt bondage. In response, emigrants began dutifully stating to local authorities when they applied for passports that "they travel under their own initiative and had not been encouraged by anyone else." They also claimed that they had received a loan from a neighbor on which they paid minimal interest. After receiving such statements, local authorities could issue travelers passports.[122]

The prominence of emigration agents in southeastern European governments' anti-emigration discourse should not be taken as proof of the agents' malign influence. Political discourse turned the emigration agent into a rhetorical figure through which salient concerns and fears could be articulated. First, emigration agents often served as scapegoats used by governments to hide their failure to improve economic conditions enough so that people would not feel compelled to go abroad to find work. The frequent government and press reports of poor, naïve emigrants who were defrauded by agents were also a discursive strategy to recast facilitating emigration as an illegal endeavor that deserved public condemnation. Emigration agents' success challenged the modern state by assisting people who were supposed to belong to a particular territorial realm to leave.

Conclusion

Emigration contributed to the globalization of southeastern Europe. It integrated the region's societies into the global labor market and it motivated governments to extend their purview across the ocean. Yet individual governmental responses to emigration differed. Divergences were rooted in different concepts of state and nation and in different institutional power arrangements. The local availability of land and agricultural developments influenced this as well. Beyond the establishment of specific rules of exit, emigration pushed governments to seek ways to extend their sovereignty beyond state borders in order to maintain control over their citizens. Attempts to maintain control over emigrants changed how state machineries operated.

Emigration engendered specific transnational bureaucratic connections because regimes of emigration became entangled with regimes of immigration. The Hungarian government's requests that US authorities reign in émigré organizations' anti-Hungarian propaganda demonstrate the emergence of a transatlantic policy field. Sending countries also extended welfare provisions to their citizens abroad, who at the same time were subject to state policies of their host countries. Fluid movements and individual agency clashed with official notions of sovereignty predicated on unambiguous borders and territory. Nicole Phelps shows that US diplomats in Austria-Hungary often represented in court proceedings naturalized immigrants who, on visits in Austria-Hungary, had been taken into custody because Habsburg authorities accused them of shirking military service. Actually, the United States and Austria-Hungary had signed a naturalization treaty in 1870 to prevent such difficulties, yet the two governments tended to interpret it differently.[123] Such difficulties in transnational bureaucratic interactions gave rise to ideas for creating international regulations for emigration. After the First World War, the International Labour Organization of the League of Nations would try to deal with this problem on the supranational level.

Another impact of emigration on the state's business concerned the expansion of diplomatic functions. Defending the interests of their citizens in the destination countries, diplomats took welfare functions upon themselves. Interventionist modern states' domestic policies gradually became elements of foreign policy.[124] The eyes of the state followed its emigrants, and the emigrants turned to their home country if they were in need. The emerging welfare state found it hard to accept that its citizens interacted in transnational social spaces that did not necessarily come under its sovereignty.

At the same time, emigration deeply worried nationalist activists in a period of intense nation building and national antagonisms. Nationalists considered emigration a threat to the political, economic, social, and cultural coherence of the nation. The historian Sebastian Conrad argued that the search for particularity and a primordial identity, which was so manifest in Europe prior to the First World War, may be explained as a response to large-scale international labor mobility.[125] Southeastern European case studies exemplify the repercussions of debates about emigration on concepts of nationhood. The experience of emigration—which weakened the hold of territory on the national body—strengthened definitions of the nation in terms of blood and descent. Politicians and intellectuals believed that bonds of kinship, a shared ethnicity, and a shared language held the nation together, regardless of location. This was similar to Italy's experience, where the nation became conceptualized as a global one by the end of the nineteenth century.[126] The historian John Torpey comments that "membership rooted in descent was a means of coping with the fact that enhanced mobility made it more and more difficult to determine who belonged and who did not."[127]

The cognitive map of the nation increasingly encompassed members dispersed across the European continent and ocean, in the United States and other destinations. Political and public debates about emigration as well as constant media coverage of the emigrants' fate firmly rooted the notion of a transterritorial nation in the imagined national community. High rates of emigration among the nonhegemonic nationalities of the Dual Monarchy strengthened their sentiment of national discrimination. The idea of communality rooted in descent and culture not only underwrote the continuous concern of the nation for "its" emigrants but also for other dislocated sisters and brothers who lived in unredeemed territories claimed by the nation. Each southeastern European country before 1914 felt that it was not yet complete but that it had a natural claim on further territories because of the alleged ethnic composition of those territories' populations. Speaking about emigrants in a national way also strengthened the nationalist claims on neighboring people, on whom very similar notions of ethnic affinity were projected. If their territories could not be incorporated, then at least the people could serve as a source of immigration for the strengthening of their "true motherland." Beginning in the nineteenth century, Balkan states were supportive of co-ethnic immigration—immigration by members of their own ethnic group living outside their national borders—while remaining hostile to the entry of people deemed "alien."

One of the many paradoxes of nationalism is that it successfully adapted an ideology based on the concept of specific territories and the loyalty of populations living on these territories to a social reality increasingly characterized by transnational social relations. Yet the politics of the territorialization of power and the state's transnational outreach were not contradictory. The modern state aims at controlling both territory and bodies, and these two fields of state sovereignty can be physically disconnected. It is of little surprise that national elites' attempts to turn emigration into a tool to develop state and nation would become more pronounced after 1918, when southeastern Europe experienced a new wave of nation building. It is important to remember, however, that these efforts built on established ideas and an entrenched groundwork of policy and regulations. The continuity of these practices reaches into the present.

Notes

Archival research for this article was supported by travel grants of the German Research Foundation (Deutsche Forschungsgesellschaft). I want to thank the participants in the workshop "The Balkans as Europe," in Vienna, January 31 to February 1, 2014, for their comments on an earlier version of this paper, in particular the workshop organizer, Timothy Snyder, and the attendees Ivo Banac and Holly Case, as well as the anonymous reviewers of the manuscript. I also am grateful to

Brittany Lehman for her support with the language and her many helpful comments on the contents of the paper.

1. Letter from the Foreign Ministry to the Interior Ministry, October 4, 1913, no. 2842(2), Ministry of Internal Affairs (hereafter MUD), Archive of Montenegro, Cetinje (hereafter ACG).

2. Letter from the Foreign Ministry to the Interior Ministry, November 12, 1913, no. 3315(2), MUD, ACG.

3. For Poland, Germany, and Italy see Donna R. Gabaccia, Dirk Hoerder, and Adam Walaszek, "Emigration and Nation Building during the Mass Migrations from Europe," in *Citizenship and Those Who Leave: The Politics of Emigration and Repatriation*, ed. Nancy L. Green and François Weil (Urbana: University of Illinois Press, 2007), 63–90.

4. Nancy L. Green and François Weil, "Introduction," in Green and Weil, *Citizenship and Those Who Leave*, 1.

5. Mark I. Choate, *Emigrant Nation: The Making of Italy Abroad* (Cambridge, MA: Harvard University Press, 2008).

6. Philipp Ther, *Die dunkle Seite der Nationalstaaten: "Ethnische Säuberungen" im modernen Europa* (Göttingen: Vandenhoeck & Ruprecht, 2011); Justin McCarthy, *Death and Exile: The Ethnic Cleansing of Ottoman Muslims, 1821–1922* (Princeton, NJ: Darwin Press, 1995).

7. Wolfgang Höpken, "Flucht vor dem Kreuz? Muslimische Emigration aus Südosteuropa nach dem Ende der osmanischen Herrschaft (19./20. Jahrhundert)," *Comparativ* 6, no. 1 (1996): 1–24.

8. Tara Zahra, *The Great Departure: Mass Migration from Eastern Europe and the Making of the Free World* (New York: W. W. Norton, 2016), 17.

9. Edvin Pezo, *Zwangsmigration in Friedenszeiten? Jugoslawische Migrationspolitik und die Auswanderung von Muslimen in die Türkei (1918 bis 1966)* (Munich: R. Oldenbourg Verlag, 2013).

10. On the Kingdom of SHS/Yugoslavia, see Vesna Đikanović, *Iseljavanje u sjedinjene Američke države: Jugoslovenso iskustvo 1918–1941* (Belgrade: Institut za Noviju Istoriju Srbije, 2012); Aleksandar R. Miletić, *Journey under Surveillance: The Overseas Emigration Policy of the Kingdom of Serbs, Croats and Slovenes in Global Context, 1918–1928* (Berlin: LIT Verlag, 2012); Ulf Brunnbauer, "Emigration Policies and Nation-building in Interwar Yugoslavia," *European History Quarterly* 42, no. 4 (2012): 602–27; on socialist Yugoslavia, Othmar N. Haberl, *Die Abwanderung von Arbeitskräften aus Jugoslawien: Zur Problematik ihrer Auslandsbeschäftigung und Rückführung* (Munich: R. Oldenbourg Verlag, 1978); Vladimir Ivanović, *Geburtstag pišeš normalno: Jugoslovenski gastarbajteri u Austriji i SR Nemačkoj* (Belgrade: Institut za Savremenu Istoriju, 2012).

11. Zahra, *The Great Departure*, 6.

12. Aristide R. Zolberg, "The Exit Revolution," in Green and Weil, *Citizenship and Those Who Leave*, 14; John C. Torpey, *The Invention of the Passport: Surveillance Citizenship and the State* (Cambridge: Cambridge University Press, 2000), 57–92.

13. For France, see Torpey, *Invention of the Passport*, 53.

14. Charles Tilly, "Migration in Modern European History," in *Human Migration: Patterns and Policies*, ed. William H. McNeill and Ruth S. Adams (Bloomington: Indiana University Press, 1978), 48.

15. Charles Maier, "Transformations of Territoriality, 1600–2000," in *Transnationale Geschichte: Themen, Tendenzen, und Theorien*, ed. Gunilla Budde, Sebastian Conrad, and Oliver Janz (Göttingen: Vandenhoeck & Ruprecht, 2010), 32–56.

16. See Torpey, *Invention of the Passport*, 93–122.

17. William S. Bernard, "Immigration: History of U.S. Policy," in *Harvard Encyclopedia of American Ethnic Groups*, ed. Stephan Thernstorm (Cambridge, MA: Harvard University Press, 1980), 486–95, 490.

18. See Green and Weil, "Introduction," 3.

19. Immigration Commission, *Statistical Review of Immigration, 1820–1910*, vol. 3 of *Reports of the Immigration Commission* (Washington, DC: Immigration Commission 1911), 44.

20. Ulf Brunnbauer, "Globalizing Southeastern Europe: The Economic Causes and Consequences of Overseas Emigration up until 1914," *Jahrbuch für Wirtschaftsgeschichte / Economic history yearbook* 1 (2014): 33–63.

21. Walter Nugent, *Crossings: The Great Transatlantic Migrations, 1870–1914* (Bloomington: Indiana University Press, 1995), 153; J. D. Gould, "European Inter-Continental Emigration, 1815–1914: The Road Home—Return Migration from the U.S.A," *Journal of European Economic History* 9 (1980): 68.

22. Hans Chmelar, *Höhepunkte der österreichischen Auswanderung: Die Auswanderung aus den im Reichsrat vertretenen Königreichen und Ländern in den Jahren 1905–1914* (Vienna: VOAW, 1974), 24; Royal Hungarian Statistical Office, *Auswanderung und Rückwanderung der Länder der ungarischen heiligen Krone in den Jahren 1899–1913* (Budapest: Königliches Ungarisches Statistisches Zentralamt, 1918), appendix 5.

23. *Statistički godišnjak Kraljevina Hrvatske i Slavonije* (1905), 244; *Statistički godišnjak Kraljevina Hrvatske i Slavonije* (1906–10), 200; Josip Lakatoš, *Narodna statistika* (Osijek: Naklada R. Bačića, 1914), 64.

24. Susanne-Sophia Spiliotis, *Transterritorialität und nationale Abgrenzung: Konstitutionsprozesse der griechischen Gesellschaft und Ansätze ihrer faschistoiden Transformation* (Munich: R. Oldenbourg Verlag, 1998), 37.

25. Đoko Pejović, *Iseljavanje Crnogoraca u XIX veku* (Titograd: Istorijski institut NR Crne Gore, 1962), 449; Novica Rakočević, "Uzroci iseljavanja crnogorskog stanovništvo u 1904. godini," *Istorijski zapisi* 21/25, no. 2 (1968): 484.

26. Albania and Romania are left out from the analysis because of limited information on these cases. The Ottoman Empire is also not considered here; it generally pursued liberal emigration policies vis-à-vis its non-Muslim subjects, although voluntary emigration was technically illegal. Muslim emigration was largely prevented. See Kemal H. Karpat, "The Ottoman Emigration to America, 1860–1914," *International Journal of Middle East Studies* 17, no. 2 (1985): 175–209.

27. Staatsgrundgesetz vom 21. Dezember 1867, über die allgemeinen Rechte der Staatsbürger für die im Reichsrathe vertretenen Königreiche und Länder, Art. IV, § 2.

28. Stefan Malfèr, "Zwischen Verbot, Laisser-faire und Hilflosigkeit: Rechtliche und sozioökonomische Aspekte der österreichisch-cisleithanischen Auswanderungspolitik bis zum Ersten Weltkrieg," *Wiener Zeitschrift zur Geschichte der Neuzeit* 10, no. 2 (2010): 91.

29. Ibid., 99–101.

30. Alexander Fischel, *Die schädlichen Seiten der Auswanderung und deren Bekämpfung: Einige Worte zu einer brennenden Frage* (Vienna: O. Andreas, 1914), Vorwort.

31. Malfèr, "Zwischen Verbot, Laisser-faire und Hilflosigkeit," 103; Chmelar, *Höhepunkte der österreichischen Auswanderung*, 142–43; Eugène Richard Sensenig-Dabbous, *Von Metternich bis EU Beitritt: Reichsfremde, Staatsfremde und Drittausländer; Immigration und Einwanderungspolitik in Österreich* (Salzburg, 1998), 140–41.

32. Emperor Franz Joseph I, speech, *Stenographische Protokolle des Herrenhauses des Reichsrats, 1861–1918*, Beilage XVII, Session (1901–7), 3.

33. Chmelar, *Höhepunkte der österreichischen Auswanderung*, 140.

34. Ibid., 21.

35. "Alleruntertänigster Vortrag des treugehorsamsten Banus der Königreiche Kroatien, Slawonien und Dalmatien Dr. Ivan Baron Skerlecz von Lomnica," July 1, 1914, f. 1071, kut. 550, Iseljenički Komesarijat, Croatian State Archives, Zagreb (Hrvatski državni arhiv u Zagrebu; hereafter HDA).

36. Fischel, *Die schädlichen Seiten*, 3; Chmelar, *Höhepunkte der österreichischen Auswanderung*, 154; Malfèr, "Zwischen Verbot, Laisser-faire und Hilflosigkeit," 104.

37. Eugene Sensenig, "Brennpunkt Buchs: Vorarlbergs Stellung im Schleppnetzwerk der Monarchie," *Montfort: Zeitschrift für Geschichte, Heimat- und Volkskunde Vorarlbergs* 50, no. 4 (1998): 289.

38. Chmelar, *Höhepunkte der österreichischen Auswanderung*, 156–59.

39. "166. Verordnung des Ministers für Landesverteidigung und des Ministers des Inneren vom 25. Juli 1914," *Reichsgesetzblatt für die im Reichsrate vertretenen Königreiche und Länder*, July 26, 1914, 169.

40. Royal Hungarian Statistical Office, *Auswanderung und Rückwanderung*.

41. James D. Whelpley, *The Problem of the Immigrant* (London: Chapman & Hall, 1905), 37. For an English translation of the Hungarian law, see ibid., 252–69.

42. Ibid., 252–69.

43. Julianna Puskás, *From Hungary to the United States, 1880–1914* (Budapest: Akadémiai Kiadó, 1982), 93–94.

44. Royal Hungarian Statistical Office, *Auswanderung und Rückwanderung*, 167.

45. See Ladislaus Schneider, *Die ungarische Auswanderung: Studie über die Ursachen und den Umfang der ungarischen Auswanderung* (Pozsony: Angermayer, 1915), 53.

46. Puskás, *Hungary to the United States*, 96.

47. Monika Glettler, *Pittsburgh–Wien–Budapest: Programm und Praxis der Nationalitätenpolitik bei der Auswanderung der ungarischen Slowaken nach Amerika um 1900* (Vienna: Österreichische Akademie der Wissenschaften, 1980), 312.

48. Puskás, *Hungary to the United States*, 97.

49. *A magyar szent korona országainak kivándorlása és visszavándorlása 1899–1913* (Budapest, 1918), 47; Ervin Dubrović, *Merika: Iseljavanje iz srednje Europe u Ameriku, 1880–1914* (Rijeka: Muzeja Grada Rijeka, 2008), 100.

50. Leopold Caro, *Auswanderung und Auswanderungspolitik in Österreich* (Leipzig: Duncker & Humblot, 1909), 11; Puskás, *Hungary to the United States*, 98, 102; Dubrović, *Merika*, 107.

51. Caro, *Auswanderung und Auswanderungspolitik*, 12; Dubrović, *Merika*, 103.

52. "Der Poolvertrag," *Pester Lloyd*, March 24, 1911; Puskás, *Hungary to the United States*, 100, 103.

53. Caro, *Auswanderung und Auswanderungspolitik*, 11.

54. "Der Poolvertrag."

55. Booker T. Washington, with Robert E. Park, *The Man Farthest Down: A Record of Observation and Study in Europe* (Garden City, NY: Doubleday, Page, 1912), 225–26.

56. Glettler, *Pittsburgh–Wien–Budapest*, 319.

57. Ibid., 108–39.

58. *Stenografski zapisnici Sabora kraljevine Hrvatske, Slavonije i Dalmacije, 1901–1906*, vol. 2, part 1, January 16–February 22, 1902 (Zagreb: Tisak Kralj. Zemaljske Tiskare, 1902), 463–6; Ibid., vol. 5, part 1, January 12–February 13, 1905 (Zagreb: Tisak Kralj. Zemaljske Tiskare, 1905), 294–99; ibid., vol. 1, March 12–May 23, 1910 (Zagreb: Tisak Kralj. Zemaljske Tiskare, 1910), 807; *Stenografski zapisnici Sabora kraljevine Hrvatske, Slavonije i Dalmacije, 1913–1918*, vol. 1, December 27, 1913–March 4, 1914 (Zagreb: Tisak Kralj. Zemaljske Tiskare, 1914), 572.

59. Trpimir Macan, "Stjepan Radić i iseljeničko pitanje," *Dubrovnik* 3, no. 5 (1992): 148–51. Radić's demographic fears were unfounded; see Lakatoš, *Narodna statistika*, 27, 41.

60. *Stenografski zapisnici Sabora kraljevine Hrvatske, Slavonije i Dalmacije, 1908–1913* (Zagreb: Tisak Kralj. Zemaljske Tiskare, 1910), 807.

61. Laza Horvat, *Naše iseljeničko pitanje ili šta nam je Amerika dala i donela* (Zagreb: Srpska Štamp., 1912), 13 (emphasis in original).

62. "Naredba kr. hrv.-slav.-dalm. zemaljske vlade, odjela za unutarnje poslove," April 5, 1901, f. 79, k. 2962, no. 18560, HDA.

63. Artur Benko Grado, "Razvitak naše državne iseljeničke službe," *Jutarnji list* 28, no. 9952 (1939): 21.

64. "Allerunthertänigster Vortrag des treugehorsamsten Banus der Königreiche Croatien, Slavonien und Dalmatien, Theodor Grafen Pejacsevich de Vöröcze," f. 1071, kut. 549, Iseljenički Komesarijat, HDA.

65. "XXV svečane zaključne saborske sjednice od 7. studenoga 1911," *Stenografski zapisnici Sabora kraljevine Hrvatske, Slavonije i Dalmacije, 1910–1915*, vol. 2 (Zagreb: Tisak Kralj. Zemaljske Tiskare, 1911), Prilog 7k., 1–10.

66. Neven Budak, "Dva izvještaja zanimljiva za povijest našeg iseljeništva u Kanadi i SAD (god. 1913. i 1924.)," *Radovi* 24 (1991): 238.

67. Artur Grado Benko, "Naredba bana kraljevina Hrvatske, Slavonije i Dalmacije od godine 1909. glede odpremanja osoba u prekomorske zemlje (1909)," f. 790, k. 3, doc. 112, no. 8391, HDA; Ivan Balta, "Slavonski arhivski i novinski zapisi o hrvatskim iseljenicima u SAD-u u razdoblju od 1905. do 1910. godine," *Društvena istraživanja* 12, no. 5 (2003): 781.

68. Artur Grado Benko, "Naredba kr. povjerenika u kraljevinama Hrvatskoj i Slavoniji" (November 26, 1913), f. 790, kut. 179, no. 82458, HDA.

69. Chmelar, *Höhepunkte der österreichischen Auswanderung*, 24–25.

70. Zemaljska Vlada, Odjel za unutarnje poslove, f. 79, k. 2962 (emigration to Brazil), HDA; f. 78, k. 2517 (emigration of peasants to Brazil), Vlada, HDA.

71. Letter from the Vice *Župan* of Požega to the Provincial Government, February 17, 1897, f. 79, k. 2962, Vlada, HDA.

72. Pejović, *Iseljavanje Crnogoraca*, 444.

73. Ibid., 134–49.

74. Ibid., 453–54; Đoko Pejović, "Uzroci masovnog iseljavanja stanovništva iz Crne Gore (1878–1916)," *Istorijski zapisi* 15/19, no. 2 (1962): 240.

75. Telegram from Brigadier Todor M. Vuković to Minister G. V. Vrbić, Kolašin, October 14, 1882, fasc. 45, no. 3317, MUD, ACG.

76. Ministarstvo unutrašnjih dela, broj 1715 (November 27, 1882), fasc. 45, no. 3940(1), MUD, ACG.

77. Pejović, *Iseljavanje Crnogoraca*, 408–13.

78. Radoslav M. Raspopović, *Diplomatija Crne Gore 1711–1918* (Podgorica, 1996), 418.

79. Miloš Jagodić, "The Emigrations of Muslims from the New Serbian Regions, 1871–1878," *Balkanologie* 2, no. 2 (December 1998): 99–122; Dietmar Müller, *Staatsbürger auf Widerruf: Juden und Muslime als Alteritätspartner im rumänischen und serbischen Nationscode; Ethnonationale Staatsbürgerschaftskonzepte, 1878–1941* (Wiesbaden: Harrasowitz, 2005), 134.

80. Radoš Trebješanin, "Naseljavanje crnogorskog stanovništva u Jablanici i Toplici od 1880. do 1906. godine," *Leskovački zbornik* 19, no. 125–57 (1979): 145–46. The Montenegrin settlers enjoyed a bad reputation in Serbia: They were said to be engaged in smuggling and other criminal activities. The authorities also considered them lazy and unruly.

81. Letter from the Montenegrin prime minister to Serbian Prime Minister Nikola Pašić, June 22, 1907, fasc. 5, doc. 340, Ministerski Savet, ACG.

82. Naredba Ministrog Vojnog, broj 6. Svim vojnim vlastima (October 31, 1911), fasc. 121, no. 4972(1), MUD, ACG.

83. Raspis svim plemenskim kapetanima (November 1, 1911), fasc. 138, no. 3315(1), MUD, ACG.

84. For example, "Protivu odlaženija na rad u Ameriku," *Glas Crnogorca*, February 18, 1906; "Vraćeni Crnogorci," *Glas Crnogorca*, May 6, 1906.

85. "Iseljavanje," *Glas Crnogorca*, April 7, 1907.

86. "Umro Velimir Čelović," *Glas Crnogorca*, June 26, 1871.

87. Nikola Novaković, "Čikago," *Glas Crnogorca*, April 9, 1894.

88. Vladimir Stojanović, "Knez Miloš Obrenović i problemi balkanskih migracija u Srbiji posle Drugog ustanka," *Zbornik istorijskog muzeja Srbije* 5 (1968): 36; see Holm Sundhaussen, *Historische Statistik Serbiens 1834–1914: Mit europäischen Vergleichsdaten* (Munich: R. Oldenbourg Verlag, 1989), 136; Tihomir R. Đorđević, *Arhivska građa za naselja u Srbiji u vreme prve vlade kneza Miloša, 1815–1839*, *Srpski etnografski zbornik*, vol. 37 (Belgrade: Grafički Zavod Makarije, 1926).

89. *Zbornik zakona i uredba u knj. Srbiji*, vol. 14 (Belgrade, 1862), § 55 and 73, quoted in Pejović, *Iseljavanje Crnogoraca*, 205.

90. *Zastava*, May 15, 1880, f. 79, k. 443, HDA; Branko Peruničić, "Prilog pručavanju migracije stanovništva," *Istorijski zapisi* 13/17, no. 2 (1960): 331.

91. Knja**ž**eska kancelarija (A/1) (1815–39), Arhiv Srbije; Policajno odeljenje (1839–1914), Ministarstvo unutrašnjih dela.

92. Visokoj kr. zemaljskoj vladi odjelu za unutarnje poslove (June 30, 1880), f. 79, k. 443, no. 14.064 (2471), HDA; letter from the town of Ruma (probably from the Župan) to the Banus in Zagreb, April 3, 1881, f. 78, kut. 172, sv. 6, Vlada, HDA; letter from the district captain in Nova Gradiška to the provincial headquarters in Zagreb, March 18, 1881, f. 78, kut. 172, sv. 6; copy of a letter from the Austrio-Hungarian ambassador to Serbia to the foreign ministry in Vienna, April 27, 1881, f. 78, kut. 172, sv. 6–413.

93. Modruško-riječka županija, f. 101, kn. 1–3, HDA; f. 78, kut. 375, sv. 4-4, Vlada, HDA.

94. Sundhaussen, *Historische Statistik*, 172.

95. Jelenko Petrović, *Pečalbari: Naročito iz okoline Pirota* (Belgrade: Štamparija "Tipografija," 1920), 6.

96. B. Mintses, *Preselenicheskijat vŭpros v Bŭlgarija* (n.p., [1928]), 7.

97. See Wolfgang Höpken, "Die Emigration von Türken aus Bulgarien (I): Die Emigration 1878 bis 1951," *Südosteuropa* 38, no. 10 (1989): 608–37; Theodora Dragostinova, *Between Two Motherlands: Nationality and Emigration among the Greeks of Bulgaria, 1900–1949* (Ithaca, NY: Cornell University Press, 2011).

98. Bŭlgarsko diplomatichesko agenstvo v Viena, f. 304k, op. 1, a.e. 621, folio 33, Central State Archives, Sofia (hereafter CDA).

99. Copy of the instruction from the Ministry of Interior to the district captain of Šumen (October 21, 1906), folio 36, Bŭlgarsko diplomatichesko agenstvo v Viena, CDA; "Ukaz za utvŭrzhdavane 'Zakon za dopŭlnenie na Zakona za zadgranichnite pasporti' s cel ogranichavane emigracijata v Amerika," *Dŭrzhaven vestnik*, November 28, 1906.

100. *Stenografski dnevnici na XIII ONS*, V RS, XXV 3 (December 3, 1907), 504–10; *Stenografski dnevnici na XIII ONS*, V RS, XXIX 3 (December 10, 1907), 675–80.

101. "Zakon za emigracijata," *Dŭrzhaven vestnik*, January 14, 1908, 2–5.

102. *Migracionni dviženija na bŭlgarite: 1878–1941* (Sofia, 1993), 532.

103. Veselin Trajkov, *Istorija na bŭlgarskata emigracija v Severna Amerika* (Sofia: Universitetsko Izdatelstvo Sv. Kliment Ohridski, 1993), 21.

104. Immigration Commission, *Emigration Conditions in Europe*, vol. 4 of *Reports of the Immigration Commission* (Washington, DC: Immigration Commission, 1911), 397.

105. Ioanna Laliotou, *Transatlantic Subjects: Acts of Migration and Cultures of Transnationalism between Greece and America* (Chicago: University of Chicago Press, 2004), 59; Theodore Saloutos, *The Greeks in the United States* (Cambridge, MA: Harvard University Press, 1964), 38.

106. Louis J. Cononelos, *In Search of Gold Paved Streets: Greek Immigrant Labor in the Far West, 1900–1920* (New York: AMS Press, 1989), 57–58.

107. Quoted in Immigration Commission, *Emigration Conditions in Europe*, 397.

108. Quoted in ibid., 398.

109. Laliotou, *Transatlantic Subjects*, 71.

110. Ibid., 54.

111. See Marios Papakyriacou, "Formulations and Definitions of the Greek National Ideology in Colonial Egypt (1856–1919)" (PhD diss., Free University of Berlin, 2012).

112. On the *padrone* system, see Immigration Commission, *Emigration Conditions in Europe*, 391–408; Saloutos, *Greeks in the United States*, 48–56.

113. Saloutos, *Greeks in the United States*, 45; Sensenig-Dabbous, *Von Metternich bis EU Beitritt*, 145; Fischel, *Die schädlichen Seiten*, 5; Malfèr, "Zwischen Verbot, Laisser-faire und Hilflosigkeit," 100; Chmelar, *Höhepunkte der österreichischen Auswanderung*, 141; Puskás, *Hungary to the United States*, 93; *Stenografski zapisnici Sabora kraljevine Hrvatske, Slavonije i Dalmacije, 1897–1902*, 99.

114. Copy of the Royal Hungarian Decree on the Postal and Telegraph Services by the Minister of Trade, f. 79, k. 1935, br. 2517, HDA.

115. See for example Letter from the Ministry of Foreign Affairs to the Ministry of the Interior, October 4, 1913, fasc. 137, doc. 2842(2), MUD, ACG.

116. Quoted in Fischel, *Die schädlichen Seiten*, 1.

117. "Der Poolvertrag," *Pester Lloyd*, March 24, 1911.

118. Sensenig-Dabbous, *Von Metternich bis EU Beitritt*, 167.

119. Sensenig, "Brennpunkt Buchs," 284–86; Chmelar, *Höhepunkte der österreichischen Auswanderung*, 89.

120. "Zemljovid, Europe i Amerike; Vozin red!," f. 1619, kut. 2, Iseljenički Muzej, HDA.

121. Sensenig, "Brennpunkt Buchs," 289.

122. Letters no. 734 and no. 735, from the captain of Ljubotinj, December 7, 1911, in fasc. 122, doc. 5613(2) and doc. 5614(2), MUD, ACG.

123. Nicole M. Phelps, *U.S.-Habsburg Relations from 1815 to the Paris Peace Conference: Sovereignty Transformed* (New York: Cambridge University Press, 2013), 131.

124. I would like to thank Holly Case for this suggestion.

125. Sebastian Conrad, *Globalisierung und Nation im Deutschen Kaiserreich* (Munich: Beck, 2006), 10.

126. Choate, *Emigrant Nation*, 2.

127. Torpey, *Invention of the Passport*, 72.

CHAPTER FIVE

THE QUIET REVOLUTION

Consuls and the International System in the Nineteenth Century

Holly Case

Over the course of the nineteenth century, the principle of state sovereignty laid down by the 1648 Peace of Westphalia began to unravel and many European states slowly turned inside out—that is, institutions of social policy were projected outward across borders, contra the Westphalia provisions. The unlikely protagonists of this transformation were consuls posted to the Ottoman Empire and its successors. Their undertakings showed the limits of Great Powers' power and facilitated small states' entry into the international system as forces with remarkable gravity.

Serbia sent its first diplomatic mission abroad in 1804, with the outbreak of the First Serbian Uprising. It took the three-man deputation consisting of a priest, a tradesman, and a cavalryman a month to get to St. Petersburg. The Serbs were seeking support for their uprising, and one of the three men, Petar Čardaklija, was married to a Russian and so thought to give Russia a try. In his memoirs of the journey, the priest, Matija Nenadović, wrote: "Thus Columbus had set out with his band on the open sea to find America and make Europe known to her; and today we set out on the quiet Danube to find Russia—though we haven't a clue where it is, but only that we had heard about its existence from songs—to make Serbia known to Russia!"[1]

The journey was marked by broken-down wagons, blowing sand, a shortage of money, occasional gleeful encounters with expatriate Serbian tavern owners, and frequent reminders of their own inferior clothing, manners, and diplomatic skills as they met with Russian consuls along the way and statesmen in St. Petersburg. Once arrived in the Russian capital, for several days the delegation were too timid to leave the rooms where they were staying. Finally they had an audience with the tsarist foreign minister, the illustrious Polish nobleman Adam Czartoryski, who advised them to form a government, "because neither Russia nor any other state will communicate with a person, but only with a nation and a governing council [*sinod*]."[2]

Over a century later, after the collapse of the continental empires—the Habsburg, the Ottoman, and the Russian—one Austrian diplomat of South Slavic origin, Alexander Musulin von Gomirje, wrote with grudging admiration of the tenacity of Serbia's diplomacy over the course of the nineteenth century and into the twentieth. Whereas Austria-Hungary was perpetually having to run its diplomacy in secret and could never rely on the backing of the Dual Monarchy's disparate elements for its foreign policy initiatives, "There was nothing quite as goal-oriented as Serbian foreign policy. . . . Despite temporary shifts . . . it barely went one step from its pre-established course."[3] Musulin von Gomirje noted that a shift had taken place in diplomacy toward emphasis on public support for the foreign policy objectives of the state. "Lucky was the country in which there was a public opinion conscious of matters of foreign policy," he wrote, speaking not merely of Serbia but above all of Austria-Hungary's primary geopolitical rival, Russia.[4]

Public Opinion and a New Diplomacy

The importance that public opinion acquired in nineteenth-century diplomacy was related to two parallel developments. One was the sense that turning public opinion in another country to favor a cause was as effective as diplomacy, and the other was the exceptional nature of consular jurisdiction in the Ottoman Empire, a feature that involved diplomacy in the realm of social policy. Together, these two developments resulted in a convergence in the interests and activities of social organizations on the one hand (missionaries, charities, advocacy groups), which increasingly sought to influence foreign policy, and foreign policy institutions (foreign ministries, diplomatic corps) on the other, which increasingly engaged in executing forms of social policy such as building and maintaining churches, schools, hospitals and other social institutions. Here I trace primarily the latter development. But first, a few words on how swaying public opinion in a foreign country came to be seen as a form of diplomacy, a retooling that brought social concerns into the mechanism of the international system.

Adam Jerzy Czartoryski was a Polish nobleman and statesman who was a close friend and adviser to the Russian tsar Alexander I and served as Russia's minister of foreign affairs from 1804 to 1806. During his tenure as foreign minister, Czartoryski drafted a ministerial act proposing the total reorganization of the boundaries of Europe, including the resurrection of an independent Poland under Russian protection. This failed plan became the seed for Czartoryski's *Essai sur la diplomatie* (Essay on Diplomacy), written in 1823 and first published in 1830, with the outbreak of the November Uprising (1830–31) against tsarist Russia.[5] During the uprising, Czartoryski served as the president of the Polish National Government before the uprising was put down by tsarist forces. When the uprising failed, he was forced into exile.[6]

The *Essai* posits the necessity of a complete overhaul of the international system, down to the very principles upon which diplomacy was based. It is organized in sections on how diplomacy actually is versus how it should be.[7] Whereas the diplomatic spirit of the time was characterized by "greed, distrust and envy," Czartoryski argued, it could, if profound reforms were to be initiated by the European cabinets, become "the noblest science and the most useful study."[8] He believed that states were effectively "masses of personified individuals" and therefore subject to natural law and entitled to the same forms of liberty and equality as individuals.[9] Most important, the *Essai* confidently asserted the "infallibility of the judgment of public opinion."[10]

During his brief tenure as president of the Polish National Government, Czartoryski initiated a public relations campaign for the Polish cause that entailed appeals to geopolitical conservatism in Austria, liberalism in France and Britain, and the propagation of philhellenic interventionist agitation on behalf of Greece.[11] Pamphlets on Poland from this period speak of the overwhelming power of public opinion.[12] The notion that international public opinion had assumed the role of an arbiter in matters of state policy and even diplomacy permeates much of the writing on geopolitical questions in the nineteenth century. "I raise my voice fearlessly before the high tribunal of public opinion," declared the émigré Polish publicist Leopold Leon Sawaszkiewicz in a pamphlet from 1840 on the "Eastern Question" as it related to the "Polish Question."[13] In an 1863 book by a Polish nobleman from Russian Poland the author similarly addressed himself to the "great court known as 'public opinion,'"[14] and noted the status of the *"question polonaise"* as a "cause célèbre . . . with public opinion as jury and Europe as judge."[15]

By the last few decades of the nineteenth century, not only publicists and activists were seeking to influence states; states, too, were proudly showcasing the approval of international public opinion of their foreign policy decisions. In an 1877 work, *Die russische Politik in der orientalischen Frage* (Russian Policy on the Eastern Question), the Russian diplomat and international law scholar Friedrich Martens wrote, "Insofar as Russia has given itself over to this mission [the improvement of the situation of Christians in the Ottoman Empire], which public opinion in all the civilized nations stood for, it is de facto fulfilling the unanimous wish of Europe."[16]

In addition to public opinion reaching into the realm of foreign policy, foreign policy institutions began to reach ever further into the realm of social policy. These two developments resulted in the "turning inside out" of states. In this chapter I explore this expansion and inversion by tracing the peculiar role played by consuls in southeastern Europe during the final decades of the nineteenth century.

The Great Convergence

Foreign policy and social policy were not formally linked within institutions of state when Czartoryski's *Essai* first appeared in 1830, because most states did not have much of a social policy at the time. By the end of the nineteenth century, however, they most certainly did, and for some European states that policy was as focused on developing social institutions abroad as it was on building them up domestically. This convergence was brought about primarily by these states' interactions with and through the Ottoman Empire, and interactions of states created in the wake of the Ottoman Empire's decline accelerated and lent shape to the process.

By the final quarter of the nineteenth century, in an attempt to secure rights of full citizenship for Jews in the Ottoman Empire and its successor states, international diaspora organizations such as the Alliance Israélite Universelle in Paris found themselves in the halls of peace conferences and concerned not only with *social* policy (schools, hospitals, shelters, and so forth) in newly minted or revamped states, but also with the redrawing of their boundaries.[17] Meanwhile missionary groups, such as the American Board of Commissioners for Foreign Missions (ABCFM), undertook lobbying work in the interest of securing independence for Ottoman territories. "Macedonia ought to be free," an ABCFM spokesperson wrote in 1903. "If it is possible for America to do aught for their freedom, it will be like the act of freeing Cuba and the Philippine Islands."[18] Institutions were adapting to a new international climate with wide-ranging implications for the way states functioned and the range of their activities both at home and abroad.

In researching the transformation of European foreign policy institutions over the nineteenth century, I offer two observations. The first is historiographical, for to date scholarship has not been able to grasp in full the quite radical nature of the transformation, indeed the revolution in the execution of foreign policy precipitated at diplomacy's lowest level—namely through consular networks—during this period. There is an irony in this, since much of the history of the young nation-states in southeastern Europe for the nineteenth century was either written by consuls or based on consular reports.[19] The fact that consuls were gathering and compiling so much information on matters of social concern—education, public health, the regulation of religious practice and institutions—is what makes these consular reports such a rich source.[20] Yet though discussions of source bias figure in studies based on these documents, the historiography seems less interested in what caused consuls to focus their energies in such areas in the first place, and even less in an appreciation of how novel and exceptional such developments were.[21]

And a further irony: Statesmen and diplomats of the time were keenly aware of the fact that consular jurisdiction, especially in the Ottoman Empire and its successors, was something exceptional, and its peculiar status inspired sustained analyses of the workings of the international system as a whole. In fact, Friedrich Martens, one of the most prominent figures in the history of international law, in 1873 wrote an entire volume on the subject, *Das Consularwesen und die Consularjurisdiction im Orient* (The Consular Entity and Consular Jurisdiction in the East).

Though the primary ostensible aim of the work was to establish "the legal basis of the special (exempt) position of the Europeans in the East and reveal the jurisdiction of the consuls in order to generate a standard for the solution of newly arising questions," it offered a sweeping political philosophy that starts with a lengthy discussion of the relationship between states in the "international community" (*Staatengesellschaft*) and the impact of a people's level of civilization and aspirations on the functioning of both the state and the international community.[22]

Martens argued that "at the present time" neither human lives nor "national relations" could be contained within borders, and that much depended on the "social power" of a given state.[23] The reference to "social power" is significant, for it is precisely the realm of social policy—education, religion, science—that fell under the purview of the consul in the East. "As a consequence states must have two types of international administrative organs: first, ones that primarily follow the purely political interests of the state; and second, ones whose particular duty consists of defending and promoting the social interests of their nationals. In actuality, envoys have turned out to be organs of international administration of the first sort, and consuls of the second."[24]

Martens's assertion relates to my second observation, which is historical rather than historiographical: namely, that during the nineteenth century, consulates and consular officials were deployed by states, new and old alike, in novel ways. There are several reasons why a blind spot continues to obscure this transformation. One is that studies of foreign ministries tend to examine their development within individual states, which obscures how the interplay between diplomatic organs and the state system altered the way foreign policy was understood and executed.[25] There is also a longstanding myth regarding nineteenth-century diplomacy that asserts, for many different states and as many different causes, that stagnation of foreign ministries and calcification of channels for the production of foreign policy was the order of the day.

This myth, I believe, was fashioned and sustained by the outbreak and outcome of the First World War, above all, by former foreign policy officials from defunct or defeated states (Austria-Hungary, Germany, the Ottoman Empire, tsarist Russia) who sought after the war to explain what went wrong, as well as Western scholars seeking to dissociate their own intellectual trajectories from failed states.[26] They placed the blame on the rigidity and inertia of foreign policy institutions in the losing countries. Of the Ottoman foreign ministry, for example, we read that there was "a highly complex body of in-bred, paper-generating clerks who scribbled away happily for generations."[27] Teddy Uldricks writes of the tsarist Russian Foreign Ministry, "Ministry officials worked at a leisurely pace and had long respites for tea."[28] As for the Ballhausplatz in Vienna, the location of the Foreign Office, we are told that over the course of the nineteenth century and into the twentieth it "hardly shows any significant changes, shifts in emphasis . . . beyond the strictly reactive. . . . It let things happen *to it* and hardly ever made its own *faits accomplis*. . . . Thus one cannot truly *write a history* of Austro-Hungarian . . . foreign policy, one can only *describe* it, because it never really changed."[29]

Nonetheless, when examining changes to foreign policy institutions in aggregate, it seems that the foreign policy activity that most challenged the precarious equilibrium in the international system as well as individual states was that executed not by foreign ministers or monarchs but by low-level diplomats from all over Europe and the United States operating in the Ottoman Empire, and particularly in southeastern Europe. And what these diplomats, mostly consuls, were doing was bending or breaking common rules of foreign policy execution, oftentimes running a new kind of high-stakes diplomacy in the form of social policy, all with the sanction of their own state and sometimes multiple others.

Because the diplomatic revolution was undertaken at the lowest level of foreign policy activity through consulates, it has escaped the attention of historians of international diplomacy, and the fallout has remained the domain of area-studies specialists working on particular countries and contexts, most notably the Balkans. The activities of consulates and consuls, though part of what scholars understand as diplomacy, have not been historicized at the level of the European state system, and their transformative role remains therefore grossly underappreciated.

One reason why diplomatic and international historians have not focused their attention on consuls—referred to by the historian of British foreign policy D. C. M. Platt as the "Cinderella service"[30]—is because historically the diplomatic establishment itself has not taken them very seriously. An Austrian diplomat noted the little rivalries between ministry and consular officials, who were tarred with the nickname "morbus Consularis," morbid consuls, on account of the difficulties they faced, which made them gloomy.[31] Consuls have not even consistently counted as diplomats—for example, generally they have not enjoyed diplomatic immunity—although in the Ottoman Empire the immunities and privileges they enjoyed were more similar or identical to those enjoyed by diplomats in other host states.[32]

The Vienna Rules of 1815 and the Aachen Protocol of 1818 established a hierarchy of diplomatic agents, dividing them into four categories with consuls at the very bottom. This hierarchy translated into a hierarchy among states, as only states with "royal honors" could enjoy ambassadorial representation.[33] This rigid hierarchy nonetheless left open a back door to the international system for Russia and the new states emerging out of Ottoman decline by giving them consular representation in the Ottoman lands. Though no one really noticed at the time, Russia entered a higher order in the European Great Power constellation when, in accordance with Article XI of the 1774 Treaty of Küçük Kaynarca following the Russo-Turkish War of 1768–74, it gained the right to consular representation in the Danubian Principalities—Moldavia and Wallachia.[34] Furthermore, the new states such as Serbia, Greece, and Romania were represented abroad primarily by consuls, so many of their foreign policy aspirations were channeled through, and even driven by, consular offices and officers.

Consuls therefore acquired an outsized significance in the Ottoman Empire and its successors.[35] In 1855, a pamphlet written by "An Anglo-Levantine" saw Britain's prestige threatened by the fact that it had failed to grasp the special role played by consuls in the Ottoman Empire: "Our diplomatic service is not of a standard commensurate with our importance amongst the family of European States. It is my humble opinion that we have for years been outmaneuvered, both by Russia and other States, and have lost all the influence which our importance as a great naval power ought to entitle us to and one of the reasons is, that our Government has never hitherto discovered that a Consul in the East has totally different duties to perform from one in a more civilized country. . . . They ought to be real diplomatists."[36] By the time the British politician William Gladstone wrote his famously inflammatory pamphlet *Bulgarian Horrors and the Question of the East* in 1876, Great Britain could boast "a network of Consulates and Vice-Consulates, really discharging diplomatic duties, all over the provinces of European Turkey."[37]

The importance of consuls in the Ottoman and former Ottoman lands in particular placed the activities of consuls increasingly at the very center of state interest. For example, during the Near Eastern Crisis in 1879, two consuls were lynched by a city mob in the Ottoman port city of Thessaloniki, and the Ilinden Uprising of 1903 escalated around the fatal shooting of a Russian consul by an Ottoman gendarme in the Macedonian town of Monastir.[38]

History of Consulates

A brief outline of the history of consulates is necessary if we are to grasp how consuls stationed in the Ottoman Empire were able to exercise such a powerful influence on the workings of the international system as a whole. That history begins in the eleventh century in Italy, where the office, which predates the permanent diplomatic post, was created to regulate and protect communities of Italian traders living and working in other countries. The earliest consuls not only possessed jurisdictional authority in seafaring and trade law but also served as governors of a sort, presiding over corporate communities whose individual members were subject not to local law but to the law of the Italian trade city whose consular official represented them.

This sort of consular post and its special jurisdictional realm spread throughout much of Europe with the rise of the Ottoman Empire, as other states beyond the Italian trade cities engaged in trade there. Nonetheless, a shift in the nature of sovereignty precipitated by the wars of religion and codified in the Augsburg Settlement in 1555 and the Treaty of Westphalia in 1648—*cuius regio, eius religio*, literally, "whoever's realm, his religion," meaning that a ruler determined his or her state's religion—served to territorialize statehood and lend a stronger geographical dimension to the concept of state sovereignty. As a result, consuls lost much of the right of special jurisdiction and their authority was limited to elaboration and enforcement of seafaring and trade law for communities living abroad.[39]

Yet the old system had a few peculiarities which would have implications for later developments. One is that consuls did not have to be citizens of the states they represented. They could, for example, be prominent merchants or traders from the very corporate communities (guilds of a sort) they were called upon to oversee.[40] The majority of Ottoman diplomats well into the nineteenth century were Greek-speaking merchants, or Phanariots.[41] When the first consular body was created in the young state of Greece by order of King Otho in 1834, the *corps consulaire* consisted mainly of men from wealthy merchant families abroad whose duties and powers extended far beyond the diplomatic norms of the time. As noted by the Greek diplomatic historian Domna Dontas, "Their extensive role finds no parallel in the diplomatic history of other nations,"[42] not least of all due to the fact that, according to Greek law of the time, "All Greeks settled in Turkey are to enjoy the same municipal liberties as those of the kingdom."[43]

The practice of choosing members of the state's dominant ethnicity living abroad to represent the state had a corollary in Habsburg diplomacy, namely, the appointment of individuals from within the state to consular and other diplomatic posts who were of the same or similar nationality as the state to which they were being posted or who had an advanced linguistic and cultural understanding of those areas. This became policy with a reform of the consular system in 1823, in accordance with which "the consulates of eminent significance should be occupied by individuals who, in addition to studying law and political science, also possess the necessary linguistic capabilities, and due to the difficult conditions in which consuls often find themselves with the sharp differences in mores and habits [*Gebräuche*] of the country, [should possess] some degree of experience and local knowledge, as well."[44] In case there was any doubt where those "consulates of eminent significance" were located, the reform legislation of 1825 specified the Ottoman Empire, where the organization of consular affairs was "of utmost importance."[45]

The first Austrian consul to Ottoman Serbia was thus a Croatian poet, Antun Mihanović, who arrived in Belgrade in August of 1836. Within a few months of his arrival, Mihanović was publishing poems in the local journal *Uranija*, one of which would later become the Croatian national anthem.[46] This practice of favoring individuals with linguistic capacities relevant to the region where they were posted continued up until the collapse of the Habsburg Monarchy.[47]

The ethnicization of diplomatic activity was accordingly driven and rein-forced by both empires and new nation-states, nudged along by the purges of the Ottoman diplomatic corps of Greek Phanariot diplomats in the wake of the Greek War of Independence in 1821, which made the Ottoman for-eign missions increasingly Turkish.[48] And as the Russian historian Teddy Uldricks notes, two Russian foreign ministers, Czartoryski and Ioannis Kapodistrias, "left Russian service to join their respective Polish and Greek causes," Czartoryski to be the first president of the short-lived Polish National Government during the failed November Uprising against Russia in 1830–31, and Kapodistrias to become the first governor of liberated Greece in 1827.[49]

Greece, when it was coming into existence in the 1820s and early 1830s, was the opposite of a state in the way states were understood in Metternich's Europe. Rather, it was an idea held mostly by individuals outside the territory of emergent Greece, an idea (the so-called megali idea, or great idea) projected from abroad by those labeling themselves Greeks, and by others. This pecu-liar reversal can be read from the evolution and early structure and person-nel of the Greek Foreign Ministry. The first Greek minister of foreign affairs, installed briefly in 1822 simultaneously with the drafting of the constitution, was Theodore Negris, from Venice. When the ministry was abolished shortly thereafter, the duties of the foreign minister were assumed by Alexander Mavrokordatos, who ran his diplomacy through the Greeks settled in London, especially the London Greek Committee.[50] The same was true of Serbia's early Foreign Ministry personnel.[51]

The other peculiarity of consular history of the modern period is that, although after Westphalia consuls lost their capacity to set up special juris-dictional realms in other Christian states, they maintained this capacity in the Ottoman Empire and elsewhere in the East. These privileges were codi-fied under agreements known as capitulations, starting with one between France and the Ottoman sultan in 1536. Other European states later signed similar agreements with the sultan, arrangements that in the nineteenth and early twentieth century were significantly extended, creating communi-ties under special jurisdiction called millets, with exemption from prosecu-tion under Ottoman law for particular Christian populations living in the Ottoman Empire.[52] A report prepared by an ad hoc commission of the Divan in Moldavia in 1857 delineated the power that capitulations bestowed on con-suls, namely their right "to exercise their own national civil and criminal juris-diction" over Christian subjects.[53]

The ostensible reason for the special jurisdiction afforded by the capitu-lations in the Ottoman Empire was outlined in a French work on the capitulatory regime from 1899: "The profound difference that separates oriental society from the European nations resulted in a special situation for foreigners who reside in the Orient, a situation which at present has no equivalent either in the Ancient or the New World."[54] This "profound difference," wrote Martens, was rooted in a disparity in the level of civilization between the Ottoman Empire and the states that operated within the law of nations (*Völkerrecht*). "Christian peoples," he wrote, were "united in a *single* Christian society . . . in that it gives a particular direction to their feelings, customs and concepts."[55] The job of the consul was to be the "protector and defender of the interests that especially bring the peoples closer together and bind them."[56] In the case of the Ottoman Empire, this meant reaching across to them over an international boundary to "bring them closer" to states like Russia.[57] "The significance of consuls is particularly clear in the Orient, where they are at once representatives of a higher culture and civilization."[58]

Consuls managed the so-called protégé system whereby "any Ottoman subject, whether Moslem or non-Moslem, could acquire the right of protection from a foreign country without being required to reside in that country."[59] The extent of the protégé system was truly vast, such that already in 1808 there were 120,000 Greek Orthodox under Russian protection.[60] In 1864 and 1871, the Ottoman Ministry of Foreign Affairs was so overwhelmed by the bureaucratic demands precipitated by the capitulations that the ministry was re-formed and expanded to include the post of provincial foreign affairs directors. These were "appointed to cope with the increasing problems created in the provinces by foreign consular representatives [and] local residents with claims to foreign nationality."[61] Although there were turf wars between the Ottoman Foreign and Interior Ministries over the activities of the provincial foreign affairs directors, it is telling of the convergence of social and geopolitical concerns that the directors were first and foremost subordinated to the Foreign Ministry, despite operating exclusively within Ottoman territory and with Ottoman subjects.[62]

Finally, another peculiarity of the capitulations was that they carried over into the new states even after these became autonomous. For their own part, Serbian and Bulgarian advocates argued vehemently for the elimination of the capitulations after they were granted independence or autonomy in 1878.[63] One advocate for Bulgaria declared in 1903, "Consular jurisdiction is at most to be maintained in the oriental lands, where the domestic organization is a very primitive one, not in a European, Christian state created by and modeled on the European powers, as is the Principality of Bulgaria."[64] It is worth noting that the capitulatory system bore many structural similarities to the way colonial mandates were established and organized after the First World War, and that arguments against them were cast in similar terms.[65]

Southeastern Europe at the Vortex

One of the most controversial provisions of the Treaty of Küçük Kaynarca of 1774, ending the Russo-Turkish war of 1768–74, was that it allowed Russia to establish consular posts in the Danubian Principalities, in Bucharest and Iaşi. The enhancement of Russian influence in the region resulting from these posts did not sit well with the Western Great Powers, especially France, which sought to block the provisions in a series of gestures that ultimately precipitated the Russo-Turkish War of 1802–12.[66] Concern about the relationship between diplomatic representation and sovereignty proved especially pointed where Ottoman state control was slipping, leaving behind regions with ambiguous international status.

The first new state to gain full independence from the Ottoman Empire was Greece. Its consular body was officially created in 1834. Just a year later, the Greeks set up consulates in Ottoman Macedonia, where consuls were charged with representing and spreading "Hellenic interests on the ground" and "took part in promoting the Greek cause." In 1836 the Education Society was founded in Athens to oversee schooling in Ottoman Macedonia.[67] Here foreign policy emerged together with social policy, as consuls saw to the creation, staffing, and coordination of education outside the borders of the state.[68]

The novel deployment of consuls was also evident in the consular activity of Western powers in the Ottoman Empire. Great Power competition in extending "protection" to Christians and others in the Ottoman lands brought their foreign affairs squarely into the realm of social policy. Following the attacks on Jews in the Damascus Affair of 1840, the US consul in Alexandria and envoy in the Ottoman Empire, David Porter—ignoring a key principle of consular jurisdiction—initiated a defense of Jews who were not and had never been US citizens nor under US protection in accordance with the capitulations.[69] In 1861 British consuls intervened to halt the expulsion from Serbia of Jews who were being targeted as "secret agents of the Turks."[70]

Further initiatives were taken against the persecution of Jews in the Danubian Principalities. In 1870, Benjamin F. Peixotto was named US consul to Bucharest; Peixotto's Jewish faith was itself intended as a diplomatic signal. In 1872, he was instructed "to address a note to the minister of foreign affairs of the principalities, in which you will . . . do anything which you discreetly can, with a reasonable prospect of success, toward preventing a recurrence or continuance of the persecution" of Jews.[71] It was clear to all parties involved that the actions of the US government through Peixotto were a violation of the principle of nonintervention in the domestic affairs of other states. As a result, that same year, the US secretary of state explained himself as follows, inviting other states to follow the US example: interference of this kind was justified "when guarantee and consideration of justice appear to have been set at defiance. . . . You will not be backward in joining a similar protest, or other measure which the foreign representatives there may deem advisable, with a view to avert or mitigate further harshness toward the Israelite residents in, or subjects of, the principalities."[72]

Given the important role assigned to consuls as the unspoken vanguard of a new diplomacy, with time it became increasingly important to have especially competent and well-trained specialists on the ground in the Ottoman Empire to fill consular positions and back home in the key sections of the Foreign Ministry. In the Dual Monarchy, for example, the more important units of the foreign ministry were the political sections, wherein "the greatest share in formulating the objectives of foreign policy fell."[73] The first among these was the Balkan Section (Section I), dedicated to the Balkans, Turkey, and Russia.[74] By far the largest Habsburg consular contingent was active in the Ottoman Empire and its successors, especially Greece.[75] An 1859 reform, brought about under the influence of Habsburg consuls in the Ottoman Empire, moved consular administration from the Trade Ministry to the Foreign Ministry.[76] This move furthered the institutional transfer of certain aspects of Habsburg social policy into the realm of foreign policy.

It was also the case that the most talented Foreign Ministry staff started out their careers working in the Ottoman and post-Ottoman southeastern Europe sections, most notably the Austrian Joseph von Schwegel, who advised Gyula Andrássy on Balkan matters during the latter's tenure as foreign minister (1871–79) and the Russian foreign minister, Aleksandr Izvol'skiĭ, during the Bosnian annexation crisis of 1908.[77] Prior to becoming Russia's foreign minister, Izvol'skiĭ's first appointments were in the Ottoman Empire, Romania, and Bulgaria.[78]

The focus of European states' diplomatic energies on southeastern Europe was also reflected in the institutions created during the late eighteenth and early nineteenth centuries to train future Foreign Ministry staff and members of the diplomatic corps. Paris founded the School of Oriental Languages in 1795 so that France could send competent directors to consular posts in the Middle East.[79] In Vienna, in 1754, Empress Maria Theresa founded the Oriental Academy, which was the premier institution for training future diplomats and foreign policy experts and later became the Diplomatic Academy of Vienna.

In terms of their socioeconomic background, area knowledge, and linguistic expertise, the consular corps in many countries was in a state of flux over the course of the nineteenth century, their status and role marked by frequent reforms and inquiries. States also tracked each other's practices and reform efforts. An 1835 report from the Select Committee on Consular Establishment prepared for the British House of Commons focused heavily on the views and propositions of statesmen and consular staff operating in the Ottoman Empire. The British consul-general in Egypt proposed that

> in framing new regulations for the consulates, much light might be obtained from the French *ordonnances*, which form a complete code for the guidance of their consuls in the Ottoman empire, and though many of their provisions have become obsolete, and others inapplicable from the greater degree of personal liberty enjoyed by the French nation now than when those *ordonnances* were formed, they are still in force, and point out the course to be pursued by their consuls in almost every possible contingency. These *ordonnances* are printed, and may therefore be consulted, should it be considered useful.[80]

Reform drives in the consular establishment to account for the growing significance of the capitulations left their mark on the nature of states' diplomatic corps, and especially their *corps consulaire*. One feature that set consular posts apart, according to a Russian statesman writing in 1807, was that consuls should be drawn from "families rather above than below the midline of the social hierarchy" and should have a solid command of "Latin, French and German," a knowledge of which will help them easily acquire "Italian, Spanish, English, Danish, Swedish, etc.," but concluded that "the Eastern languages are a thing unto themselves."[81]

As the century progressed, however, consular posts were increasingly filled by upwardly mobile members of the middle class who either grew up speaking the needed languages or distinguished themselves at the new training venues for their skills in acquiring them. The historian Helmut Rumpler, an expert on the Habsburg Empire, has observed a marked increase in the number of non-aristocratic diplomats serving the Habsburgs over the course of the nineteenth century. "Entry to the diplomatic service" had the effect of softening "social differences," he wrote.[82] And "An Anglo-Levantine" argued in 1855 that consuls should be "well acquainted with the language, character, and institutions of the people amongst whom they are to reside; and their functions will not be entirely commercial, as at Marseilles or Hamburg, as they will be called much more frequently to act the diplomat."[83]

So even as foreign policy institutions were taking on ever more social political concerns, a minor social revolution was brewing within the consular establishment that was altering its profile and therefore its concerns. This development paralleled what some saw as the key to the success of the younger nations' diplomatic efforts, namely, their less socially stratified societies. "In Serbia there is neither a nobility nor a favored class," wrote Gustav Rasch in 1867.[84] This made these nations more likely to take education, skill, and experience into account when selecting members of their consular corps, who were for them the diplomatic elite.

To answer the need for greater professionalization, the new states in southeastern Europe initiated a series of reforms and expansions of their foreign ministries. Greece reorganized its consular service in 1877 such that "career diplomats were appointed to the new posts in the Balkan consulates, for . . . the Greek government considered it essential to compete with its northern neighbors for supremacy in regions that might succeed in throwing off Turkish rule."[85] Greek consuls were therefore actively involved in fomenting "rebellions in various regions of European Turkey."[86] Another review and series of revisions to consular law were undertaken in the last years of the nineteenth century, again with Greece's position in Ottoman Macedonia in mind.[87]

At about the same time, and just after gaining autonomy from the Ottoman Empire, Bulgaria established a diplomatic presence with agents in Serbia, Romania, and Istanbul.[88] The Serbian Foreign Ministry was also quick to undertake expansion and reform. The first Serbian consulates were opened in 1886 and 1887 in Skopje and Thessaloniki, followed a year later by another in Bitola, in Macedonia, and another the next year in Priština, Albania.[89] A further institutional transformation came in 1889, when a department of the Serbian Ministry of Education, the Department for Serbian Schools and Churches Outside Serbia, was dissolved, and its activities transferred to the Ministry of Foreign Affairs, in part as the permanent Education Commission of the Ministry of Foreign Affairs, a kind of advisory council made up of "professionals in the Macedonian question."[90] The commission itself was part of the Secret Propaganda Section, which was to "concern itself exclusively with problems of Serbian propaganda, be it in Macedonia or in Old Serbia (the sanjak of Kosovo and Metohija)."[91]

The Secret Propaganda Section came into existence at the behest of Serbian consuls who, already engaged in setting up and maintaining Serbian schools and churches in the areas where they operated, proactively sought greater coordination of their activities. Above all, the consul in Skopje at the time, Vladimir Karić, called for the creation of an office in Belgrade to coordinate consular activity.[92] The mandate of the Secret Propaganda Section was the preservation and in many cases the creation of Serbian schools, churches, and patriotic organizations in areas outside of Serbia—that is, where its consulates were active.[93] Nor did the consuls let up the pressure once the section was created: In 1891 two of them proposed a consular conference to discuss shared goals and concerns and pushed for the Serbian Foreign Ministry to provide consuls with the resources to run a census in Macedonia.[94]

What was true of Serbia was also true of Greece, which used its consuls in the region, and specifically school and church projects, to create a base for territorial expansion.[95] The official government periodical in Bulgaria, *Dŭrzhaven Vestnik* (State Newspaper), from 1891 includes the founding document of the state-sponsored propaganda organization St. Kiril and Methodius in Sofia. The organization had as its mission to "favor the nationality, faith and enlightenment of all Bulgarians living outside the principality" by opening schools "in poor districts," building or repairing churches in those districts, and supplying them with clergy.[96]

The activities of the Serbian consuls were themselves a result of the June 28, 1881, secret treaty between Serbia and Austria-Hungary, according to which Austria-Hungary promised to support Serbian territorial aspirations in the southeast in exchange for Serbia's promise not to undertake similar agitation in Bosnia and Herzegovina, a territory then under Austro-Hungarian occupation.[97] Austro-Hungarian consular activity in the region thus had the aim of encouraging maximum ethnic competition between the new nation-states in nearby Macedonia precisely in order to prevent nationalist activists from neighboring Serbia from agitating in Bosnia and Herzegovina. This demanded creativity and individual initiative on the part of Austro-Hungarian consular staff, who were often given very broad directives and left to work out particular strategies on their own.[98]

The extent of independent Austro-Hungarian consular involvement in the region can be illustrated with an anecdote: During a trip through the Ottoman Empire's remaining holdings in Europe in the spring of 1887, a Habsburg army officer, Moritz Auffenberg-Komarów, who had participated in the military occupation of Bosnia in 1878, described his encounter with the Austro-Hungarian consul general in Thessaloniki, who "assured me, that the conditions were ripe for the Austrians to march in, and that one even anticipated it."[99] Austro-Hungarian diplomats were also conscious of the fact that other states were letting their diplomatic representatives in the region off the leash. As was observed by Musulin von Gomirje, who made his career in the Oriental Section of the Habsburg Foreign Ministry, Russian diplomats in the

Balkans "from ambassador down to the smallest vice-consul, made policy on their own initiative."[100] In 1890 Friedrich Engels wrote, "The Russian diplomatic corps forms, so to speak, a modern Jesuit order, [one] powerful enough in case of necessity to overcome even the whims of the Tsar."[101]

Turning the State Inside Out and Outside In

Consular activity in southeastern Europe reveals the extent to which states were turning themselves inside out, how institutions of social policy were being projected outward across borders, and outside in, in that foreign policy methods were being deployed at home by nationalist activists as much as statesmen. Here it is worth noting the parallel between Serbian, Bulgarian, and Greek activities in Ottoman Macedonia and the simultaneous efforts of German nationalists within Austria—specifically, Bohemia and the Slovene lands—to conceptualize and push the boundaries of a "language frontier," as described in Pieter Judson's *Guardians of the Nation*.[102] A similar correlation can be observed between the activities of French, Austrian, American, and other foreign missionaries in southeastern Europe and the structure of nationalist activism there. In Ottoman Macedonia in 1900, "the Supreme Committee" of Macedonian militant *komites* sent a group of individuals "nicknamed 'the wandering apostles' because of the sometimes multiple aspect of their mission: create a committee, a passage for transport of weapons, and raise the state of mind in a certain village."[103] When the two phenomena are juxtaposed, the distinction between foreign policy strategy and domestic social policy fades the more rapidly, for territorialization and on-the-ground advocacy looked very similar, even to the extent of diplomats' and nationalists' focus on schooling and placing experts on the ground to promote the interests of a particular national-ethnic community.

The process by which states were turning inside out is exemplified by the careers of two Habsburg bureaucrats, Benjamin von Kállay and Stojan Novaković. Benjamin von Kállay began his career in the Austro-Hungarian Foreign Ministry just after the *Ausgleich*, the Compromise, which created the Dual Monarchy. From 1868 to 1875 he was the head consul in Belgrade, then for several years was a member of the Hungarian Parliament, and then the governor in Bosnia (1882–1903). He also wrote several books on Serbs, Russia's "eastern ambitions," Muslims in Bosnia, and Hungary's position "between East and West." Kállay was not unique in moving from a foreign policy career to domestic governance; his vita was comparable to that of other individuals such as Heinrich Müller von Roghoj, who completed his studies at the Oriental Academy and served in the consulates in Beirut, Cairo, and Constantinople in the 1870s before being transferred to the regional government (*Landesregierung*) of Sarajevo in 1879.[104] His trajectory thus took him from a diplomatic career abroad to administration of a territory under Austro-Hungarian control, where the expertise he had gained during the former was especially well suited to governing first Sarajevo and later the whole of occupied Bosnia and Herzegovina.

The vita of Mustafa Reşid Paşa (1800–1858) offers an example of a state turning outside in. Reşid Paşa began his career as a diplomat in Paris and London and rose to become foreign minister and ultimately grand vizier of the Ottoman Empire. As grand vizier he was the primary champion of the *Tanzimat* (reform) initiative and introduced social reforms, including the abolition of slavery, the guarantee of religious equality, and the creation of an Ottoman Academy of Sciences. A poem from one Ottoman statesman, Fuad Paşa, to another, Ali Paşa, told of the merging of the functions of the foreign minister and the grand vizier achieved by Reşid Paşa: "Foreign affairs are the heart of the state; all business lies there."[105]

Another example of states turning outside in can be seen in the career of the Serbian diplomat, statesman, and historian Stojan Novaković, whose achievements also highlight the emergent tight bond between domestic social policy, especially education, and foreign policy for a state in the process of turning inside out. Novaković served three times as minister of education between 1873 and 1883, before being sent to Constantinople as the Serbian envoy. During his tenure there he ushered through a diplomatic convention with the Ottoman Empire that allowed for the creation of Serbian consulates on Ottoman territory, in what are now Macedonia and Kosovo. In 1895 he became Serbia's foreign minister, and set as his ministry's mission "that it work with all available means on Serbian religious education propaganda and on the enhancement of Serbian national consciousness in Turkey."[106]

Novaković was operating under the ideational influence of the *Načertanije*, or "program," of 1844 of a former Serbian foreign minister, Ilija Garašanin, which had called for the "expansion of its national territory and liberation from political tutelage" of Serbs then under Ottoman rule.[107] One of the items in that document was the necessity of bringing young Serbs from Bosnia and other areas where they lived outside of Serbia to work for the state service.[108] For Novaković, the trajectory was from education to its export in planning for a future expanded Serbian state with an imported officialdom.

That statesmen were preoccupied with squaring the social-geopolitical circle by not merely moving personnel but also by softening state boundaries is evident from a further item in Garašanin's *Načertanije,* namely the goal of a regional federation, a dream Novaković and Kállay also periodically shared. All three men believed that regional federation was the only way to address the social and geopolitical questions of the nineteenth century in one stroke. These ideas were inspired, at least in part, by Czartoryski, who believed that small states had a role to play in the international system but were too weak to stand alone, so therefore should unite in federative arrangements.[109]

So it was that the transformation taking place in foreign ministries over the nineteenth century irrevocably muddled the institutional distinction between the domestic social versus foreign policy affairs of states. We find an institutional confession of sorts, testifying to the importance of consular work and the changes it had wrought, in the reorganization of the German Foreign Office following World War I. The way the German Foreign Office was structured prior to the War belied the important role being assumed by consuls and consulates during the second half of the nineteenth century. The office had two sections, a political department (Department I), and one for economic policy and the consular service (Department II). Foreign Secretary Herbert von Bismarck once said that Department I did all the "important and fine work," and only the "bulk work stays in Department II."[110]

Among other changes, the so-called Schüler Reform (named for Edmund Schüler, the head of personnel and administration in Department I) consisted of the unification of the diplomatic and consular careers (earlier these had been strictly divided), the introduction of a regional system (like that in Austria, Great Britain, and Russia), and the opening of the foreign service to men from the world of commerce and industry, and also politics and science—nonaristocrats. One historian has noted that with the reforms "the Foreign Office" conceded that "international politics were confronted with economic and social questions to a degree hitherto unknown." Schüler's reforms were inspired in large part by his friend Ludwig Roselius, previously consul general to Bulgaria.[111] The primary "reform concern" for Germany at that point was "above all the concern for a large German diaspora. Only a country whose foreign nationals are at the same time also entirely or predominantly its citizens can limit itself solely to the basic protection of [state] interests. The care of the millions of these fellow Germans [*Volksgenossen*] cannot be left to particular parties or associations, but become an essential component of official German foreign policy."[112] Important lessons had been learned, not only about the structure of institutions but about how to make an external issue into a

territorial one by placing social policy in the hands of foreign policy institutions, effectively turning the state inside out.

Notes

I would like to express my gratitude to the anonymous reviewers, as well as the many scholars who have offered useful feedback on this project following presentations at the Institute for the Human Sciences (Institut für die Wissenschaften vom Menschen, IWM) in Vienna, the Imre Kertész Kolleg in Jena, the International History Workshop at Columbia University, and the New York Kruzhok. I would also like to thank the institutions that have supported my research, among them the Imre Kertész Kolleg, the Andrew W. Mellon Foundation's New Directions Fellowship, the Center for European and Mediterranean Studies at NYU, Cornell University, and the IWM.

1. Matija Nenadović, *Memoari prote Matije Nenadovića* (Belgrade: Srpska Književna Zadruga, 1893), 125.

2. Ibid., 212.

3. Alexander Musulin von Gomirje, *Das Haus am Ballplatz: Erinnerungen eines österreich-ungarischen Diplomaten* (Munich: Verlag für Kulturpolitik, 1924), 198.

4. Ibid., 62.

5. Adam Czartoryski, *Essai sur la diplomatie, manuscrit d'un philhellène: publié par M. Toulouzan* (Paris: F. Didot, 1830). A second edition, Adam Czartoryski, *Essai sur la diplomatie, par le prince Adam Czartoryski* (Paris: Amyot, 1864), was published in 1864, during the January uprising. On the year when the essay was written, 1823, see ii.

6. In Britain he was responsible for the creation of the Literary Association of the Friends of Poland. He spent most of the rest of his life in France, where he died in 1861.

7. The form of Czartoryski's argument is likely as significant as its context, for this strategy of juxtaposition was common among religious reformers of the Central European pre-Reformation, who juxtaposed images and descriptions of the Roman Church with those of the primitive church in order to demonstrate the former's deviation from the latter's teachings. See Howard Kaminsky et al., "Master Nicholas of Dresden: The Old Color and the New; Selected Works Contrasting the Primitive Church and the Roman Church," *Transactions of the American Philosophical Society*, New Series 55, no. 1 (1965): 1–93.

8. Czartoryski, *Essai sur la diplomatie*, 23, 418–19.

9. Ibid., 157.

10. Ibid., 85. It is interesting to note that by the 1850s, the fickleness of public attention to the Polish question was already apparent, as was the decline in support—especially among liberal Germans—for Polish aspirations. And the 1864 edition asserts that public opinion in Britain has little effect on policymaking, a pessimism that is not present in the 1830 edition. See Czartoryski, *Essai sur la diplomatie, par le prince Adam Czartoryski*, 235. The near unanimous support of European public opinion for the 1830 uprising had not, after all, resulted in intervention by the Great Powers. In fact, the *Essai* closes with a rather pathetic whimper: "Notre voix est trop faible, trop isolée pour en éveiller même l'espérance" (Our voice is too weak, too isolated to even awaken hope). Czartoryski, *Essai sur la diplomatie*, 418. Still, there were those who still believed in the transformative capacity of public opinion. Around the time the second edition of the *Essai* appeared, the Frenchman Alfred Briosne, *Remaniement de l'Europe, réflexions sur la question polonaise* (Paris: E. Dentu, 1865), wrote on the Polish question, highlighting the "impotence of diplomacy" to prevent war, and stating that public opinion of "civilized Europe" should be able to participate in international debates "irrespective of their nationality" in the interest of peace (19).

11. See Endre Kovács, *A lengyel kérdés a reformkori Magyarországon* (Budapest: Akadémiai Kiadó, 1959), 114–15; Oliver Schulz, *Ein Sieg der zivilisierten Welt? Die Intervention der europäischen Grossmächte im griechischen Unabhängigkeitskrieg (1826–1832)* (Münster: LIT Verlag, 2011), 52–53. Note also the subtitle of Czartoryski's *Essai*: "*manuscrit d'un philhellène.*"

12. *Un mot sur la question polonaise en 1829* (Paris: Alexandre Mesnier, 1829), 8. One pamphleteer wrote of the "Gewalt [force] der öffentlichen Meinung." See *Ueber die polnische Frage* (Paris: Carl Heideloff, 1831), 3. Attempts to sway public opinion in favor of Poland go back further than the origin of the Polish question as a matter of public discussion and debate, and indeed began in earnest during the negotiations of the Congress of Vienna. One result was a pamphlet by Henry Brougham, *An Appeal to the Allies, and the English Nation, in Behalf of Poland* (London: J. Harding, 1814). Brougham had advised a Polish envoy of sorts (Biernacki, sent to London by Czartoryski in 1814) to "enlist the interest and sympathy of prominent journalists, poets, and other writers on behalf of Poland, so as to induce them to write in her favour." See Adam Jerzy Czartoryski, *Memoirs of Prince Adam Czartoryski and his Correspondence with Alexander I: With Documents Relative to the Prince's Negotiations with Pitt, Fox, and Brougham, and an Account of his Conversations with Lord Palmerston and other English Statesmen in London in 1832*, ed. Adam Gielgud (London: Remington, 1888), 257–58.

13. Leopold Leon Sawaszkiewicz, *Why the Eastern Question Cannot Be Satisfactorily Settled: Or, Reflexions on Poland and France* (London: J. Ridgway, 1840),

iv. On Sawaszkiewicz, see *Polski Słownik Biograficzny* [Polish biographical dictionary], s.v. "Sawaszkiewicz, Leopold Leon."

14. Baron Fedor Ivanovich Fircks, *La Question polonaise au point de vue de la Pologne, de la Russie et de l'Europe* (Paris: E. Dentu; Bruxelles: L'Office de Publicité; Berlin: Librairie B. Behr, 1863), 85.

15. Ibid., 5–6.

16. Friedrich Martens, *Die russische Politik in der orientalischen Frage: eine historische Studie* (St. Petersburg: Verlag der Kaiserlichen Hofbuchhandlung H. Schmitzdorff, 1877), 3–4.

17. Carole Fink, *Defending the Rights of Others: The Great Powers, the Jews, and International Minority Protection, 1878–1938* (Cambridge: Cambridge University Press, 2004).

18. Cited in Andrea Despot, *Amerikas Weg auf den Balkan: Zur Genese der Beziehungen zwischen den USA und Südosteuropa 1820–1920* (Wiesbaden: Harrassowitz, 2010), 68. Other countries' missionaries were also broadly presumed to be using schools and churches as sites of spreading sedition among Christian subjects of the Ottoman Empire. See, for example, Nasīm Susa, *The Capitulatory Régime of Turkey: Its History, Origin, and Nature* (Baltimore: Johns Hopkins Press, 1933), 143, 146.

19. See, for example, Béni Kállay, *A szerbek története 1780–1815* (Budapest: A Magyar tudományos akadémia könyvkiadó-hivatala, 1877). Kállay, a Hungarian, was the Dual Monarchy's consul in Belgrade from 1868 to 1875 (his German name was Benjamin von Kállay). Another example is the famous orientalist Joseph von Hammer-Purgstall, who attended the Oriental Academy in Vienna, was later posted to Istanbul, and then served as consul in Iaşi (Danubian Principalities) from 1806 to 1807. Among his works is a ten-volume history of the Ottoman Empire, *Geschichte des osmanischen Reiches*, 10 vols. (Pest: C. A. Hartleben, 1827–33).

20. See, for example, Bülent Özdemir, "Being a Part of the Cinderella Service: Consul Charles Blunt at Salonica in the 1840s," in *Frontiers of Ottoman Studies: State, Province, and the West*, ed. Colin Imber and Keiko Kiyotaki (London: I. B. Tauris, 2005), 1:241.

21. See, for example, J. Milojkovic-Djuric, "Benjamin von Kallay: Consul and Historian in Serbia from 1868 to 1875," in *East European Quarterly* 36, no. 4 (2002): 417–40.

22. Fedor Fedorovich Martens, *Das Consularwesen und die Consularjurisdiction im Orient*, translated from Russian by H. Skerst (Berlin: Weidmannsche Buchhandlung, 1874), iv, 9.

23. Ibid., 11, 13. "Exempt," *eximirt* in the original, is now spelled *eximiert*.

24. Ibid., 25.

25. Although one edited volume exists that includes chapters on the evolution of various foreign ministries, it is not comparative, but a parallel rendering with only a few scattered references to developments in other states. See Zara Steiner, ed., *The Times Survey of Foreign Ministries of the World* (London: Times Books, 1982).

26. See Nicole M. Phelps, *U.S.-Habsburg Relations from 1815 to the Paris Peace Conference: Sovereignty Transformed* (New York: Cambridge University Press, 2013), 279–80.

27. Sinan Kuneralp, "The Ministry of Foreign Affairs under the Ottoman Empire and the Turkish Republic," in Steiner, *Times Survey of Foreign Ministries*, 497.

28. Teddy J. Uldricks, "The Tsarist and Soviet Ministry of Foreign Affairs," in Steiner, *Times Survey of Foreign Ministries*, 522.

29. Georg Schmid, "Der Ballhausplatz 1848–1918," *Österreichische Osthefte* 23 (1981): 23, 25 (emphasis in original).

30. Valerie Cromwell, "The Foreign and Commonwealth Office," in Steiner, *Times Survey of Foreign Ministries*, 554. In his 1971 book *The Cinderella Service*, the British historian D. C. M. Platt wrote, "To a diplomat the consular official was regarded as a maid of all work" and "treated as second-class citizens within their own department." Cited in Bülent Özdemir, "Being a Part of the Cinderella Service: Consul Charles Blunt at Salonica in the 1840s," in *Frontiers of Ottoman Studies: State, Province, and the West*, ed. Colin Imber, Keiko Kiyotaki and Rhoads Murphey (London: I. B. Tauris, 2005), 2:242.

31. Musulin von Gomirje, *Das Haus am Ballplatz*, 138.

32. F. Borel, *De l'origine et des fonctions des consuls* (St. Petersburg: Imprimeur du Département des Affaires Étrangères, 1807), 54.

33. Otto Reinfried Schifferdecker, "Die Organisation des auswärtigen Dienstes im alten und neuen Reich" (PhD diss., Heidelberg University, 1932), 104–5.

34. This is evidenced by the fact that, although the so-called Eastern question was not formulated as such until the 1820s, many retrospectively dated its origins to the 1774 treaty and Russia's emergence as a force to be reckoned with in the region. See, for example, Dr. Richard Roepell, *Die orientalische Frage in ihrer geschichtlichen Entwickelung, 1774–1830* (Breslau: Verlag von Trewendt & Granier, 1854), 15; L. Carl Brown, *International Politics and the Middle East: Old Rules, Dangerous Game* (Princeton, NJ: Princeton University Press, 1984), 21–30. See also A. W. Brian Simpson, *Human Rights and the End of Empire: Britain and the Genesis of the European Convention* (Oxford: Oxford University Press, 2001), 111–13.

35. According to the Swiss legal historian Johannes Berchtold in *Recht und Gerechtigkeit in der Konsulargerichtsbarkeit: Britische Exterritorialität im Osmanischen Reich 1825–1914* (Munich: R. Oldenbourg Verlag, 2009), "die Konsuln im Osmanischen Reich und insbesondere auf dem Balkan diplomatische und nicht so sehr traditionell konsularische Funktionen ausübten" (92n37; consuls in the Ottoman Empire and especially in the Balkans carried out diplomatic and not so very traditional consulary functions). Özdemir, "Being a Part of the Cinderella Service," writes that consuls wielded the rights given them by the capitulations "not for the economic reasons such as stimulating trade activities by giving certain privileges to the merchants, but for the political and diplomatic objectives by which they could put pressure upon the local authorities and to a certain degree become independent" (244).

36. An Anglo-Levantine [pseud.], *Our Consuls in the East: A Parliamentary Inquiry into Their Proceedings Imperative* (London: A. M. Pigott, 1855), 9–10.

37. William Ewart Gladstone, *Bulgarian Horrors and the Question of the East* (London: John Murray, 1876), 20.

38. Mark Mazower, "Travellers and the Oriental City, c. 1840–1920," *Transactions of the Royal Historical Society* 12 (2002): 104; Keith Brown, *The Past in Question: Modern Macedonia and the Uncertainties of Nation* (Princeton, NJ: Princeton University Press, 2003), 63; Gladstone, *Bulgarian Horrors*, 37–38.

39. Schifferdecker, "Die Organisation des auswärtigen Dienstes," 23–24.

40. Of the Ottoman Empire, Carter V. Findley, "The Foundation of the Ottoman Foreign Ministry: The Beginnings of Bureaucratic Reform under Selim III and Mahmud II," *International Journal of Middle East Studies* 3, no. 4 (October 1972), writes: "It appears, in fact, that the consular appointments which began to be recorded in a special register in 1802 really represent, not so much an innovation on the part of the sultan, as the extension of official recognition to a system already in existence in a de facto way among certain classes of his subjects. Traian Stoianovich has pointed out that it was traditional by this time for Orthodox Balkan merchants trading outside the empire to be 'organized into companies or merchant guilds, with a "consul" or "Richter" at their head to smooth out discords and promote the business of the entire "company"'" (396).

41. See Christine Philliou, *Biography of an Empire: Governing Ottomans in an Age of Revolution* (Berkeley: University of California Press, 2010), 5–37.

42. Domna Dontas, "The Greek Foreign Ministry," in Steiner, *Times Survey of Foreign Ministries*, 262.

43. Edouard Driault and Michel Lhéritier, *Histoire diplomatique de la Grèce de 1821 à nos jours* (Paris: Les Presses universitaires de France, 1925), 2:112.

44. J. Dr. Joseph Piskur, *Oesterreichs Consularwesen* (Vienna: Druck und Verlag von Carl Gerdold's Sohn, 1862), 14–15.

45. Ibid.

46. Bogdan Popović, *Istorija Ministarstva inostranih dela Srbije* (Belgrade: Glasnik, Diplomatska akademija, 2005), 77. In doing so, he belied the claim of the Austrian diplomat of Croatian origin, Freiherr Alexander Musulin von Gomirje, in *Das Haus am Ballplatz*, that "Croatian literature has no interrelation with that of the Kingdom of Serbia" (18).

47. Among the Austro-Hungarian diplomats of this sort were the two particularly important ones, Alexander Musulin von Gomirje, a Croat from the military frontier (*Militärgrenze*), the cordon sanitaire between the Habsburg and Ottoman Empires, and Benjamin von Kállay, whose mother was a Serb.

48. Sinan Kuneralp, "Ministry of Foreign Affairs," 499.

49. Uldricks, "Tsarist and Soviet Ministry," 519.

50. Dontas, "The Greek Foreign Ministry," 260.

51. Popović, *Istorija Ministarstva Inostranih Dela Srbije*, 15.

52. Carter V. Findley, *Bureaucratic Reform in the Ottoman Empire: The Sublime Porte, 1789–1922* (Princeton, NJ: Princeton University Press, 1980), 22.

53. Isidore Loeb, *La Situation des israélites en Turquie, en Serbie et en Roumanie* (Paris: J. Baer, 1877), 30.

54. Francis Rey, *La Protection diplomatique et consulaire dans les échelles du Levant et de Barbarie avec des documents inédits tirés des Archives du Ministère des affaires étrangères* (Paris: L. Larose & Forcel, 1899), 1.

55. Martens, *Das Consularwesen*, 38–39.

56. Ibid., 14.

57. Ibid., 42.

58. Ibid., 594.

59. Susa, *Capitulatory Régime*, 96–97.

60. Victor Roudometof, *Nationalism, Globalization, and Orthodoxy: The Social Origins of Ethnic Conflict in the Balkans* (Westport, CT: Greenwood Press, 2001), 36.

61. Findley, *Bureaucratic Reform*, 189. The writer Halid Ziya Uşaklıgil worked in the Izmir Mesalih-i Ecnebiye Müdüriyeti and wrote unfavorably of his experiences. See Halid Ziya Uşaklıgil, *Kırk yıl* (Istanbul: İnkılâp Kitabevi, 1987), 354–56. The Ottoman leadership was convinced that the capitulations were the source of many state woes and therefore unilaterally abolished all of them between the outbreak of World War I and the Ottoman Empire's entry into it. Findley, *Bureaucratic Reform*, 333. Kuneralp, "Ministry of Foreign Affairs," writes that a "Department of Nationalities, known in French as the Bureau des Sujetions [was]

established in 1869 to check on the real nationality of a great number of individuals living in Turkey who claimed to have foreign nationality in order to benefit from the advantages given by the Capitulations to foreign nationals. . . . [The Department] had branches in all the main provincial centres" (501).

62. Findley, *Bureaucratic Reform*, 263.

63. Jovan Ristić appealed to the Great Powers to lift the capitulations for Serbia. See Popović, *Istorija Ministarstva Inostranih Dela Srbije*, 122–23.

64. Raphael Caleb, *Die Konsulargerichtsbarkeit in Bulgarien auf Grund der Capitulationen mit der Türkei* (Strasbourg: C. & J. Goeller, 1903), 12–13.

65. See, for example, Susa, "Memorandum Read by the Turkish Delegate at the Lousanne Conference at the Meeting of December 2, 1922, of the Commission on the Regime of Foreigners," in Susa, *Capitulatory Regime*, 332–43.

66. V. A. Ulianitskii', "Istoricheskii' ocherk russkikh konsul'stv za granicei," in *Sbornik Moskovskago Glavnago Arkhiva Ministerstva Inostrannikh Dyel*, vypusk 6-i, Izdanie Komissii' Pechataniia Gosudarstvennnikh Gramot i Dogovorov (Moscow: Tipografiia G. Lissnera i A. Geshelia, 1899), 295–96; Radu R. Florescu, "Romania, Relations with," in *Encyclopedia of Russian History*, ed. James R. Millar (New York: Macmillan Reference USA, 2004), 3:1292. It is interesting to note that Russia had set up a consulate in the Polish-Lithuanian Commonwealth in 1763. See Ulianitskii', "Istoricheskii' ocherk," 265.

67. Fikret Adanır, *Die makedonische Frage: Ihre Entstehung und Entwicklung bis 1908* (Wiesbaden: Franz Steiner Verlag, 1979), 102. On later administrative oversight of the Foreign Ministry over the Society for the Propagation of Greek Letters, see Gennadius Library Archives (Athens, Greece), Archeio Stefanou Dragoumē, Fak. 30.3, Epistoles, poikila (1887–92), Poikila: Syllogos pros diadosin ellēnikōun grammatōun (kanonismos scheseōun symvouliou tou syllogou me to ypourgeio Exōuterikōun), eggr. 74.

68. The Dante Alighieri Society in Italy, established much later, in 1889, also maintained close ties to the Italian Foreign Ministry. It had as its *implicit* aim "to keep alive the irredentism among the Italian populations still under the rule of the Austro-Hungarian Empire." See Enrico Serra, "The Ministry of Foreign Affairs," in Steiner, *Times Survey of Foreign Ministries*, 305–6.

69. Despot, *Amerikas Weg*, 73.

70. Loeb, *La Situation des israélites*, 40–43.

71. Despot, *Amerikas Weg*, 76–78.

72. Ibid.

73. Helmut Rumpler, "The Foreign Ministry of Austria and Austria-Hungary 1848–1918," in Steiner, *Times Survey of Foreign Ministries*, 55.

74. Musulin von Gomirje, *Das Haus am Ballplatz*, 135.

75. On the distribution as of 1862, see Piskur, *Oesterreichs Consularwesen*, 20–30. On Britain, see "Report from the Select Committee on Consular Establishment, Together with the Minutes of Evidence and Appendix," *House of Commons Papers*, 1835 (499), 6:116–18.

76. Piskur, *Oesterreichs Consularwesen*, 19.

77. Rumpler, "Foreign Ministry of Austria," 56. Julius Zwiedeneck-Südenhorst, who started out as head of the Oriental Section, later took charge of all political sections.

78. See W. M. Carlgren, *Iswolsky und Aehrenthal vor der bosnischen Annexionskrise: Russische und österreichisch-ungarische Balkan Politik 1906–1908* (Uppsala: Almqvist & Wiksells boktr, 1955), 68. See also A. P. Izvol'skii', *Mémoires de Alexandre Iswolsky, ancien ambassadeur de Russie à Paris (1906–1910)* (Paris: Payot, 1923).

79. Georges Dethan, "The Ministry of Foreign Affairs since the Nineteenth Century," in Steiner, *Times Survey of Foreign Ministries*, 204.

80. "Report from the Select Committee on Consular Establishment," 6:199.

81. Borel, *De l'origine et des fonctions des consuls*, 73, 81.

82. Rumpler, "Foreign Ministry of Austria," 54–55.

83. Anglo-Levantine [pseud.], *Our Consuls in the East*, 9–10.

84. Gustav Rasch, *Die Völker der unteren Donau und die orientalische Frage* (Breslau: J. U. Kern, 1867), 93.

85. Dontas, "Greek Foreign Ministry," 264.

86. Ibid.

87. Gennadius Library Archives (Athens, Greece), Archeio Stefanou Dragoumē, Fak. 44–45, esp. Ypofak. 45.1, Meletē proxenou Fōukiōunos me titlo: "Ē alētheia peri tou proxenikou kladou ēmōun" (1898), eggr. 13, 1–94.

88. Elena B. Statelova, Radoslav D. Popov, and Vasilka A. Tankova, *Istorija na bălgarskata diplomacija: 1879–1913 g.* (Sofia: Fondacija Otvoreno Obštestvo, 1994), 7.

89. Popović, *Istorija Ministarstva Inostranih Dela Srbije*, 134. Two more consulates opened in 1897 and 1899, in Serez and Prizren, but both werre short-lived.

90. Ibid., 136. The so-called Prosvetni Odbor (Education Committee) had been active in establishing schools in Macedonia and "Old Serbia" and securing for them teachers and textbooks since 1868. See Andrew Rossos, *Macedonia and the Macedonians: A History* (Stanford: Hoover Institution Press, 2008), 75. The Ministry of Education had earlier supported and funded propaganda organizations such as the Družtvo Sv. Save (Society of St. Sava), which with the reform were placed under the auspices of the foreign ministry. Arhiv Srbije, Belgrade

(hereafter AS), MID-PP, red. 26(I)/1891, Pismo od predsednika družtva Sv. Save, Nikolajević, February 21, 1891.

91. See Kliment Džambazovski, ed., *Građa za Istoriju Makedonskog Naroda iz Arhiva Srbije: Graga za Istorijata na Makedonskiot Narod od Arhivot na Srbija*, vol. 4, bk. 3, *1888–1889* (Belgrade: Arhiv Srbije, 1987), 11.

92. See Mihailo Vojvodić, *Stojan Novaković i Vladimir Karić* (Belgrade: Clio, 2003), 149.

93. Plans and protocols for opening Serbian schools were prepared by the consul in Bitolj for consuls in other areas of Macedonia and Old Serbia in 1889. See AS, MID-PP, f. IV, 1889, dok. od konsulata u Bitolju, 5. jula 1889; 3. dok. od 12. jula 1889.

94. AS, MID-PP, red. 8/1891, Konferencija Konsula predlažu Karić i Botić—Ministarstvo Inostranih Dela, 23. Feb. 1891 u Beogradu. Similarly, the Bulgarian Exarchate at the time was also keen on taking a census. See AS, MID-PP, red. 78/1891. On differing ethnic distributions offered in statistics of Serbia, Greece and Bulgaria, see Valery Kolev and Christina Koulouri, eds., *The Balkan Wars* (Thessaloniki: Center for Democracy and Reconciliation in Southeast Europe, 2005), 42.

95. On the activities of Greek consuls in Macedonia, see Dontas, "The Greek Foreign Ministry," 262.

96. *Dŭrzhaven Viestnik*, August 30, 1891, 4–7. It is important to note, however, that since Bulgaria was not fully independent, its representatives abroad were generally referred to as agents at this time.

97. *Pregled razvoja medjunarodno-pravnih odnosa jugoslovenskih zemalja od 1800 do danas* (Belgrade: Institut za međunarodnu politiku i privredu, 1953), 89–90; Alfred F. Pribram, *Die politischen Geheimverträge Österreich-Ungarns, 1879–1914* (Vienna: W. Braumüller, 1920), 19.

98. Musulin von Gomirje, *Das Haus am Ballplatz*, 145–47, wrote that a necessary trait of a good diplomat was *Phantasie*, not least because the overall mission in Macedonia in particular seemed impossible: "[Wir] waren zunächst bemüht, in Mazedonien und Albanien erträgliche Zustände zu schaffen und durch entsprechende Reformen die Situation zu bessern, ohne daß diese Reformen so weit gehen sollten, die Existenz der Türkei zu gefährden" (We were first concerned with bringing about bearable conditions in Macedonia and Albania and with improving the situation by means of appropriate reforms, without these reforms going so far as to endanger the existence of Turkey).

99. Moriz Auffenberg-Komarów, *Aus Österreichs Höhe und Niedergang: Eine Lebensschilderung* (Munich: Drei Masken Verlag, 1921), 64.

100. Musulin von Gomirje, *Das Haus am Ballplatz*, 61.

101. Cited in Uldricks, "Tsarist and Soviet Ministry," 519.

102. Pieter M. Judson, *Guardians of the Nation: Activists on the Language Frontiers of Imperial Austria* (Cambridge, MA: Harvard University Press, 2006), 19–65.

103. Nadine Lange-Akhund, *The Macedonian Question, 1893–1908, from Western Sources* (Boulder, CO: East European Monographs, 1998), 102.

104. *Österreichisches Biographisches Lexikon 1815–1950*, s.v. "Müller von Roghoj, Heinrich."

105. Cited in Findley, *Bureaucratic Reform*, 151.

106. Vojvodić, *Stojan Novaković*, 21–55, 150.

107. Popović, *Istorija Ministarstva Inostranih Dela Srbije*, 107–8.

108. D. Stranjaković, "Kako je postalo Garašaninovo *Načertanije*," *Spomenik (Srpska kraljevska akademija)* 91 (1939): 76–102.

109. Czartoryski, *Essai sur la diplomatie*, 301–3. On Czartoryski's influence on Kállay, see J. Milojkovic-Djuric, "Benjamin von Kallay: Consul and Historian in Serbia from 1868 to 1875," *East European Quarterly* 36, no. 4 (2002): 434.

110. Kurt Doß, "The History of the German Foreign Office," in Steiner, *Times Survey of Foreign Ministries*, 229.

111. Ibid., 236–37.

112. Schifferdecker, "Die Organisation des auswärtigen Dienstes," 67–68.

CHAPTER SIX

THE HOLLOW CROWN

Civil and Military Relations during
Serbia's "Golden Age," 1903–1914

John Paul Newman

The Balkans played a sensational—if not always fully understood—part in
the outbreak of the First World War. When, in June 1914, a Bosnian Serb
nationalist shot and killed the Habsburg heir, Archduke Franz Ferdinand, and
his wife, Sophie Chotek, Duchess of Hohenberg, he also delivered to Austria-
Hungary a casus belli against its regional rival, Serbia. But the consequent
diplomatic crisis turned this Balkan imbroglio between Austria-Hungary and
Serbia into a Europe-wide concern. During the "July days" that followed
the assassination, Europe's leaders activated a series of interlocking military
mobilizations and counter-mobilizations, thereby triggering, in the space of
barely a month, a global conflict unprecedented in its destructive capacities,
the first war to be called a "world war."[1] The rival armies dashing toward the
Belgian coast in August 1914, the static sinews of trenches cut into the soil of
Flanders, the besieged fortresses of Galicia, the Battles of the Marne, Verdun,
Tannenberg, Caparetto, and Gallipoli—Princip is often presented as the hap-
less "trigger" of all this, a mere pretext for the warring rivalries of the European
great powers to break out into hostilities.[2] Thus are the Balkans relegated to
the periphery of Europe once again.

Explosive events garner more attention than slow-burning historical pro-
cesses. The history of the prewar era in Europe was pockmarked with minor
eruptions from the Balkan "powder keg." The region was the Gordian knot of

that taxing diplomatic entanglement of the late nineteenth century, the great Eastern Question, which begged an answer from the European powers as to how best to manage the obvious decline of the Ottoman Empire. Informed observers in 1914 would also have recalled an earlier sensational regicide in these parts: that of Aleksandar Obrenović, the ruling Serbian monarch, in a palace coup in Belgrade in 1903. The grisly details of this killing had shocked Europeans.[3] So, too, had the atrocities carried out by the national armies of the Balkan alliance (Serbia, Montenegro, Greece, and Bulgaria) in the Balkan wars of 1912–13. (These conflicts were soon eclipsed by the First World War itself, but for a brief time they were front-page news throughout much of Europe, and were the subject of a detailed and assiduously compiled report commissioned by the Carnegie Endowment for International Peace.)[4] Few Europeans, however, properly understood Balkan affairs in the years before 1914. Regional expertise remained the preserve of a handful of eccentric and often politically engaged intellectuals such as R. W. Seton-Watson, James Bourchier, and Edith Durham.

Yet the years between 1903 and 1914, a brief but defining period framed by two sensational acts of regicide, are crucial to understanding the Balkan roots of the First World War, and for understanding the relationship between the Balkans and the rest of Europe. The assassination of Franz Ferdinand in 1914 and the diplomatic crisis it caused could not have happened without the killing of Aleksandar Obrenović in 1903. The regicide and the coup of 1903 realigned Serbia's international alliances—away from Austria-Hungary and toward Russia. The European dimensions of this new shift of allegiance became obvious in July 1914. The coup also brought into Serbian domestic politics a powerful and influential militarist factor whose crowning achievement would be the assassination of the Habsburg heir in 1914. Thus, both the Sarajevo assassination itself and its fatally amplified consequences can be traced backward to its forerunner of 1903. In order to understand the roots of the war, it is necessary to look more closely at this short period of accelerated events in Serbia.

In this chapter my intention is to keep Serbia and the Balkans at the heart of the story of the origins of the First World War by delving deeper into the domestic affairs of the Serbian state between 1903 and 1914, and especially into the relations between the country's civilian leaders and certain militarist groups that were implicated in the regicides of both 1903 and 1914. It is telling that the same militarist clique was involved in the regicides of both 1903 and 1914: a group of Serbian army officers informally led by Dragutin "Apis" Dimitrijević, known to its opponents as Unification or Death and to posterity as the Black Hand. Apis and his allies were representative of a strain of militarism that was prominent in Serbia in the first decade of the twentieth century, one that was largely unrestrained by constitutional checks and whose adherents had a proprietary attitude toward the state's domestic and foreign matters and vied for supremacy in national affairs with the country's elected politicians.

This militarism is a memento mori frequently hidden in the picture of Serbian history in the years before the outbreak of the war, not only because the bigger European narrative misses the region's finer details but also because Serbian histories themselves have knowingly understated the influence of the military factor in domestic politics. Until recently, the dominant, though not the exclusive, interpretation of national history in the decade or so before the First World War is that of a "Golden Age" during which the state was governed along enlightened, constitutional, and democratic lines. According to the adherents of the Golden Age interpretation, the end of Obrenović rule in 1903 supposedly ushered in a period of liberalization and political modernization in Serbian history that was rudely cut short by the Austro-Hungarian attack of 1914. In this interpretation, militarist groups are usually idealized on terms they themselves set: as benign guardians of the nation's best interests.

This perception has been remarkably persistent, and its formulation began soon after 1918, when many Serbs, disappointed with the failures of the common South Slav state, looked back upon an idealized and almost mythic past in which the Serbs had supposedly been united behind a common goal and a common purpose.[5] These tropes were subsequently resurrected in the so-called Serbian National Revival of the 1980s, as many Serbian intellectuals publicly rejected the official and obviously politicized myths of the ruling Yugoslav League of Communists and replaced them with their own "counter-myths," typically ones that exclusively emphasized themes of Serbian sacrifice and heroism.[6] The First World War and its origins was a prime candidate for such revisionism.[7] Yet even when the nationalist revival was at its highest tide, in the 1990s, there existed in Serbia a group of scholars who pointed out the darker realities of the Golden Age of 1903–14.[8] This chapter continues the interrogation of Serbia's Golden Age, starting with a study of the longer-term roots of the military strains that would play such a decisive role in the years immediately preceding the outbreak of the First World War.

The Origins of Militarism in Serbia, 1804–1903

The origins of the hypertrophied militarism and the civil-military tensions so prominent in Serbia at the beginning of the twentieth century can be traced in part to the origins of the Serbian state. The Serbian state of the nineteenth century was born in armed uprising against the Ottomans (1804), and it was thus in armed struggle that the Serbian national revolution found its purest form.[9] It was only natural that the military would enjoy a privileged position in the institutional and national culture of Serbia. The exalted role of the Serbian army was to deliver the people from the purgatory of empire and into national emancipation via armed struggle. Its officers were aware of their important role in the nationalizing mission: Their raison d'être was the "liberation" of all "unredeemed lands," or irredenta; they remained true to this goal, and they were impatient with civilian meddling and restraint.[10]

Because of its revolutionary heritage, the Serbian army as an institution came to define itself through its anti-imperial traditions: The *hajduk* (irregular peasant infantry bands); the peasant uprisings of the early nineteenth century; Karadjordje, "Black George," the leader of the 1804 uprising and, in fact, a veteran of the imperial Austrian army; and Karadjordje's fellow insurgents— these were the supposed tributaries of the Serbian army. But this institutional culture obscured the Serbian army's numerous foreign debts: modern military science in Serbia was largely an import from western Europe, adapted and suited to local circumstances. The historian Dimitrije Djordjević has outlined a four-stage process of modernization and development to which Balkan armies of the nineteenth century adhered, and this schema can be usefully applied to the Serbian case. The first stage, typically lasting from the end of the eighteenth century until the 1830s, sees the beginning of revolutionary national armies in the Balkan peasant uprisings that were a feature of this period. The second period, from the 1830s until the 1860s, sees the installation of professional standing armies in the region. Third, this is followed by a "double standard" of development in both territorial, popular army units *and* standing armies. Finally, there is a period lasting from the 1880s until the beginning of the First World War, during which Balkan armies were organized, equipped, and trained to western European models and standards.[11] In Serbia, Djordjević's first period began with the First Serbian Uprising of 1804 and continued until the beginning of the Second Serbian Uprising in 1815, during which time most able-bodied men were armed and fought.[12] Miloš Obrenović, leader of the Second Serbian Uprising (1815–17) and the first Prince of Serbia, initiated the second phase of development, establishing a small army of paid soldiers recruited from across the land.[13] Then, in 1861, the Law on the Organization of the National Army of 1861 created a large popular national army to complement the existing standing army, thus ushering in Djordjević's "fourth period." By 1883 the Serbs had a large standing army in which every Serbian male between the ages of twenty and fifty was required to serve for a period of two years. By the beginning of the twentieth century the Serbian army could mobilize 250,000 to 300,000 men.[14] The Serbs had, in effect, a modern national army whose institutional organization would have been the envy of many more developed western European states. As the army professionalized, its officer corps emerged as a powerful national elite, sufficiently well organized to rival the country's civilian politicians—the latter being an elite group that was itself in the process of formation in the nineteenth century.[15]

The ultimate goal of both military and political elites in nineteenth-century Serbia was essentially the same: to recruit the peasant masses to the Serbian cause and to reclaim—"redeem"—national lands from the Ottomans and the Habsburgs. Serbia in the nineteenth and early twentieth centuries was a "nationalizing state" whose institutions were committed to inculcating people with a sense of national identity and loyalty.[16] The task ahead had been set out by Ilija Garašanin, Serbia's minister of the interior, later prime minister, in his secret *Načertanije*, an "outline" or "blueprint," drawn up in 1844 but not widely disclosed until much later. This policy document called for the unification of all Serbs into one state to create a Great Serbia whose realization would complete the process of national liberation that had begun with the First Serbian Uprising of 1804.[17] Nationalizing agenda of the kind laid out in the *Načertanije* were quite typical of all Balkan states before the First World War. As Mark Biondich has noted, the Balkan countries had in common "a commitment to the nationalist project, the homogenization of their societies, and the ideology of irredenta."[18] But more than this, the goal of national integration was typical of states throughout Europe in the latter part of the nineteenth century. Both Germans and Italians had similar designs toward the unification of their national groups into a single state, both saw the difficulties of inculcating putative national groups with a sense of national identity, and both saw national and nationalizing institutions such as the army as potential vehicles that would carry them toward this goal. In this respect the Serbians were programmatically European, applying a modernizing and nationalizing template to the specific circumstances of the region.

A common destination does not imply a common route, however, and in Serbia there were important differences between civil and military elites over the direction and tempo of the proposed national revolution. Civilian leaders tended to be more patient and flexible, willing to bend to the expediencies of diplomacy; the military elite was frequently bullish and uncompromising in its pursuit of the nationalizing mission. Importantly, the military was ready to act decisively and aggressively if internal or external opponents threatened this mission. The Serbian military elite, represented by the army's officer corps, came to regard itself as the guardian of state interests; for many professional soldiers in Serbia the country's civilian leadership was answerable to the army, not vice versa. It was a kind of "institutional extremism" whereby the officers of the Serbian army demanded an ever-accelerating drive toward national liberation, a goal to which all other concerns were subordinated.[19] This institutional extremism impinged upon the civilian leaders of Serbia, who were unable to fully tame the army and its officers in the years before the war.

The May Coup, 1903

The palace coup that begins the critical period in Serbian history at the start of the twentieth century was a sensational demonstration of a self-confident and largely autonomous military acting as watchdogs over national life. Its details are well known: On a May night in 1903, a small group of army officers, who enjoyed broad support throughout the officer corps of the Serbian army, invaded the royal palace of Aleksandar Obrenović with the intention of finding and killing the king.[20] After some hours of stumbling around the palace's corridors and rooms, the king was discovered, along with his wife, Draga Mašin, hiding in a bedroom closet. The royal couple was set upon by the conspirators with sabers, after which the mutilated corpses were defenestrated and left to lie in the palace courtyard until the following morning.

The immediate trigger for this bloody business, which came to be called the May Coup, was King Aleksandar's marriage to Draga Mašin, a commoner, a widow, and a society woman with a shady past. King Aleksandar was also the army's chief of staff, so for the officer conspirators, who became known as the regicides, the king's unseemly marriage and his impolitic behavior was damaging to the prestige of the army. In addition to Aleksandar's embarrassing marriage there were other concerns that underpinned the regicides' actions and shored up support for their conspiracy. Aleksandar's autocratic rule was becoming increasingly unpopular throughout the country, especially his abrogation of the country's constitution and his curtailment of free speech.[21] The May Coup was thus a vivid demonstration of how the army and its officers were prepared to remove and replace Serbia's leaders if they deemed it necessary. They themselves defined the national interest and acted in its name, and in the name of all those who opposed Aleksandar's rule.

But even more was at stake than this: Aleksandar, like his father, King Milan, had been apathetic about claims on Serbia's national irredenta, preferring instead to cultivate good relations with the country's imperial neighbors, especially Austria-Hungary. This unambitious foreign policy meant that by the beginning of the twentieth century Serbia was looking less and less like a dynamic force of national revolution. Such lethargy was obviously at odds with the regicides and with the officer corps of the army more generally, since they were fully committed to maintaining the momentum of Serbia's national emancipation. The institutional extremism of the Serbian army tolerated no obstacles, even when they came in royal form. The May Coup clearly showed what fate awaited those who were indifferent or opposed to the national cause. Abroad, the lurid details of the coup prompted outrage in the chancelleries of Europe, and especially on the part of British observers, who were shocked that a monarch—even a Balkan monarch—could be thus abused while his assassins escaped without punishment.[22] This, then, was the curtain raiser of Serbia's putative Golden Age.

In post-coup Serbia, Petar Karadjordjević, the exiled claimant, replaced Aleksandar Obrenović on the Serbian throne, the last switch in a century of rivalry between the two dynasties. Petar was a man of liberal and libertarian tastes (he was responsible for translating John Stewart Mill's essay "On Liberty" into Serbian) who ruled as a constitutional monarch. Under Petar, unlike under Aleksandar, party political life was allowed to thrive: post-1903 Serbian governments would be dominated by the People's Radical Party (Narodna radikalna stranka), a powerful and well-organized political force with mass electoral support whose program was rooted in the traditions of Serbian agrarian socialism. Radical Party doctrine called for the political and constitutional freedoms supposedly enjoyed by Serbians within Serbia to be extended to all Serbs living under foreign rule.[23] The urgency of the nationalizing mission was restored; Serbia's post-1903 rulers had an appetite for state aggrandizement that their predecessors lacked. Soon after the coup, the Radicals and Petar steered Serbia away from the Austrian tutelage cultivated so assiduously by the Obrenovićs and moved the country into the orbit of tsarist Russia. A fateful realignment indeed, not just for Serbia and Austria-Hungary, but ultimately for the whole of Europe.[24] There was at this stage nothing inevitable about a showdown, military or otherwise, between the two states; nevertheless, as Jonathan Gumz has shown, the differences between Serbia, the nationalizing state, and Austria-Hungary, the "anational," bureaucratic empire, were now more clearly delineated than ever.[25]

The liberal and constitutional trappings of Karadjordjević's Serbia concealed some unpleasant facts about the sources of power in the country. Despite benefiting from its consequences, neither Petar nor the Radicals had been involved in the May Coup, and when the regicides handed over the reins to the parliament and the new king, they made sure to maintain their own autonomy and, potentially, their ability to act against the new regime. The regicides' interests were enshrined in Serbia's new constitution of 1903, which acknowledged the regicides as the "saviors of the nation."[26] The democratic and liberal institutions of the Serbian state thus bore the scars of their violent birth: Militarism remained the country's primal curse. Power struggles between the civilian and military elites of post-coup Serbia became an important feature of the country's political landscape. On the one hand, the country's new government curbed the influence of the regicides and their allies by retiring a number of their most prominent supporters from the army. On the other hand, from 1906 onward, the Ministry of the Army was continually headed by a regicide or by one of their allies, meaning that the influence of the conspirators reached into the very heart of democratic politics.

These rivalries were in fact three-cornered, between the regicides, the government, and the king himself, who realized that his own fate could match that of his unfortunate predecessor. What is more, these rivalries played out in the context of worsening relations between Serbia and Austria-Hungary. The Serbian state's change of dynasty and its new foreign alignments after 1903 caused concern in Vienna. After the May Coup, antagonisms between Austria-Hungary and Serbia had flared up repeatedly; indeed, the two countries were in a state of economic war in 1906–11, waging a battle over tariffs known as the Pig War.[27] Later, in 1909, Austro-Hungarian authorities accused members of the Croat-Serb Coalition, a South Slav political party in the Croatian *sabor* (assembly), of spying for Serbia, leading to two sensational trials, the Zagreb High Treason Trial and the Friedjung Trial.

The Annexation of Bosnia and the Proliferation of Militarism in Serbia

The most serious confrontation between the two states, however, occurred in 1908, following Austria-Hungary's annexation of Bosnia. Austria-Hungary's move on Bosnia had been prompted by uncertainty after the Young Turk revolution in the Ottoman Empire. The annexation itself did little more than confirm de jure what had been in place de facto since the Habsburg occupation of 1878: Austria-Hungary's control of Bosnia at the expense of the Ottomans.[28] But it also made Habsburg authority of the province a permanent and apparently irreversible fact, much to the consternation of the nationalizers within Serbia.

The domestic reactions to the annexation crisis in Serbia threw into sharp relief the differences between the country's civilian leaders and their militarist counterparts. After some protest and saber rattling, the Radical government resigned itself to the Austro-Hungarian fait accompli, at least for the time being. The annexation of Bosnia had caused a shift in official Serbia's foreign policy aims. Even though the eventual incorporation of Serb-populated Habsburg lands into Serbia remained a long-term goal, its immediate realization seemed impossible.

It was now expedient for Serbia's civilian leaders to redirect nationalist energies southward, toward the more plausibly attainable Ottoman lands, since Ottoman control in the Balkans at that time was far weaker than Habsburg control in Bosnia and looked as if it would only weaken further. For years groups of Christian bandits had operated in these parts; known to the Ottomans as *komitadji* ("committee men," members of rebel bands), they referred to themselves as *četnici*, a term derived from the Serbian word *četa*, meaning troop or military unit.[29] At the beginning of the twentieth century, activists in Serbia, hoping to coordinate and strengthen the national character of such banditry, had organized a *četnik* executive committee based in Belgrade but with sub-branches in other parts of Serbia (the largest was in Vranje), which recruited young men into the *četnici* and organized their activities in Ottoman lands to the south.[30] Soon the Serbian government was giving financial and material support to these groups. The change of dynasty and government in Belgrade after the May Coup of 1903 created more amenable conditions for the *četnik* executive committee. Expediency sometimes dictated that official Serbia distance itself from such guerrilla groups; nevertheless, the Serbian state shared the committee's interest in turning acts of banditry into more concerted anti-imperial guerrilla action, and the *četnici* came to serve as an auxiliary of the Serbian state's nationalization drive in the Ottoman Balkans.

The regicides, however, took the Bosnian annexation far less lightly than their civilian counterparts, and Vienna's perceived encroachment on Serbian irredenta, as well as persistent rivalries with the civilian government and the ever-worsening relations in Bosnia, prompted the regicides to create their own association. This was Unification or Death, the Black Hand, formed in May 1911.[31] The Black Hand was a clandestine organization that took as inspiration the secret German and Italian societies of the nineteenth century (the Black Hand's journal was titled *Piedmont*), societies that had been instrumental in realizing German and Italian unification. The leaders of the Black Hand, including, of course, Apis, cloaked their society in a mantle of arcane symbols and secret underground meetings. The society's seal showed a skull and bones, a knife, a bomb, and a vial of poison. Initiates of the Black Hand stood in front of a real knife, bomb, and vial of poison while swearing fealty to the organization's primary goal: the incorporation of all Serbs currently living under imperial rule into the extended borders of an enlarged Serbian kingdom, the "unification" of Unification or Death. According to Wayne Vucinich, the Black Hand was a "powerful and nefarious influence" in Serbia, increasing the existing power of the regicides in the royal court, the parliament, and in the various post-1903 governments.[32]

Such was the concern caused by Apis and his allies that Crown Prince Aleksandar Karadjordjević, King Petar's son, began to cultivate a rival militarist clique of his own, the so-called White Hand, a loosely organized cabal of officers loyal to Aleksandar and headed by Colonel (later General) Petar Živković. The White Hand was Aleksandar's bulwark against the ever-powerful officers of the Black Hand, a means of securing his succession should Apis and his cohort decide to act against the Karadjordjević dynasty as they had against Aleksandar Obrenović. Although lacking the formal organization and constitution of the Black Hand, the White Hand exerted a powerful influence of its own, its members being well positioned both in the army and in the royal court. Živković was especially close to Aleksandar and would remain so until the latter's death, in 1934.[33]

As David MacKenzie has shown, militarist societies and groups in Serbia proliferated in the years before the outbreak of the First World War: The Austro-Hungarian annexation of Bosnia in 1908 caused a surge in patriotic and nationalistic sentiment throughout the Serbian lands.[34] Along with the Black Hand, the annexation prompted the creation of societies such as National Defense (Narodna odbrana, formed in 1908), a patriotic association committed to protecting Serbian interests in the annexed provinces. National Defense's central committee was located in Belgrade, but the society also had around 220 local committees in villages and towns throughout Serbia. Its goal was to awaken Serbian resistance to the annexation, to recruit volunteers for guerrilla and terrorist actions in the annexed lands, and ultimately to unify all the Serbs in one state.[35]

The Balkan Wars

In Serbia, the military victories of the Balkan wars of 1912–13 have been threaded together with the war of 1914–18: the entire period is known as one continuous conflict for the "liberation and unification" of all South Slavs (liberation from imperial rule and unification into a single state).[36] Yet for many Serbs the victory of 1918 is marred because it led to the creation of Yugoslavia, a political project that many Serbs now believe to have been their undoing in the twentieth century. No such stigma attaches itself to the victories of 1912–13: These were largely Serbian affairs, and the Balkan Wars mark the apogee of the Serbian state's prowess before the outbreak of the First World War. According to Serbian patriots, the victories against the Ottoman army in the First Balkan War ended centuries of national slavery and avenged Tsar Lazar's epoch-making defeat at the Field of Blackbirds (Kosovo Polje) in 1389.[37] Upon victory in the Second Balkan War, Serbia asserted its maximalist territorial claims over much coveted lands, especially the sanjak of Novi Pazar, thereby supplanting Bulgaria as the most powerful political and military force in the region. For many Serbs, the victories of 1912 and 1913 were depicted as the final stage in the long war of national emancipation ignited in the First Serbian Uprising of 1804.[38]

And yet the all-conquering Serbian army of 1912–13 was in reality utterly removed from the peasant militias of Karadjordje, the ragtag guerillas and mercenaries responsible for temporarily driving the Ottoman Empire's janissaries out of Serbia at the beginning of the nineteenth century. Since then, the Serbian army had become a force to be reckoned with: still largely a peasant army but headed by a professional officer corps; modern and well equipped and trained in line with the cutting edge of European military sciences.[39] The Serbian army mobilized over 400,000 soldiers in 1912 from a population of 2,945,950.[40] The impressive military performances of the Serbian army in 1912–13 and, for that matter, in 1914–15 are a testament to the fairly rapid and successful process of modernization and development that had transformed the armed forces of Serbia into a highly effective instrument of war. And given the importance of mobilization and organizational matters throughout Europe in the weeks before and after the outbreak of the First World War, there were perhaps many important lessons to be learned from the case of Serbia in 1912.

Živojin Mišić, a colonel of the Serbian army who was promoted to general for his conduct in the Balkan Wars, interpreted the mobilization of 1912 as a *levée en masse* which proved that "in the whole of our nation, particularly in the army, there prevailed a great spirit [*veliko raspoloženje*] for this war. Nobody doubted its successful outcome."[41] The author Isidora Sekulić claimed that the victories of 1912 and 1913 had "resurrected" the Serbian nation, that her people were no longer mired in a "slave mentality" brought on by centuries of Turkish rule.[42] Natalija Zrnić, a Serbian woman living in

Vranje, a town in the south of Serbia, wrote in her diary following her country's victories in the First Balkan War: "We ran out on the street. . . . Then the Royal Guard started playing near the monument. . . . Everybody was running toward the monument happy and excited. The band first played the Serbian national anthem, then 'Hej Sloveni,' followed by the Bulgarian, Russian, and Montenegrin anthems."[43]

As Jeffrey Verhey has shown in his insightful study of popular responses to the outbreak of the First World War in Germany, images of national euphoria and national unanimity are potent centripetal forces.[44] The defining image of the Balkan Wars in Serbia is of a unified nation rising up triumphantly and in its entirety against its enemies. Yet just as the notion that Germans were uniformly enthusiastic about the outbreak of the First World War is problematic, so too is the idea that Serbians and Serbia were unified in the era of the wars before the Great War. It is largely a myth that ignores the fissures within the country at the time, and these fissures must be exposed if we are to fully understand the Serbian state and its behavior during the period of the Balkan Wars. In reality, civil-military rivalries in the Serbian state were most serious in the wake of the victories of 1912–13. Despite the myth of the Golden Age and the stories of national euphoria and unity, the architects of Serbia's victories were far from unified: There were deep inter- and intraparty divisions within Serbia's political classes, and deep divisions between those classes and certain sections of the army.

During 1913–14, a struggle for supremacy in the territories newly won from Bulgaria and the Ottoman Empire broke out between the army and the government. It was a conflict that went straight to the crux of civil-military relations in Serbia, threatening to topple the king and his government. At its heart was the question of whether the regions won by Serbia in the Balkan Wars should have a civil or a military administration. In the immediate aftermath of the fighting, Serbian army officers enjoyed priority in the "newly associated territories." But this situation changed in April 1913 when Interior Minister Stojan Protić issued a decree that called for the establishment of an interim civil administration, effectively "demilitarizing" authority in the regions and passing it to the hands of the civilian government.[45] This move brought the regicides, including Apis, back into the heart of Serbia's domestic politics. Many of the regicides, retired following the May Coup, were now back on the army's active list, having served during the Balkan Wars. They were once again ready to assert themselves in Serbia's politics, standing their ground over the matter of civilian or military control in the new territories, violently denouncing Protić's decision in the pages of their journal, and strategically allying themselves with politicians who opposed the Radical government.

Once again, Apis cast a long shadow over Serbia's domestic affairs: He and other Black Handers were fearful that their restored prominence, gained in the military victories of the Balkan Wars, was to be taken away from them. It looked too much like a repeat of the drama following the May Coup, when Apis and his co-conspirators, having served their purpose, were sidelined in favor of civilian authority. No doubt the ghosts of 1903 haunted all sides, for just as the Black Hand feared that the government was once again denying them a central role in the nationalizing mission, so civilian leaders looked back nervously at the fate of Aleksandar Obrenović. Indeed, the Black Hand's journal needled Protić by claiming he "saw praetorians in his sleep."[46] The civil-military tug of war was just as fierce now as it had ever been. At stake was far more than just the administration of Serbia's new territories: The outcome of the conflict between the Black Hand and the government would go some way toward deciding who really controlled the Serbian state.

As of May 1914, the civil-military struggle had assumed greater dimensions and had shifted into the sphere of democratic politics. This was partly because Apis and his officer supporters had courted, and were courted by, opposition figures who hoped to use the question of administration in the south to bring down the Radical government of Nikola Pašić. Pašić, for his part, had enlisted the support of Crown Prince Aleksandar Karadjordjević, a more powerful ally than the ailing King Petar, who in any case had passed on the royal prerogative to Aleksandar in June 1914. Pašić had a slim majority in the Serbian government and was practically forced to call a general election, steadfastly refusing to rescind Protić's decree on the interim administration and hoping that the post-election cards would fall in his favor. Had the elections taken place, the question of civil or military administration of the new territories would have been central to the electoral campaigns of all parties.

But of course the elections were never held. The Balkan Wars had set into motion a chain of events that would plunge the Serbian state into yet another conflict. Serbia's military successes and her territorial aggrandizement had also convinced a number of Habsburg South Slav youths, mainly students of the monarchy's universities and gymnasia, that Serbia could and should liberate them from imperial rule.[47] Even before the conflicts in the Ottoman Balkans, the youth movement—in reality only a small section of the Habsburg South Slav educated elite, which was itself a tiny section of the population—had come to the attention of nationalist associations in Serbia. In April 1912, Croat students of Zagreb University had visited Belgrade, where they were courted by prominent Black Handers, including Apis, Vojislav Tankosić, and *Piedmont* editor Ljuba "Cupa" Jovanović.[48] According to the author Josip Horvat, the students knew little about whom they were associating with, for the Black Handers "chatted with them amicably, as if they were amongst peers." "The majority of them [students] certainly did not know that these people were the ringleaders of the group of so-called conspirators of 1903 who got rid of the Obrenović dynasty. Still fewer could have known that those conspirators were in a latent conflict with the Serbian government and dynasty, who loved them not, but who feared them."[49] The years and months before the outbreak of the First World War were marked by a series of terrorist attacks and *Attentate* (assassination attempts) on Habsburg officials, and it was in this context of sporadic anti-Habsburg terrorism and support for unification with Serbia that Gavrilo Princip succeeded in assassinating the heir to the Habsburg throne.[50] Officers associated with the Black Hand had armed Princip and his group and had also arranged for their passage over the border from Serbia to Bosnia.

Once again, militarist groups were pushing harder toward unification than their civilian counterparts, for the Radical government of Nikola Pašić, in the middle of a closely fought election campaign, was caught largely off guard by the events in Sarajevo and the subsequent Austro-Hungarian ultimatum. But Pašić's position was a moot point for Austria-Hungary, whose leaders— and especially its military leaders—had been at odds with Serbia since 1903 and had been on a collision course with the state since its victories in the Balkan Wars.[51] The assassination of Franz Ferdinand was the casus belli of the Habsburg-Serbian war, but Austria-Hungary's underlying aim was to confront and defeat an ascendant enemy.

Golden, or Merely Gilded?

This chapter has been concerned with the Golden Age in Serbia's history, from 1903 to 1914. According to the Golden Age view of Serbian history, the Balkan Wars are a culmination of the Serbian state's political and military grandeur, a moment of unity and euphoria in which the Serbs successfully extended the constitutional and democratic freedoms of their state into unredeemed Ottoman lands. In this interpretation, the Austro-Hungarian attack of 1914 is a sudden and violent rupture in Serbian history, a cruel curtailment of the country's Periclean age. But in order to fully understand the direction of the Serbian state during this period it is also necessary to trace its militarist sources of power and the fraught relations between military and political elites. The May Coup was less a transition from autocracy to democracy than a continuation of the militarist influence in Serbia's national affairs. Because of this powerful influence, the country's politicians were unable to fully direct the trajectory of the state in the years before the First World War. It is likely that the civilian government of Serbia would have been satisfied to pause the national revolution following the victories of 1912–13, in order to consolidate territorial gains in newly acquired territories and, perhaps more important, to deal with the militarist faction, represented most threateningly by Apis and his allies. But certain militarist groups demanded that the momentum of the national revolution be maintained: They pushed for immediate satisfaction in Bosnia, and in so doing they also pushed Serbia into a far more serious conflict with Austria-Hungary. Thus, the Golden Age of 1903–14 was not a time of unity and common purpose among Serbia's rulers; quite the contrary, its close study reveals the deep divisions within the country.

Epilogue: Exorcising Apis

So it was that in 1914 Serbia, for the third time in the space of two years, went to war. At least initially, in this conflict the Serbian army fared well against the ill-disposed units of Austria-Hungary. In 1914, the Habsburg generals certainly underestimated the fighting capacities of the Serbs, all the more surprising given that those capacities were on full display during the Balkan Wars of 1912–13. When Serbia succumbed, it did so under the combined pressures of Austro-Hungarian, German, and Bulgarian attack. The civil and military institutions of the Serbian state, along with a trail of civilian refugees, made a harrowing trek across the Albanian mountains to the coast in the winter of 1915. The army and the government were eventually resettled and reconstructed at the Macedonian front in Thessaloniki. In September 1918, along with the French and British armies, the Serbs made a triumphant return home, breaking through a disintegrating Bulgarian line, pushing back into Serbia and then beyond, into the territories of the now defunct Austro-Hungarian Empire, creating the common South Slav state.[52] Princip, the schoolboy assassin, did not live to see the fulfillment of his dream for South Slav unity and liberation from Austria-Hungary: he died of tuberculosis in 1918 in Austrian internment in the fortress of Theresienstadt in Bohemia, which was used as a political prison camp during the First World War.

What of the civil-military conflict that had characterized Serbian national politics during the prewar Golden Age? This too, was recast in the forge of the world war. At Thessaloniki, the wartime Radical government set aside its differences with Crown Prince Aleksandar Karadjordjević, forming an alliance with him against Apis and the leaders of the Black Hand. Apis and a group of "co-conspirators" were charged with plotting to assassinate Aleksandar, high treason in a time of war, and a rigged trial took place in 1917.[53] There is no doubt that the charges were false: Aleksandar and the civilian leaders of Serbia were using the war and the trial as a means of disposing of a powerful and autonomous rival, checkmating a dangerous foe. Apis, the master conspirator, was at last outmaneuvered: Found guilty of high treason against the crown, he was executed by a firing squad at dawn on June 26, 1917, along with his fellow Black Hand leaders Ljubomir Vulović and Rade Malobabić. Several other members of the group were given lengthy prison sentences, and fifty-nine officers believed to be associated with the group were pensioned off. It was nothing less than a full-scale purge of the Black Hand leadership from the Serbian army's officer corps. And it worked, for the Black Hand, although still present after the war, was barely a shadow of its fearsome prewar incarnation.

The civil-military line had been settled in favor of the crown and the civilian leadership, but what now remained was an increasingly confident and powerful faction within the army that was loyal exclusively to Aleksandar, who became king of Yugoslavia in 1921 upon the death of his ailing father. This was the much galvanized White Hand camarilla of officers whom Aleksandar continued to cultivate and to promote during the 1920s, seeing them as his own praetorians answerable to and serving him and him alone. As the authority of parliamentary parties in 1920s Yugoslavia diminished in successive political crises, so Aleksandar, supported by the army, increased his authority and stature. His suspension of parliament and institution of a personal dictatorship in 1929 was the culmination of this process, but Aleksandar could not have taken absolute power into his own hands without the full backing of the army. The differences in relations between Aleksandar and the army after 1918 are striking in comparison to his father's struggles with the Black Hand before 1914, to say nothing of the unfortunate fate of Aleksandar Obrenović.

The civil-military rivalries of the Golden Age were decisively laid to rest in Yugoslavia, but this did not mean that a depoliticized army or demilitarized politics emerged in their place. With no challenge from the Black Hand or a similarly autonomous militarist faction either inside or outside the army, Aleksandar was free to dispose of political institutions as he pleased. The execution of Apis and the purging of the Black Hand in 1917 was the end of an autonomous militarist faction that had operated largely according to its own will during the Golden Age, as the Sarajevo assassination graphically demonstrated. But as one kind of civilian-military line came to an end, another began, and the roots of interwar authoritarianism in Yugoslavia lie in

Aleksandar's unopposed control of the army, which was born of the purge of 1917. Apis and the Black Hand may have been exorcised, but the militarist faction remained very much alive well after the end of the Golden Age.

Notes

1. On this topic, see Thomas Otte, *July Crisis: The World's Descent into War, Summer 1914* (Cambridge: Cambridge University Press, 2015).

2. On Princip as trigger, see, for example, Tim Butcher, *The Trigger: Hunting the Assassin Who Brought the World to War* (New York: Grove Press, 2014). Given this tendency to put the Balkans on the periphery of the First World War, Christopher Clark's somewhat revisionist study of the origins of the First World War, *The Sleepwalkers: How Europe Went to War in 1914* (London: Allen Lane, 2013), is noteworthy. Clark's stated goal is to put "Serbia and the Balkans back at the centre of the story." For Clark, Serbia is akin to a twenty-first-century rogue state in so far as it was governed by a political class operating closely with reckless militarist groups responsible for arming Princip and his fellow assassins. This civil-military union created an instability in international affairs centered in the Balkans, but whose effects were felt throughout the continent. For Clark, the Balkans are decidedly *not* peripheral: they are rather the epicenter of the great catastrophe of 1914–18. A critical take on Clark's account is supplied by Maria Todovora, "Outrages and their Outcomes," review of *The Sleepwalkers*, by Christopher Clark, *Times Literary Supplement*, January 4, 2013.

3. Wayne Vucinich, *Serbia between East and West: The Events of 1903–1908* (Stanford, CA: Stanford University Press, 1954).

4. Carnegie Endowment for International Peace, *Report of the International Commission to Inquire into the Causes and Conduct of the Balkan Wars* (Washington DC: Carnegie Endowment for International Peace, 1914).

5. See John Paul Newman, *Yugoslavia in the Shadow of War: Veterans and the Limits of State Building, 1903–1945* (Cambridge: Cambridge University Press, 2015).

6. See Jasna Dragojević-Soso, *Saviours of the Nation: Serbia's Intellectual Opposition and the Revival of Nationalism* (Montreal: McGill-Queen's University Press, 2002).

7. The publication of Dobrica Ćosić, *Vreme smrti* [A time of death] (Belgrade: Prosveta, 1972–79), a multivolume novel of the Serbia at the start of the First World War, is of decisive importance in this revival. See Dragojević-Soso, *Saviours of the Nation*, 89–93.

8. The key work of this school is Olga Popović-Obradović, *Parlamentarizam u Srbiji 1903–1914*, 2nd ed. (New Belgrade: Logistika, 2008), a forensic study of the constitutional malpractices of the Serbian state by a prominent legal historian based at the law faculty of the University of Belgrade. This work has been translated into English by Branka Magaš as *The Parliamentary System in Serbia 1903–1914* (Belgrade: Helsinki Committee for Human Rights in Serbia, 2013). See also Dubravka Stojanović, *Srbija i Demokratija 1903–1914* (Belgrade: Udruženje za Društvenu Istoriju, 2003). Stojanović's preface gives an overview of the historiographical trajectory of the "Golden Age" thesis.

9. The best English-language history of Serbia in the nineteenth century is Michael Boro Petrovich, *A History of Modern Serbia, 1804–1918* (New York: Harcourt Brace Jovanovich, 1976). On the 1804 uprising, see Wayne Vucinich, *The First Serbian Uprising 1804–1813* (Boulder, CO: Columbia University Press, 1982).

10. See Dimitrije Djordjević and Stephen Fischer-Galati, *The Balkan Revolutionary Tradition* (New York: Columbia University Press, 1981).

11. Dimitrije Djordjević, "The Role of the Military in the Balkans in the Nineteenth Century," in *Der Berliner Kongress von 1878: Die Politik der Grossmächte und die Probleme der Modernisierung in Südosteuropa in der zweiten Hälfte des 19. Jahrhunderts*, ed. Ralph Melville and Hans-Jürgen Schröder (Wiesbaden: Steiner, 1982), 318–19.

12. Petrovich, *A History of Modern Serbia*, 204. See also "Vojska," in *Narodno enciklopedija srpsko-hrvatsko-slovenačka*, ed. Stanoje Stanojević, 4 vols. (Zagreb: Bibliografski zavod, 1925–29), 4:1140; Draga Vuksanović-Anić, *Stvaranje moderne srpske vojske: francuski uticaj na njeno formiranje* (Belgrade: Vojna štamparija, 1993); Slavica Ratković-Kostić, *Evropeizacija srpske vojske: 1878–1903* (Belgrade: Vojna štamparija, 2007).

13. Ibid., 206–8.

14. Djordjević, "Role of the Military," 324.

15. Ibid., 328. See also Gale Stokes, *Politics as Development: The Emergence of Political Parties in Nineteenth-Century Serbia* (Durham, NC: Duke University Press, 1990).

16. See Rogers Brubaker, *Nationalism Reframed: Nationhood and the National Question in the New Europe* (Cambridge: Cambridge University Press, 1996), 79–106. See also Diana Mishkova, "Modernization and Political Elites in the Balkans before the First World War," *Eastern European Politics and Societies* 9, no. 1 (December 1994): 63–89.

17. On Garašanin, see David MacKenzie, *Ilija Garašanin: Balkan Bismarck* (Boulder, CO: Columbia University Press, 1985). See also David MacKenzie,

"Serbian Nationalist and Military Organizations and the Piedmont Idea, 1844–1914," *Eastern European Quarterly* 16, no. 3 (September 1982): 323–44.

18. Mark Biondich, *The Balkans: Revolution, War, and Political Violence since 1878* (Oxford: Oxford University Press, 2011), 62.

19. See Isabel V. Hull, *Absolute Destruction: Military Culture and the Practices of War in Imperial Germany* (Ithaca, NY: Cornell University Press, 2006), 1.

20. The best accounts of the palace coup are Dragiša Vasić, *Devetsto treća: prilozi za istoriju Srbije od 8. jula 1900 do 17. januara 1907* (Belgrade: Izdanje i štampa štamparije "Tucović," 1925), and Vucinich, *Serbia between East and West*.

21. The reign of Aleksandar is covered comprehensively and critically in the Serbian polymath Slobodan Jovanović's classic study, written in the interwar period, *Vlada Aleksandra Obrenovića* (Belgrade: Geca Kon, 1929–31, 3 vols).

22. Vucinich, *Serbia between East and West*, 80.

23. See Vladimir Stojančević, "Pašićevi pogledi na rešavanje pitanja Stare Srbije i Makedonije do 1912. godine," in *Nikola Pašić: Život i delo; zbornik radova sa naučnog skupa u Srpskoj akademiji nauka i umetnosti, Beograd, 16. i 17. oktobar 1995. godine, i Zadužbini "Nikola Pašić," Zaječar, 19. oktobar 1995. godine*, ed. Vasilije Krestić (Belgrade: Kultura, 1997), 281.

24. The Serbian Academy of Arts and Sciences has now digitized and uploaded the Serbian kingdom's diplomatic papers for the 1903–14 period. They are available at http://diplprepiska.mi.sanu.ac.rs/.

25. Jonathan Gumz, *The Resurrection and Collapse of Empire in Habsburg Serbia, 1914–1918* (Cambridge: Cambridge University Press, 2009), 7.

26. See Popović-Obradović, *Parlamentarizam u Srbiji 1903–1914*.

27. See Vladimir Čorović, *Odnosi izmedju Srbije i Austrougarske u XX veku* (Belgrade: Državna štamparija Kraljevine Jugoslavije, 1936), and Samuel Williamson, *Austria-Hungary and the Origins of the First World War* (London: Macmillan, 1991).

28. See Robin Okey, *Taming Balkan Nationalism: The Habsburg "Civilizing Mission" in Bosnia, 1878–1914* (Oxford: Oxford University Press, 2007).

29. Milan Mijalkovski, "Četničke (gerilske) jednice Kraljevine Srbije—borci protiv terora turskog okupatora," in *Gerila na Balkanu: Borci za slobodu, buntovnici ili banditi—Istraživanje gerile i paramilitarnih formacija na Balkanu*e, ed. Momčilo Pavlović, Testsuya Sahara, and Predrag J. Marković (Belgrade: Institute of Contemporary History, Faculty for Security Studies, 2007).

30. On the *četnici*, see Aleksa Jovanović, "Četnički pokret u južnoj Srbiji pod Turcima," in *Spomenica dvadesetpetogodišnjice oslobođenje južne Srbije*, ed. Aleksa Jovanović (Skopje: Štamparija "Južna Srbija" Milana Đ. Ilića, 1937). See also MacKenzie, "Serbian Nationalist and Military Organizations," 334.

31. The best study of the Black Hand in English is David MacKenzie, *The "Black Hand" on Trial: Salonika, 1917* (Boulder, CO: East European Monographs, 1995). See also Vasa Kazimirović, *Crna Ruka: Ličnosti i događaji u Srbiji od prevrata 1903. do Solunskog procesa 1917. godine* (Novi Sad: Prometej, 2013).

32. Vucinich, *Serbia between East and West*, 104.

33. Ivo Banac, *The National Question in Yugoslavia: Origins, History, Politics* (Ithaca, NY: Cornell University Press, 1988), 146.

34. MacKenzie, "Serbian Nationalist and Military Organizations," 334.

35. Bogomir A. Bogić, *Ciljevi Narodne odbrane* (Belgrade: printed by the author, 1934).

36. Newman, *Yugoslavia in the Shadow*. See also Danilo Šarenac, *Top, vojnik, i sećanje: Prvi svetski rat u Srbiji 1914–2009* (Belgrade: Planeta Print, 2014); Olga Manojlović Pintar, *Arheologija sećanja: spomenici i identiteti u Srbiji, 1918–1989* (Belgrade: Udruženje za društvenu istoriju, 2014).

37. See James Pettifer, "After the Golden Age? The Journalism of the Balkan Wars," in *War in the Balkans: Conflict and Diplomacy before World War One*, ed. James Pettifer and Tom Buchanan (London: I. B. Tauris, 2016).

38. See, for example, Béla Király, "East Central European Society and Warfare in the Era of the Balkan Wars," in *East Central European Society and the Balkan Wars*, ed. Béla Király and Djordjević (Boulder, CO: East European Monographs, 1987), 6.

39. Stanoje Stanojević, ed., *Narodno enciklopedija srpsko-hrvatsko-slovenačka* (Zagreb: Bibliografski zavod, 1925–29), s.v. "Vojska."

40. Borislav Ratković, "Srpska vojska u balkanskim ratovima 1912–1913 i u prvom svetskom ratu 1914–1918," *Vojnoistorijski glasnik* 43, no. 1–2 (1993): 56.

41. Živojin Mišić, *Moje uspomene* (Belgrade: Fondacija "Vojvoda Živojin Mišić" Institut za suvremenu istoriju, 2010), 220.

42. Isidora Sekulić, *Zapisi o mome narodu* (Novi Sad: Stylos, 2001), 66–67.

43. Jill A. Irvine and Carol S. Lilly, eds., *Natalija: Life in the Balkan Powder Keg, 1880–1956* (Budapest: Central European University Press, 2008), 149.

44. Jeffrey Verhey, *The Spirit of 1914: Militarism, Myth, and Mobilization in Germany* (Cambridge: Cambridge University Press, 2000).

45. See MacKenzie, "Stojan Protić's Final Decade and Serbia's Radical Party," *East European Quarterly* 42, no. 3 (September 2008): 223.

46. *Pijemont*, January 5, 1914, cited in ibid., 224.

47. See Mirjana Gross, "Nacionalne ideje studentske omladine u Hrvatskoj uoči i svjetskog rata," *Historijski zbornik* 21–22 (1968–69): 75–143; Vladimir Dedijer, *Sarajevo 1914* (Belgrade: Prosveta, 1966), published in English as *The Road to Sarajevo* (London: Macgibbon & Kee, 1967).

48. Josip Horvat, *Pobuna omladine 1911–1914* (Zagreb: SKD "Prosvjeta," 2006), 149–51.

49. Ibid., 150.

50. On these attacks, see ibid.

51. As Samuel Williamson has noted, by the end of the Balkan Wars, Serbia had become the "most persistent threat" that Austria-Hungary faced. See Williamson, *Austria-Hungary and the Origins of the First World War*, 103.

52. On the First World War in Serbia, see Andrej Mitrović *Serbia's Great War 1914–1918* (London: Hurst, 2007), a slightly abridged translation of the author's Serbian-language original, *Srbija u prvom svetskom ratu* (Belgrade: Stubovi kulture, 2004).

53. MacKenzie, *The "Black Hand" on Trial*.

CONTRIBUTORS

ULF BRUNNBAUER is director of the Leibniz Institute for East and Southeast European Studies in Regensburg and holds the chair of the Department of the History of Southeastern and Eastern Europe at the University of Regensburg. He has a PhD in history from the University of Graz (Austria) and a Habilitation from the Free University of Berlin. His research deals mainly with the social history of southeastern Europe in the nineteenth and twentieth century, with a special interest in the history of migration, labor, and family relations. His most recent books are *Globalizing Southeastern Europe: Emigrants, America, and the State since the Late Nineteenth Century* (Lexington, 2016) and *The Ambiguous Nation: Case Studies from Southeastern Europe in the 20th Century*, coedited with Hannes Grandits (Oldenbourg, 2013).

HOLLY CASE is an associate professor of modern European history at Brown University. Her first book, *Between States: The Transylvanian Question and the European Idea during World War II*, was published in May 2009. She is currently completing a book on the "Age of Questions" (the age when such questions as the Eastern, Jewish, Polish, woman, and worker questions first emerged) spanning the nineteenth and twentieth centuries.

DESSISLAVA LILOVA is associate professor at Sofia University. Her fields of study include national identity, imagined geographies, and entangled histories of modernity. She was the Andrew Mellon and Fernand Braudel Fellow at the Maison des sciences de l'homme (Paris), a guest researcher at the Institut für die Wissenschaften von Menschen / Institute for Human Sciences (Vienna) and the Georg Eckert Institut (Braunschweig), and recipient of fellowships at Collegium Budapest and the Center for Advanced Studies (Sofia). Her book on Bulgarian historiography in the nineteenth century was published in 2003. Her articles have appeared in scholarly volumes and journals in Bulgaria, Greece, France, Austria, Germany, Hungary, and Brazil.

JOHN PAUL NEWMAN is senior lecturer of twentieth-century European history and director of European studies at Maynooth University, Ireland. He is the author of *Yugoslavia in the Shadow of War: Veterans and the Limits of State Building, 1903–1945* (Cambridge University Press, 2015), and the coeditor (with Mark Cornwall) of *Sacrifice and Rebirth: The Legacy of the Last Habsburg War* (Berghahn, 2016), and (with Julia Eichenberg) *The Great War and Veterans' Internationalism* (Palgrave Macmillan, 2013). Until September 2011, he was an ERC Postdoctoral Research Fellow working on the project "Paramilitary Violence after the Great War," to which he contributed a case study of violence in the Balkans.

ROUMIANA PRESHLENOVA is professor at the Institute of Balkan Studies and Centre of Thracology at the Bulgarian Academy of Sciences in Sofia. She teaches in the Faculty of History at Sofia University "St. Kliment Ohridski." Her areas of interest include Balkan history in the nineteenth and twentieth centuries (nationalism, identities, education, international relations, and the role of Central Europe in Balkan modernization). Among her recent publications are monographs on higher education in Austria-Hungary and the Bulgarians, 1879–1918 (Sofia, 2008) and Austria-Hungary and the Balkans, 1878–1912 (Sofia, 2017), and the edited volume *Looking West, Feeling East: Impacts, Values and Loyalties in South-Eastern Europe* (Sofia, 2015).

DOMINIQUE KIRCHNER REILL (PhD in history from Columbia University) is currently associate professor in modern European history at the University of Miami. She is also an editor for the journal *Contemporary European History* published by Cambridge University Press and a series editor for Purdue University Press's Central European Studies. Her first monograph, *Nationalists Who Feared the Nation: Adriatic Multi-nationalism in Habsburg Dalmatia, Trieste, and Venice*, was published by Stanford University Press in 2012 and was awarded the Austrian Studies Book Prize. The title received an honorable mention for the Smith Award. Currently she is completing her new monograph tentatively titled "Rebel City: Fiume's Challenge to Wilson's Europe."

TIMOTHY SNYDER is the Richard E. Levin Professor of History at Yale University and a permanent fellow at the Institut für die Wissenschaften vom Menschen / Institute for Human Sciences (Vienna). His most recent books include *The Road to Unfreedom: Russia, Europe, America* (2018); *On Tyranny: Twenty Lessons from the Twentieth Century* (2017); *Black Earth: The Holocaust as History and Warning* (2015); and *Bloodlands: Europe between Hitler and*

Stalin (2010). His work has received the Arts and Letters Award for Literature from the American Academy of Arts and Letters, the Hannah Arendt Prize, and the Leipzig Book Prize for European Understanding.

KATHERINE YOUNGER is a research associate for the Ukraine in European Dialogue program at the Institut für die Wissenschaften vom Menschen / Institute for Human Sciences (Vienna). She completed her PhD in history at Yale University in 2018. Her dissertation focused on the Greek Catholic (Uniate) Church in the nineteenth century and its place in European international relations.

Index

Rochester Studies in East and Central Europe

Series Editor: Timothy Snyder, Yale University

Additional Titles of Interest

Polish Cinema in a Transnational Context
Edited by Ewa Mazierska and Michael Goddard

Literary Translation and the Idea of a Minor Romania
Sean Cotter

Coming of Age under Martial Law:
The Initiation Novels of Poland's Last Communist Generation
Svetlana Vassileva-Karagyozova

Revolution and Counterrevolution in Poland, 1980–1989:
Solidarity, Martial Law, and the End of Communism in Europe
Andrzej Paczkowski
Translated by Christina Manetti

The Utopia of Terror: Life and Death in Wartime Croatia
Rory Yeomans

Kyiv as Regime City: The Return of Soviet Power after Nazi Occupation
Martin J. Blackwell

Magnetic North: Conversations with Tomas Venclova
Ellen Hinsey and Tomas Venclova

Witnessing Romania's Century of Turmoil: Memoirs of a Political Prisoner
Nicolae Margineanu
Edited by Dennis Deletant

Plebeian Modernity:
Social Practices, Illegality, and the Urban Poor in Russia, 1906–1916
Ilya Gerasimov

Making Martyrs: The Language of Sacrifice in Russian Culture from Stalin to Putin
Yuliya Minkova

A complete list of titles in the Rochester Studies in East and
Central Europe series may be found on our website, www.urpress.com.

This collection of essays places the Balkans at the center of European developments, not as a conflict-ridden problem zone, but rather as a full-fledged European region. Contrary to the commonly held perception, contributors to the
volume argue, the Balkans did not lag behind the rest of European history, but
rather anticipated many (West) European developments in the decades before
and after 1900.

In the second half of the nineteenth century, the Balkan states became fully
independent nation-states. As they worked to consolidate their sovereignty,
these countries looked beyond traditional state formation strategies to alternative visions rooted in militarism or national political economy, and not only succeeded on their own terms but changed Europe and the world beginning in
1912–14. As the Ottoman Empire weakened and ever more kinds of informal
diplomacy were practiced on its territory by more powerful states, relationships
between identity and geopolitics were also transformed. The result, as the contributors demonstrate, was a phenomenon that would come to pervade the
whole of Europe by the 1920s and 1930s: the creeping substitution of ideas of
religion and ethnicity for the idea of state belonging or subjecthood.

"Innovative, well written for a broad audience, and timely, *The Balkans as Europe,
1821–1914* offers fresh insight about the region, in ways that demand attention
from specialists in other areas. The contributors advance a coherent set of inter-
pretations—all pointing to the modernity and relevance of Balkan models for
other parts of Europe and the world. This is cutting-edge work."

—Jeremy King, Mount Holyoke College

"*The Balkans as Europe, 1821–1914* is a timely, superbly documented, and truly
persuasive contribution to the symbolic geography of Europe. It challenges and
transcends the semantically dubious and politically supercilious characterization
of the Balkans as a marginal, underdeveloped backwater, fiercely nationalist and
devoid of civil society. The volume is a strong and necessary refutation of fro-
zen (and condescending) conceptualizations which contrast the Habsburg legacies (often idealized) with the inescapable 'Balkan ghosts.'"

—Vladimir Tismaneanu, University of Maryland

CONTRIBUTORS: Ulf Brunnbauer, Holly Case, Dessislava Lilova, John Paul
Newman, Roumiana Preshlenova, Dominique Kirchner Reill, Timothy Snyder

TIMOTHY SNYDER is Richard C. Levin Professor of History at Yale University. KATHERINE YOUNGER is a research associate at the Institute for Human Sciences (IWM) in Vienna, Austria.

www.ingramcontent.com/pod-product-compliance
Lightning Source LLC
Chambersburg PA
CBHW020809100426
42814CB00014B/391/J